2021 SUPPLEMENT
FIFTEENTH EDITIONS

MODERN CRIMINAL PROCEDURE
BASIC CRIMINAL PROCEDURE

AND

ADVANCED CRIMINAL PROCEDURE

■ ■ ■

Yale Kamisar
Clarence Darrow Distinguished University Professor Emeritus of Law
University of Michigan
Professor Emeritus of Law, University of San Diego

Wayne R. LaFave
David C. Baum Professor Emeritus of Law
and Center for Advanced Study Professor Emeritus
University of Illinois

Jerold H. Israel
Alene and Allan F. Smith Professor Emeritus
University of Michigan
Emeritus Ed Rood Eminent Scholar in Trial Advocacy and Procedure
University of Florida, Fredric G. Levin College of Law

Nancy J. King
Lee S. & Charles A. Speir Professor of Law
Vanderbilt University Law School

Orin S. Kerr
Professor of Law
University of California, Berkeley

Eve Brensike Primus
Yale Kamisar Collegiate Professor of Law
University of Michigan

AMERICAN CASEBOOK SERIES®

WEST
ACADEMIC
PUBLISHING

American Casebook Series is a trademark registered in the U.S. Patent and Trademark Office.

© 2019, 2020 LEG, Inc. d/b/a West Academic
© 2021 LEG, Inc. d/b/a West Academic
    444 Cedar Street, Suite 700
    St. Paul, MN 55101
    1-877-888-1330

West, West Academic Publishing, and West Academic are trademarks of West Publishing Corporation, used under license.

Printed in the United States of America

ISBN: 978-1-64708-896-5

UNITED STATES SUPREME COURT CHART

UNITED STATES SUPREME COURT
1940–1985

Timeline: 1940 — 1945 — 1950 — 1955 — 1960 — 1965 — 1970 — 1975 — 1980 — 1985

Seat (start)	Succession (1940–1985)
Hughes 1930	Stone → Vinson → Warren → Burger
Frankfurter 1939	Goldberg → Fortas → Blackmun
Black 1937	Powell
McReynolds 1914	Byrnes → Rutledge → Minton → Brennan
Douglas 1939	Stevens
Murphy 1940	Clark → Marshall
Reed 1938	Whittaker → White
Stone 1925	Jackson → Harlan → Rehnquist → Scalia
Roberts 1930	Burton → Stewart → O'Connor

1985–PRESENT

Timeline: 1985 — 1990 — 1995 — 2000 — 2005 — 2010 — 2015 — 2020

Seat	Succession (1985–Present)
Burger	Rehnquist → ROBERTS
Blackmun	BREYER
Powell	Kennedy → KAVANAUGH
Brennan	Souter → SOTOMAYOR
Stevens	KAGAN
Marshall	THOMAS
White	Ginsburg → BARRETT
Scalia	GORSUCH
O'Connor	ALITO

The publishers wish to acknowledge that the above chart was developed from a suggestion by Dean Joe E. Covington of the University of Missouri Law School.

PREFACE

This Supplement to the fifteenth editions of *Modern Criminal Procedure, Basic Criminal Procedure* and *Advanced Criminal Procedure* contains all significant cases decided by the United States Supreme Court since publication of those fifteenth editions. It also includes a number of lower court cases and citations to, or extracts from, recent academic commentary. This volume also contains Appendices A through C, containing selected provisions from the U.S. Constitution and U.S. Code, and all provisions of the Federal Rules of Criminal Procedure.

Following the 2020 Supplement, Wayne LaFave joined Yale Kamisar as a retired contributor to this project. Wayne's quips and comments, as well as his substantive contributions, will be sorely missed.

JEROLD H. ISRAEL
NANCY J. KING
ORIN S. KERR
EVE BRENSIKE PRIMUS

July 2021

ACKNOWLEDGMENTS

Excerpt from the following article appears with the kind permission of the copyright holder.

PRISONERS OF POLITICS: BREAKING THE CYCLE OF MASS INCARCERATION by Rachel Elise Barkow, Cambridge, Mass.: The Belknap Press of Harvard University Press, Copyright © 2019 by the President and Fellows of Harvard College.

Capers, I. Bennett, Citizenship Talk in THE CAMBRIDGE HANDBOOK OF POLICING IN THE UNITED STATES (T. Lave & E. Miller eds.). Copyright © 2019 by Cambridge University Press.

Carbado, Devon W., From Stopping Black People to Killing Black People: The Fourth Amendment Pathways to Police Violence, 105 Calif. L. Rev. 125 (2017). Copyright © 2017 by Devon Carbado.

Davis, Angela J., Reimagining Prosecution: A Growing Progressive Movement, 3 UCLA Crim. Just. L. Rev. 1 (2019). Copyright © 2019 by the UCLA Criminal Justice Law Review.

Eaglin, Jessica M., To "Defund" The Police, 73 Stanford L. Rev. Online 120 (2021). Copyright © 2021 by Jessica Eaglin.

Fryer, Daniel, Race, Reform, & Progressive Prosecution, 110 J. Crim. L. & Criminology 769 (2020). Copyright © 2020 by the Journal of Criminal Law & Criminology.

TABLE OF CONTENTS

UNITED STATES SUPREME COURT CHART.. III

PREFACE V

ACKNOWLEDGMENTS..VII

TABLE OF CASES XIII

PART 1. INTRODUCTION

CHAPTER 2. SOURCES OF CRIMINAL PROCEDURE LAW..............................3
§ 1. *THE INCORPORATION DOCTRINE*...3

CHAPTER 3. SOME GENERAL REFLECTIONS ON THE
    CONSTITUTIONALIZATION OF CRIMINAL PROCEDURE...........................5
§ 1. *INSTITUTIONAL COMPETENCE* 5
    Rachel Elise Barkow—Prisoners of Politics: Breaking the Cycle of Mass
        Incarceration 5
    Angela J. Davis—Reimagining Prosecution: A Growing Progressive
        Movement..6
    Daniel Fryer—Race, Reform, & Progressive Prosecution 7
§ 2. *RACIAL INJUSTICE*...9
    I. Bennett Capers—*Citizenship Talk in* The Cambridge Handbook of
        Policing in the United States 9
    Devon W. Carbado—From Stopping Black People to Killing Black People:
        The Fourth Amendment Pathways to Police Violence 14
§ 4. *MISDEMEANORS* 17
§ 5. *REMEDIES FOR GOVERNMENT MISCONDUCT* 17
    Scott Calvert & Dan Frosch—Police Rethink Policies as Cities Pay
        Millions to Settle Misconduct Claims 17
§ 6. *POLICE DEPARTMENT HIRING AND TRAINING* 18
§ 7. *THE MOVEMENT TO DEFUND THE POLICE*.......................................18
    Jessica M. Eaglin—To "Defund" The Police....................................18
    Bernard Starr—The Alternative to Defunding the Police: Increase
        Funding for Vetting to Keep Racist and Violent Cops Out 21

CHAPTER 4. THE RIGHT TO COUNSEL...23
§ 1. *THE RIGHT TO APPOINTED COUNSEL AND RELATED PROBLEMS* 23
    A. *THE RIGHT TO APPOINTED COUNSEL IN CRIMINAL PROCEEDINGS*.....23
§ 2. *THE RIGHT TO APPOINTED COUNSEL IN PROCEEDINGS OTHER THAN
    CRIMINAL PROSECUTIONS: THE CONTINUED VITALITY OF THE* BETTS
    VS. BRADY *APPROACH*..23
    A. *PROBATION AND PAROLE REVOCATION HEARINGS: JUVENILE
        COURT PROCEEDINGS; PARENTAL STATUS TERMINATION
        PROCEEDINGS; CONTEMPT HEARINGS*...23

CHAPTER 5. THE PERFORMANCE OF COUNSEL 25
§ 6. *CLIENT CONTROL* 25

PART 2. POLICE PRACTICES

CHAPTER 6. ARREST, SEARCH AND SEIZURE 29
§ 2. *PROTECTED AREAS AND INTERESTS* 29
    B.   *PREMISES* 29
    C.   *MOVEMENTS AND LOCATION* 29
    D.   *NETWORKS* 35
    E.   *NON-FOURTH AMENDMENT CONSTITUTIONAL PROTECTIONS* 36
    F.   *SEIZURES* 36
        Torres v. Madrid 37
§ 4. *SEARCH WARRANTS* 43
    B.   *EXECUTION OF THE WARRANT* 43

CHAPTER 7. WARRANTLESS AND LESSER-GROUNDS SEARCHES AND
    SEIZURES 45
§ 1. *WARRANTLESS ARRESTS AND SEARCHES OF THE PERSON* 45
    Mitchell v. Wisconsin 46
§ 2. *WARRANTLESS ENTRIES AND SEARCHES OF PREMISES* 48
§ 3. *WARRANTLESS SEIZURES AND SEARCHES OF VEHICLES AND
    CONTAINERS* 48
§ 4. *STOP AND FRISK* 50
    A.   *POLICE ACTION SHORT OF A SEIZURE* 50
    B.   *GROUNDS FOR TEMPORARY SEIZURE FOR INVESTIGATION* 53
        Kansas v. Glover 53
    C.   *PERMISSIBLE EXTENT AND SCOPE OF TEMPORARY SEIZURE* 56
    E.   *PROTECTIVE SEARCH* 57
§ 6. *CONSENT SEARCHES* 57
    A.   *THE NATURE OF "CONSENT"* 57

CHAPTER 9. POLICE INTERROGATION AND CONFESSIONS 59
§ 3. *APPLYING AND EXPLAINING* MIRANDA 59
    A.   *WHEN ARE THE* MIRANDA *RIGHTS TRIGGERED?* 59
    D.   *INVOKING THE* MIRANDA *RIGHT TO COUNSEL* 60
§ 5. *THE VOLUNTARINESS TEST REVISITED* 60
    B.   *THE DEFINITION OF VOLUNTARINESS POST-*MIRANDA 60
    C.   *THE ADDITION OF A THRESHOLD INQUIRY* 61
    D.   *THE PROBLEM OF FALSE CONFESSIONS* 62

CHAPTER 11. INVESTIGATION BY SUBPOENA 63
§ 2. *CHALLENGES TO THE GROUNDING AND SCOPE OF THE SUBPOENA* 63
    C.   *APPLYING THE OVERBREADTH PROHIBITION* 63

CHAPTER 12. THE SCOPE OF THE EXCLUSIONARY RULES 65
§ 2. *THE "FRUIT OF THE POISONOUS TREE"* 65
    A.   *FOURTH AMENDMENT VIOLATIONS* 65

PART 3. THE COMMENCEMENT OF FORMAL PROCEEDINGS

CHAPTER 13. PRETRIAL RELEASE..69
§ 1. THE RIGHT TO BAIL; PRETRIAL RELEASE PROCEDURES 69
    A.   STATE AND FEDERAL BAIL SYSTEMS.......................................69
    B.   CONSTITUTIONAL LIMITS ON PRETRIAL RELEASE PROCESS................69

CHAPTER 14. THE DECISION WHETHER TO PROSECUTE 71
*§ 1. THE OFFICE OF PROSECUTOR AND THE NATURE OF THE DECISION
WHETHER TO PROSECUTE* 71

PART 4. THE ADVERSARY SYSTEM AND THE DETERMINATION OF GUILT OR INNOCENCE

CHAPTER 22. GUILTY PLEAS...75
*§ 2. REJECTED, KEPT AND BROKEN BARGAINS; UNREALIZED
EXPECTATIONS* 75
§ 3. THE ROLE AND RESPONSIBILITY OF DEFENSE COUNSEL 75
    Garza v. Idaho..75

CHAPTER 23. TRIAL BY JURY..79
§ 1. RIGHT TO JURY TRIAL 79
    Ramos v. Louisiana 79
§ 2. JURY SELECTION 82
    B.   SELECTING THE JURY FROM THE VENIRE: VOIR DIRE...............82

CHAPTER 25. THE CRIMINAL TRIAL..85
§ 2. CONFRONTATION AND TESTIMONIAL HEARSAY 85

CHAPTER 26. REPROSECUTION AND DOUBLE JEOPARDY.................87
§ 4. REPROSECUTION BY A DIFFERENT SOVEREIGN 87
    Gamble v. United States..87

CHAPTER 27. SENTENCING..89
§ 1. INTRODUCTION TO SENTENCING 89
    B.   TYPES OF SENTENCES 89
§ 2. ALLOCATING AND CONTROLLING SENTENCING DISCRETION 89
    C.   APPELLATE REVIEW 89
§ 3. CONSTITUTIONAL LIMITS ON SENTENCING PROCEDURE................89
    D.   JURY TRIAL AND BURDEN OF PROOF 89
        United States v. Haymond 90

CHAPTER 28. APPEALS..93
§ 1. THE DEFENDANT'S RIGHT TO APPEAL..93
§ 4. REVIEW FOR CLAIMS NOT RAISED ON TIME 93
    Greer v. United States; United States v. Gary 93
§ 5. THE HARMLESS ERROR RULE 96
    B.   CONSTITUTIONAL ERROR..96

CHAPTER 29. POST-CONVICTION REVIEW: FEDERAL HABEAS CORPUS.......97
§ 5. RETROACTIVITY—WHICH LAW APPLIES? 97

**APPENDIX A. SELECTED PROVISIONS OF THE UNITED STATES
    CONSTITUTION**...99

APPENDIX B. SELECTED FEDERAL STATUTORY PROVISIONS 103
Wire and Electronic Communications Interception and Interception of Oral
    Communications...103
Stored Wire and Electronic Communications and Transactional Records Access 121
Searches and Seizures 128
Bail Reform Act of 1984 130
Speedy Trial Act of 1974 (as Amended)..139
Jencks Act...144
Litigation Concerning Sources of Evidence 145
Criminal Appeals Act of 1970 (as Amended)...146
Crime Victims' Rights..146
Jury Selection and Service Act of 1968 (as Amended)..149
Habeas Corpus 155
Privacy Protection Act of 1980 165
Guidelines...169
Foreign Intelligence Surveillance Act...172

**APPENDIX C. FEDERAL RULES OF CRIMINAL PROCEDURE FOR THE
    UNITED STATES DISTRICT COURTS**...181

TABLE OF CASES

The names of principal cases and major Note cases (see *A Guide for Readers*) are in bold type. For Commonwealth v. ____, People v. ___, State v. ___, and United States v. ___, see the name of the other party. For "ex. rel" (including cases starting with the name of a government), "Ex parte," and "In re," see the name following that introductory procedural phrase.

This table includes only pages on which the discussion of the case is accompanied by a full citation to the case (both case name and reporter) or a partial citation (typically the case name followed by a page cross-reference to the primary discussion).

Alabama v. Shelton, 90
Apodaca v. Louisiana, 79
Baker, State v., 60
Bobadilla v. State, 75
Bousley v. United States, 97
Boustani, United States v., 69
Bowe, State v., 61
Brewster v. Beck, 42
Brower v. County of Inyo, 40
Brown, United States v., 17, 57
Buzzard, United States v., 57
Cady v. Dombrowki, 50
California v. Hodari D., 38
Caniglia v. Strom, 50
Correa, United States v., 29
Countess of Rutland's Case, 39, 41
Cunningham, United States v., 49
Diaz v. Commonwealth, 85
Dixon, United States v., 30
Dozier v. United States, 52
Dye, State v., 75
Edwards v. Vannoy, 97, 98
Florida v. Bostick, 42
Flowers v. Mississippi, 83
Ford v. Wainwright, 97
Forrester, United States v., 35
Foster v. City of Indio, 56
Gamble v. United States, 87
Gary, United States v., 93
Garza v. Idaho, 25, **75**, 93
Genner v. Sparks, 38
Gooch, United States v., 48
Greer v. United States, 93
Hammond, United States v., 34
Haymond, United States v., 23, **90**
Hood, United States v., 35
Humphrey, In re, 70
Jacobsen, United States v., 42
Jamison v. McClendon, 61
Jemison, People v., 85
Jones v. Mississippi, 97
Kansas v. Glover, 53
Kennedy v. Louisiana, 97
Knapp, United States v., 49
Knights, United States v., 17, 50
Lang, State v., 49
Lange v. California, 48

Lee v. City of Chicago, 42
Long, Commonwealth v., 45
Lora, Commonwealth v., 45
Mabry, United States v., 42
Matsumoto, State v., 60
McCarthy, Commonwealth v., 30
Miller v. Alabama, 97
Mitchell v. Wisconsin, **46**, 57
Montgomery v. Louisiana, 97
Moore, State v., 45
Navas, United States v., 49
New York v. Belton, 49
Nicholl v. Darley, 38
Peery v. City of Miami, 42
Pina, United States v., 48
Place, United States v., 42
Plessy v. Ferguson, 82
Puentes-Hurtado, United States v., 75
Ramirez, United States v., 43
Ramos v. Louisiana, 3, **79**, 97
Randall, State v., 58
Rehaif v. United States, 93
Richmond, United States v., 29
Robey v. Superior Court,, 49
Roper v. Simmons, 97
Sacramento, County of v. Lewis, 39
San Antonio Indep. Sch. Dist. v. Rodriguez, 70
Santana, People v., 48
Soldal v. Cook County, 36
Stegall, United States v., 50
Symes v. United States, 48
Tate v. Short, 70
Taylor v. City of Saginaw, 29
Timbs v. Indiana, 3, 89
Torres v. Madrid, 37
Walker v. City of Calhoun, Georgia, 70
Welch v. United States, 97
White, United States v., 50

2021 SUPPLEMENT TO FIFTEENTH EDITIONS

MODERN CRIMINAL PROCEDURE
BASIC CRIMINAL PROCEDURE

AND

ADVANCED CRIMINAL PROCEDURE

PART 1

INTRODUCTION

■ ■ ■

CHAPTER 2

SOURCES OF CRIMINAL PROCEDURE LAW

■ ■ ■

§ 1. THE INCORPORATION DOCTRINE

15th ed., p. 26; replace footnote 13 with the following:

¹³ [T]he only [other] rights not fully incorporated are (1) the Third Amendment's protection against quartering of soldiers; (2) the Fifth Amendment's grand jury indictment requirement; [and] (3) the Seventh Amendment right to a jury trial in civil cases[.] * * *

We have never decided whether the Third Amendment * * * applies to the States through the Due Process Clause. * * * Our governing decisions regarding the Grand Jury Clause of the Fifth Amendment and the Seventh Amendment's civil jury requirement long predate the era of selective incorporation.

[The Supreme Court recently incorporated the Eighth Amendment's prohibition on excessive fines in *Timbs v. Indiana*, 139 S.Ct. 682 (2019), and the Sixth Amendment right to a unanimous jury verdict in *Ramos v. Louisiana*, 140 S.Ct. 1390 (2020). For further discussion of *Ramos, see* Supp. pp. 79 & 97.]

15th ed., p. 26; delete footnote 14.

CHAPTER 3

SOME GENERAL REFLECTIONS ON THE CONSTITUTIONALIZATION OF CRIMINAL PROCEDURE

■ ■ ■

§ 1. INSTITUTIONAL COMPETENCE

15th ed., p. 40; before Section 2, add:

RACHEL ELISE BARKOW—PRISONERS OF POLITICS: BREAKING THE CYCLE OF MASS INCARCERATION
Pp. 1–11 (2019).

Few people would want to establish air pollutant limits or workplace safety conditions by popular vote. Instead, most people prefer to trust experts with specialized knowledge to set policies based on studies of what maximizes public safety and an analysis of the costs and benefits of different courses of action. This is now the well-established path for just about every public health and safety area in American life because we recognize that the typical voter lacks the requisite data and knowledge to make the best decisions in these areas. We understand that we would get inferior outcomes if instead we relied upon the emotional preferences of the body politic or politicians' intuitive guesses about what is likely to work.

Yet that is precisely what we do when it comes to decisions about public safety and crime control. We do not rely on experts or use studies and rational assessment to minimize crime. Instead, criminal justice policy in the United States is set largely based on emotions and the gut reactions of laypeople. We have been doing this for decades, with the public and politicians reacting to stories or panics about crime with ill-informed laws and punitive policies that extend far beyond the high-profile event that sparked them and without much thought about whether the response will promote public safety. * * *

[As a result,] many of America's criminal justice policies have little to no effect on crime. They take limited public funds that could be better spent on more effective measures for improving public safety. Even worse, many of our crime policies *increase* the risk of crime instead of fighting it—all while producing racially discriminatory outcomes and devaluing individual liberty. * * *

We have these ill-considered policies because we have a pathological political process that caters to the public's fears and emotions without any institutional safeguards or checks for rationality to make sure these policies work or are the best approach to combatting crime. * * *

[If this is going to change, one] critical avenue of institutional reform is to create expert agencies and commissions that are charged with using data and facts to make and recommend policies that maximize public safety. * * * [T]hese agencies should be subject to statutory requirements to stay within certain prison population caps and expenditure limits, which in turn will give these agencies the ability to produce better outcomes and push back against ill-informed populist impulses when those impulses would balloon the prison population or cost too much. These agencies should also be required to have diverse members who are attuned to all the

5

relevant interests in criminal justice administration and who are well connected to key legislators so that their policies will have political support. Of course agencies will still be susceptible to some populist pressures, but these design traits will maximize their ability to resist them. Indeed, we know from the experience of expert criminal justice agencies that already exist that they can and have been successful in making fundamental changes to criminal justice policies that have resulted in better public safety outcomes, lower incarceration rates, cost savings, and far less human misery. The U.S. Sentencing Commission, for example, is not particularly well designed to resist political pressures and has often been used by Congress as just another avenue for increasing punishments. But even that agency was able to reduce more than 30,000 drug sentences retroactively based on its evaluation of data and recidivism studies. * * * It could have been even more effective with a better design, as we have seen in states that have more successful sentencing commissions. We need to empower more agencies to make important criminal policy decisions and design them so that their expertise, not ill-informed emotional responses, guides their policy-making.

ANGELA J. DAVIS—REIMAGINING PROSECUTION: A GROWING PROGRESSIVE MOVEMENT
3 UCLA Crim. Just. L. Rev. 1, 4–5 & 22 (2019).

Prosecutors are the most powerful officials in the criminal justice system. Thus, their discretionary decisions—especially their charging and plea-bargaining decisions—play a very significant role in contributing to mass incarceration and unwarranted racial disparities. Police officers have a tremendous amount of discretion on the street but ultimately only have the power to bring an individual to the courthouse door. It is the prosecutor who decides whether and to what extent that individual will become a part of the criminal justice system.

Prosecutors decide whether an individual will be charged with a crime, and the standard for charging—probable cause—is very easily met, allowing prosecutors to "pile on" charges that they may not be able to prove at trial. This phenomenon, known as "overcharging," gives the prosecutor an advantage at the plea-bargaining stage of the process. An individual facing a long list of charges will be highly motivated to accept a plea bargain that requires him to plead guilty to one or more charges—even if he is not guilty or has a valid defense—just to avoid the possibility of a jury convicting him of all of the charges.

The charging and plea-bargaining decisions are entirely controlled by prosecutors. Just as a prosecutor may decide to "pile on" unmeritorious charges, he may decide to forego charges altogether even if there is evidence to support a conviction. A prosecutor may offer a plea bargain but is not required to do so. He may decide to give one individual a break while prosecuting another similarly situated individual arrested for the same offense. Likewise, prosecutors may offer a better deal to one individual than to another who is similarly situated. This vast discretion in the charging and plea bargaining process often results in unwarranted racial disparities. The disparities may be the result of implicit bias or the result of race neutral factors that have a racial impact. Regardless of the cause, the result is the same: unfair treatment of black and brown people in the criminal justice system.

However, just as the power and discretion of prosecutors have contributed to mass incarceration and racial disparities in the criminal justice system, that same power and discretion may be used to institute reforms to correct these injustices. Many prosecutors aggressively pursue charges in as many cases as possible, seek high cash bail, and advocate for lengthy prison sentences. But a prosecutor instead could use her power and discretion to institute policies and practices that would reduce the incarceration rate and unwarranted racial disparities. . . . In recent years, a growing number of elected prosecutors have chosen this path, attempting to balance the pursuit of public safety with the reduction of the prison and jail population. . . .

Progressive prosecutors are committed to reducing mass incarceration and racial disparities in the criminal justice system. There are several ways prosecutors can achieve these goals. Opposing cash bail can reduce the jail population. Foregoing charges in certain categories of cases and implementing diversion programs may reduce the incarceration rate. Diversion programs that do not require guilty pleas (and hence convictions) make it easier for participants to find employment and housing. Likewise, diversion programs that do not require the payment of fees and fines or impose other difficult conditions are more likely to reduce the number of people in prisons and jails. Prosecutors who commit never to charge juveniles as adults, even when the law permits them to do so, keep juveniles out of the criminal justice system and help to reduce the disproportionate number of black and brown youths tried in adult court. Prosecutors who refuse to seek the death penalty take an important step towards ending the well-documented racial disparities in the implementation of the death penalty. . . .

DANIEL FRYER—RACE, REFORM, & PROGRESSIVE PROSECUTION
110 J. Crim. L. & Criminology 769, 771–72, 779–80, 787–800 (2020).

Our penal society is shaped by longstanding stereotypes of black criminality, a complex relationship between racial capitalism and carceral punishment, and a general desire to promote white supremacy. Thus, although the recent movement of "progressive prosecution" is lauded as the solution to the flaws of our system, we may be skeptical about the potential reach of these prosecutors who are viewing issues in a new light. This is not to say that the movement isn't promising. Yet endorsements encouraging those "concerned about how the criminal justice system treats African-Americans" to focus their energy on electing prosecutors should be met with caution. . . . To the extent prosecutors have a lot of power, it is because other actors permit them to have it. . . .

Since contact with other officials in the criminal justice system is often procedurally antecedent to prosecutors, it makes intuitive sense that these other officials hold more power than prosecutors. For example, police are "first movers" who typically have to make a decision before prosecutors get involved. And legislatures could prevent cases from falling on prosecutors' desks by decriminalizing conduct. Indeed, . . . prosecutorial power [is] contingent on prosecutors' ability to make recommendations that others—police, juries, judges, and parole boards—follow. . . . Rather than viewing prosecutors as having unilateral power to affect mass incarceration and racial justice, it instead appears that prosecutors have a *contingent power*—that is, one that is dependent on other criminal justice officials assisting them in attaining their goals. . . .

Although progressive prosecutors may reduce the rate at which people are sentenced, without compliance from the police officers the movement may not do much to change the everyday racial mistreatment encountered by persons outside of the courtroom.

Or consider a situation where legislatures decide not to defer to prosecutors. They may reduce prosecutor offices' budgets, reduce the discretion that prosecutors have in cases, or even—following what is done in several jurisdictions—permit police officers to litigate cases themselves. Further, a legislature dissatisfied with the way a local prosecutor's office is handling cases could follow Pennsylvania's example and give the State Attorney General's office concurrent jurisdiction over those cases. Similarly, a governor may reassign cases from a progressive prosecutor's office to another office that is not so progressive. And the DOJ—which is staffed via presidential appointment—could pursue federal charges against offenders who would ordinarily be prosecuted locally. The real issue with treating prosecutorial power as unilateral is that it fails to realize the ways other officials are able to diminish the power of the prosecutors when they refuse to defer. The power to create the problems does not entail the power to fix them. . . .

The upshot of all this is that reformists should move beyond the assumption that prosecutorial power is unilateral and advance a goal that simultaneously targets all powerful criminal justice officials. A prosecutor with a tenuous relationship to other criminal justice officials (legislators, police, judges, parole boards, etc.) may not be as effective as one who has a strong relationship with them. The point is not that reformists should not continue to push for progressive prosecutors. The point is that reformists should appreciate the importance of other criminal justice officials as they continue to advance reform. . . .

I [also] want to challenge a second assumption that advocates of progressive prosecution appear to hold: that black Americans would be the beneficiaries of the reform progressive prosecutors advance. . . . Many of the aims frequently articulated by progressive prosecutors appear to contain tools that are just as likely to exacerbate racial inequalities in our criminal justice system. . . .

At first sight, it seems obvious that progressive prosecution would alleviate the racial injustice in our criminal justice system. "[T]here are unwarranted racial disparities at every step of the criminal process . . . . Black men are six times as likely to be incarcerated as white men, and Latino men are twice as likely to be incarcerated as white men." In addition, for those born in 2001, the lifetime probability of incarceration for black boys is estimated to be 32%, for Latino boys it is 17%, and for white boys it is 6%. And the decisions from prosecutors—from charging, to plea bargaining, to sentencing recommendations—"play a very significant role in contributing to mass incarceration and unwarranted racial disparities." . . .

[But,] we need to distinguish more clearly between when prosecutors are seeking to correct mass incarceration and when they are seeking to correct racial injustice. Although there is some overlap between the two, they also come apart. For example, one could implement policies that decarcerate the population without addressing any of the structural racism on which our criminal justice system is built. . . .

When we look at some of the policies of progressive prosecutors, it becomes clear that the movement may not even remain neutral in its effect on the racial injustice in our system. Rather, the policies advanced have the potential to undermine racial inequality and perpetuate racial disparities.

Take diversion, for example. Diversion programs are often thought to be the "hallmarks of progressive prosecution." They allow defendants the opportunity to avoid incarceration if they meet certain conditions. Once a participant completes the program, charges are dismissed, and the participant avoids a criminal conviction and all of its collateral consequences. . . . However, "[e]very defendant charged with a misdemeanor or nonviolent felony [does] not receive diversion." "Eligibility is determined by a detailed assessment of each defendant that includes an examination of his criminal record, background, lifestyle, and other relevant factors." . . . "[A]ny discretionary screening decision in the American criminal justice system raises concerns about racial bias and other pernicious factors." Since diversion requires prosecutors to exercise their discretion, we are likely to see the same bias and false beliefs that infect other areas of the criminal process. For example, "[p]olls suggest that the majority of white people think that blacks are violent." And one's potential to be violent is likely to be one of the "relevant factors" considered when making a decision to place someone in diversion. The likely consequence is that those who are white and viewed as if they "do not belong in prison" are offered these diversion programs more often than those who are black and viewed as violent. . . .

Moreover, a diversion program based on race-neutral policies would be unreasonable if it fails to consider the effects that racial injustice had on an offender's prior arrest, charging, or sentencing. And many prosecutors' offices have diversion programs designed for first-time offenders. But progressive prosecutors will likely confront offenders who have prior offenses because of racially-charged policing and prosecution from a prior administration. . . . The point here is that any neutral criteria used for these programs are likely to exacerbate the problems that have already plagued black individuals who end up in the criminal justice system because racial inequality is already an essential part of it. . . .

[A]s we move forward with these programs, we have to consciously avoid placing the burden on the least well off. A decarceration program that does not deliberately seek racial justice could be counterproductive and perpetuate harms against black Americans. . . .

Perhaps the most worrisome aspect of focusing on decarceration without an eye on racial injustice is not that there would be a continued overenforcement of prosecution in racially-marginalized communities, but that there may be a disproportionate *underenforcement* of prosecution in these communities. . . . One of the consequences of our unjust social system is that not only do blacks disproportionately end up as defendants, blacks also disproportionately end up as victims. Any progressive movement seeking to right the wrongs of our justice system must note that certain crimes disproportionately affect black people in vulnerable communities. . . . We cannot forget that leniency is sometimes regarded as the common way in which a state expresses that black lives don't matter. . . . If progressive prosecutors want to achieve successful reform, a simultaneous attack on both mass incarceration and the neglect of injuries to those in marginalized communities must be central to their agenda.

§ 2. RACIAL INJUSTICE

15th ed., p. 42; before the Notes and Questions, add:

I. BENNETT CAPERS—*CITIZENSHIP TALK IN* THE CAMBRIDGE HANDBOOK OF POLICING IN THE UNITED STATES

Cambridge Law Handbooks, pp. 473–490 (T. Lave & E. Miller eds. 2019).

Blue on black police violence is not new; though the ubiquity of smartphone cameras and other video recordings have certainly rendered such violence visible. We watch the dying moments of Eric Garner being placed in a chokehold and crying, "I can't breathe," and wonder again about the wisdom of aggressive police tactics and escalation. We watch the footage of Shakara, the foster student who was flipped out of her desk by a school resource officer for failing to put away her cell phone fast enough, and wonder about the school to prison pipeline. We remember Michael Brown shot by a police officer in Ferguson, Missouri—the only surveillance footage is from before the encounter, but images of police shootings are by now so familiar that we imagine we have seen the rest—and think about residential segregation. We see the video of Sandra Bland being dragged from her car following a traffic violation simply for declining to put out her cigarette, and have conversations about unfettered police authority. We see the video of Scott Wilson, prostrate on the ground, and wonder how a person could be shot in the back after being pulled over for a broken tail light. We wonder too what would have happened if a bystander hadn't caught the image of the police shooting on his phone, including the image of the police planting evidence, especially since the officer claimed he shot in self-defense, and everyone knows that a police officer's word is truer than a civilian's, especially if the police officer is white and the civilian is black, especially if the civilian is dead, and probably especially in the South. Indeed, such images and the role they play in countering police narratives reminds us why Lolita Buckner Innis describes cameras as equivalent to a "white witness."

And these are just some of the names. Now, images of police violence seem so ubiquitous that many of us barely notice. . . . Still, we watch the videos on social media and online. We note the news stories. Indeed, the news stories, made newsworthy by the presence of video, appear so frequently that *The Huffington Post* now devotes an entire section to police brutality. The repetition is numbing, but still we watch. . . .

I have not yet mentioned that I am a black man, though by now it may be obvious. Since I believe "the subject position is everything in my analysis of the law," I'll again make it very clear. I am a black man. Unfortunately, I am a black man in a country where race and policing seem inseparable.

[Right now,] in barbershops and hair salons, in churches and yes, prisons [and mostly in] homes[,] black and brown parents [are having "the talk"] with their children, especially boys, about how to "act" around the police. And about how to come back home.

It is this far more intimate talk that is the focus of this brief essay, and that provides the impetus for the argument I want to make. My argument is that the talk is incomplete, at least to my way of thinking. After all, there is a crucial aspect to policing that is entirely absent from most talks: the role the Supreme Court has played in enabling racialized policing and blue on black violence.

For starters, then, I want to argue for adding to the talk: it is not only the police we should prepare our children for. It is also the Court, the supposed protector of individual rights, because the truth is it is very unlikely the Court will "have their backs." It has not had their backs for some time. Thus, the first goal of this chapter is to broaden the talk.

[An additional goal] returns to "the talk," [and] urges others who are not black or brown or shielded in blue to really listen to the talk, and in turn change *their* talk. I am thinking here of the Court, which all too often engages in talk that unfairly valorizes the police, that elevates the police, that confers upon them a type of immunity that enables racialized policing while at the same time reducing citizens to citizen subjects. I am thinking too of the police themselves, who too often hear the Court's talk as granting them "above the law" status. As in a game of telephone, the police in turn promote that talk among themselves to justify a top-down policing, to justify a warrior mentality, to justify taking literally the notion of a *war* against crime. Too many police hear the Court's talk and use it to justify talk among themselves and to citizens that says "Whose streets? Our streets!" Lastly, I am thinking of the rest of us—everyday citizens. Perhaps by acknowledging the talk so many black and brown parents have with their children, every day citizens will be spurred to engage in another type of talk: one that is about equal citizenship, and about "mak[ing] America what America must become"—"fair, egalitarian, responsive to the needs of all of its citizens, and truly democratic in all respects, including its policing." Or at least that is the hope.

The Talk

Black parents know the talk. Black sons know the talk. Eric Holder, the country's first African-American Attorney General, received the talk from his father. And Eric Holder in turn gave it to his son. The talk has even come up in a Supreme Court opinion. Dissenting in Utah v. Strieff, a case which in effect gave police officers carte blanche to stop individuals to conduct warrant checks even when officers lack probable cause or reasonable suspicion, Justice Sotomayor referenced the talk in arguing that the majority's decision would have a disproportionate impact on black and brown people, compounding the already existing problem of racialized policing. She stated, "For generations, black and brown parents have given their children 'the talk'—instructing them never to run down the street; always keep your hands where they can be seen; do not even think of talking back to a stranger—all out of fear of how an officer with a gun will react to them."
. . .

To be clear, what has become known as the talk is not limited to black and Latino kids. The "talk" extends to some Muslim American families. And as the country becomes increasingly mixed race, more and more whites are giving the talk to their children of color. . . .

But perhaps because I am a black man writing "against a sharp white background," to borrow from Zora Neale Hurston, it is my own talk, the one my own parents gave to me, that has most informed my thoughts about policing. This is what they instructed me on how I should "act" if accosted by the police:

Don't run. Say, "Yes, sir," or "No, sir." Don't talk back. Keep your head down, don't look them in the eye. That's disrespectful. Say, "Yes, sir," or "No, sir." "Yes, ma'am," or "No, ma'am" if it's a lady cop. Don't act smart. Don't get smart. Just keep your head down and be deferential. Don't ask how come or why. Don't run. If they let you go, say "Thank, you." Don't show your color. Don't act black. A cop will kick your ass in a second, you hear? Don't talk back. Do whatever they say, you hear? Unless he asks you something, shut your mouth and keep it shut. Don't start talking about rights. Definitely don't start talking about black power. What were you doing wearing baggie pants and a hoodie in the first place? What were you doing walking/driving on that side of town any old way? What were you doing looking at his badge number and name? You don't have rights, you hear? Don't run. And you best say, "Yes, sir," or "No, sir."

My point here is not to seek commiseration, or understanding, or even demand 40 acres and a mule. It is simply to make salient to most Americans something that is matter of fact, routine, and inescapable for those of us who are black and brown. It is part of the "pools of knowledge" common to black and brown folk. Indeed, black and brown folk know that police violence is merely the most visible and final byproduct of a system of unequal policing. After all, as I have written elsewhere, every police shooting "begins with a look, a suspicion, an encounter. We can do little to address racialized police violence, if we do nothing to address the far broader issue of racialized looks and encounters." And even if most men of color will never be the victims of police violence, especially those of us cloaked by class privilege, few of us can escape racialized policing. Not Eric Holder, the former US Attorney General. Not Republican Senator Tim Scott. Not astrophysicist Neil DeGrasse Tyson. Not Harvard Professor and PBS staple Henry Louis Gates, Jr. And certainly not professors of law.

Here is the thing though: the talk says too little. After all, the unequal policing that we face is inextricably linked to the almost unfettered discretion the Court has given police, and to the Court's repeatedly tipping the scales to favor the police. In short, it is not just a talk about policing that is urgent, but also a talk about the Court.

Court Talk

African-Americans in particular have long looked to the Court as a protector of their rights. As on *their* side. Indeed, in the legal academy, this view contributed in part to the formation of the Critical Race Theory movement. Many scholars who now identify at Critical Race Theory scholars initially aligned themselves with the Critical Legal Studies movement. It was the Critical Legal Studies movement's disdain for rights that prompted many African-American and Latino scholars to leave Critical Legal Studies and form Critical Race Theory.

Even outside legal academia and ivory towers, the narrative of the Court being a protector of rights was a common one. And continues to be. For many African-Americans, the Court is forever associated with Brown v. Board of Education, the case that sounded the death knell of de jure school segregation. Even when it comes to race and policing, many blacks, especially older ones, are likely to think of the Court as their defender. Even if many older African-Americans do not know the names of Warren Court cases from the 1960s that attempted to level the playing field between minorities and the police—think Duncan v. Louisiana, or Miranda v. Arizona, or even

Gideon v. Wainwright—they likely recall the politics of the time. Richard Nixon, after all, ran a law-and-order campaign in which appointing justices to combat the Court's anti-law enforcement decisions was a crucial part.

But in reality, the Court's role in protecting individual rights vis-à-vis the police is not so laudable. Indeed, one reason why the "talk" remains necessary is because of the Court.

Consider just a handful of cases. There is Terry v. Ohio, which came near the end of the Warren Court era, and which played a crucial role in enabling the current state of policing. Although the practice of officers engaging in forcible stops and frisks without probable cause was not new, what was new was the issue before the Court: how such practices could possibly be consistent with the Fourth Amendment of the Constitution, which had been understood as requiring warrants and probable cause. In *Terry* itself, a detective had observed two African-American men repeatedly peering through a store window and, suspecting the two men were "casing a job, a stick-up," grabbed the men and patted them down. Both men had guns, and they were charged with carrying concealed weapons. The "problem" was that the detective did not first have probable cause to forcibly stop the men. To get around this problem, the Court, out of whole cloth, re-interpreted the Fourth Amendment to permit stops based on an entirely new standard, one that required far less than probable cause. The Court held that so long as an officer has specific and articulable facts to believe that "criminal activity is afoot," an officer can engage in a limited detention of the person. In addition, if the officer separately has reasonable suspicion that the person is armed and dangerous, the officer can couple the limited detention with a pat-down for weapons. In short, the Court gave its blessing to what is now commonly known of as stop-and-frisk. Importantly, the Court recognized that its decision was likely to have a disproportionate effect on racial and other minorities. However, faced with a choice of whether to protect the rights of minorities and furthering the goal of equality, or whether to give its blessing to this policing tool, the Court chose the latter. The end result was thus not only a decision that disadvantaged Terry, whose conviction on gun charges was upheld. The end result is also the aggressive stop-and-frisk practices that police engage in today. . . .

A recounting of the many cases that enable the current state of policing must also include Whren v. United States, in which the Court ruled that the subjective, even racist, motivations of a police officer in singling out a particular individual are largely irrelevant under the Fourth Amendment. As long as the stop itself is supported by reasonable suspicion (in the case of a stop) or probable cause (in the case of an arrest), the stop will be valid. . . .

For parents who tell their black sons especially how to behave when pulled over for a traffic violation, it is to Wren v. United States that they owe this honor, because since *Wren*, police have used traffic violations—which everyone commits—to target blacks and Hispanics. . . .

For [ ] investigatory stops, black drivers are nearly three times more likely than white drivers to be stopped, and five times more likely to have their cars searched. . . . [T]he Court itself, the nominal protector of minority rights, in fact gave its imprimatur to this type of discretionary enforcement. . . .

Some years ago, Justice Stevens observed that the Court, rather than standing up for individual rights and the rights of minorities, had become a "loyal foot soldier" of the police. It shows. . . .

If we begin with *Terry*, the Court goes from expressing some concern about the balance of power between the police and the citizen, and even concern about the racial impact of this balancing (albeit in two footnotes), to something far more one-sided. In its later cases, the deference to the police is practically absolute, so much so that in Muehler v. Mena the Court treated the handcuffing of a Latina, who was merely present in a location to be searched, for two hours as a mere "marginal intrusion." And as the Court has increased its deference to officers, it has curtailed its concern for citizens more and more. In earlier work, I referred to police practices such as racial profiling as being "citizenship-diminishing." In fact, it would have been more accurate to also include the Court. Much of the Court's criminal procedure jurisprudence is also citizenship-diminishing.

The second aspect of this criminal procedure jurisprudence is related. Rather than addressing race—so often the elephant in the room in criminal procedure cases—the Court studiously avoids race. One is reminded of the novelist Toni Morrison's observation that "the habit of ignoring race is understood to be a graceful, even generous, liberal gesture." Except one senses the Court's avoidance of race in its criminal procedure talk is far more strategic. In short, at the same time black and brown parents have been giving their children "the talk" about race and policing and equality, the Court itself has taken pains to avoid talk about race and policing and equality. . . .

When We All Talk

[I]magine[ ] what benefits might flow if those who are not black or brown or shielded in blue, instead of turning a deaf ear to the warnings black and brown parents give their children, actually listened to the talk, and in turn change *their* talk. Specifically, what might it mean for the Court to change its talk? Or the police to change theirs? Indeed, what might it mean for everyday Americans to change their talk, and to talk about equality? To be sure, this may seem overly optimistic, or even wishful thinking. . . . Still, it is a goal worth pursuing.

Consider the Court, which too often engages in talk—through its judicial opinions—that tips the scales in favor of the police and too often treats citizens, especially black and brown citizens, as citizen subjects. The Court's talk plays a critical role in marking who belongs, and who does not. Who is entitled to be treated as a regular citizen, and who can be treated as second class. Its talk also includes expectations of what it means to be a good citizen. There is language in *Miranda*, for example, that suggests the good citizen willingly answers questions put to him by a police officer; language in Schneckloth v. Bustamonte that the good citizen willingly consents to police searches; language in Illinois v. Wardlow that the good citizen does not evade the police; language in Illinois v. Lidster that individuals should react "positively when police simply ask for their help as 'responsible citizens.' " All of this has racial undertones, especially since criminal procedure cases, even when race is unsaid, are often "race" cases. All of these cases communicate that racial minorities in particular must do "citizenship" work—specifically, they must be extra deferential, acquiesce to demands, and in effect relinquish citizenship rights. As I have written recently, the "double-bind is not just that to warrant the treatment normally accorded white citizens, we must 'work' our citizenship. The double-bind is that the citizenship we must perform is that of the obedient citizen. The docile citizen. The non-problem citizen. And yes, the second class citizen."

At the same time that the Court's talk communicates what it means to be a good citizen— deferential to authority, compliant, docile—the Court's talk plays a critical role in exalting the police; the police are "always-already" deserving of deference; they have earned the right to exercise discretion. The police certainly should not be questioned. In this sense, the Court's talk socially constructs the "good cop" who, in the imagination of the Court, "cares solely about getting the bad guy off the street and bringing him to justice, is law-abiding, does not engage in racialized policing, and is certainly inclined to adhere to any constraints placed on him by the Court." Most importantly, in the Court's talk, the police and the policed are not equal. But imagine what might happen if the Court really listened to the talk that so many black and brown parents find themselves compelled to give their children, and recognized that all is not well. That unequal policing is inconsistent with our democratic project. Imagine what might happen if the Court, having heard "the talk," in turn changed its talk to emphasize rights, equality, and even the value of dissent.

For this chapter, allow me to focus on equality. Simply changing its language to valorize equality has the potential to change police-citizen encounters. [The Court has stated] that equal protection is a matter for "the Equal Protection Clause, not the Fourth Amendment." The effect was the Court engaging in something "akin to constitutional segregation"; equality may be a concern of the Fourteenth Amendment, but it is not a concern of the criminal procedure amendments. But this is not the only way to read the Fourth Amendment. One could easily read the Bill of Rights, including the Fourth Amendment, as incorporating the equality concern that animates the Fourteenth Amendment's Equal Protection Clause. So imagine how such an emphasis on equality under the law could change the outcomes [in cases] in which the Court vested the police with almost unfettered discretion to engage in unequal treatment. Imagine how it might change the dynamic in police-citizen encounters if the Court, in its decisions, included asides about the importance of the police treating all citizens equally. If it emphasized that equality, too, is implicit in the Fourth Amendment's reasonableness clause. More radical still, imagine the Court including language to remind officers that at the end of the day, they are not supermen to citizens, or overseers to citizens. In the eyes of the Constitution, they are simply this: equals.

And reimagining how the Court talks is only the beginning. Right now, the police too often interpret the Court's talk as giving them carte blanche to exercise a warrior mentality, to be authoritarian, to show "who's the man," and to act in ways that are deeply racialized. But we can also imagine the police hearing "the talk," really hearing it, and one day changing *their* talk. Part of this may happen as police departments become more diverse, especially when diverse individuals are in positions of power. Part of this may happen too as police departments internalize the Court's new language. But certainly it is possible to imagine the police shifting their talk to recast themselves as protectors of the community, not its adversary. Certainly it is possible to imagine them engaging in talk that, however aspirational, communicates that we are all in this together. That the goal is not only to make sure they're alive and unharmed at the end of the day, but also to make to make sure everyone else is alive and unharmed at the end of the day, potential crime victims and actual criminals alike. Perhaps it is even possible to imagine them chanting "Whose streets? Our streets!" and meaning something entirely different, something inclusive, and something that celebrates equality.

Lastly, the goal should be encouraging the rest of us—those who are neither black nor brown nor shielded by blue—to really hear the talk and recognize that equal citizenship cannot exist if there is unequal policing. Perhaps then, we can truly finish the project of "mak[ing] America what America must become."

DEVON W. CARBADO—FROM STOPPING BLACK PEOPLE TO KILLING BLACK PEOPLE: THE FOURTH AMENDMENT PATHWAYS TO POLICE VIOLENCE
105 Calif. L. Rev. 125, 127–31 (2017).

Why are African Americans so often the victims of police violence? Why are police officers so rarely prosecuted for the acts of violence they commit? And why, when officers are prosecuted, do judges and juries seldom hold them accountable? These are just some of the questions that people across the United States continue to ask in what we might call "post-Ferguson America."

But our collective engagement of the foregoing questions has elided an important dimension of the police violence problem: Fourth Amendment law. It permits police officers to force interactions with African Americans with little or no basis. This "front-end" police contact—which Fourth Amendment law enables—is often the predicate to "back-end" police violence—which Fourth Amendment law should help to prevent.

A report by the Missouri Attorney General reveals that black residents in Ferguson have had significant front-end contact with the police. Ferguson is roughly 67 percent black and 29 percent white. Out of 611 searches that police officers in Ferguson conducted in 2013, 562 (90 percent) were of African Americans, while 47 (8 percent) were of whites. Moreover, of the 21 searches that lasted between 16 and 30 minutes, 20 were of African Americans and 1 was of a white person. With respect to stops, the statistics, though less stark in their racial disparity, at the very least raise a question about whether the Ferguson police were engaged in racial profiling. Of 2,489 stops, 1,983 (80 percent) were of African Americans and 469 (19 percent) were of whites. When police officers stopped cars for investigatory purposes (i.e., for reasons other than traffic infractions), they likewise focused their attention on African Americans. Of such searches, 328 of 363 (90 percent) were of African Americans; only 27 (7 percent) were of whites. Finally, Ferguson police arrest records reveal a similar racial pattern. Whereas 4,632 out of 5,384 (86 percent) of the arrests were of African Americans, 686 (13 percent) were of whites. A 2015 U.S. Department of Justice report tells the same basic story.

Racially disproportionate policing is endemic elsewhere in the country, too, as recent litigation over police overuse of stops-and-frisks in New York City attests. Across the United States, police officers routinely force interactions with African Americans. Because these interactions are often the precursors to excessive force, including homicide, they should figure more prominently in our analysis of police violence.

Writing in a different context, Angela Y. Davis makes a very similar point. She observes:

> We tend to think about torture as an aberrant event. Torture is extraordinary and can be clearly distinguished from other regimes of punishment. But if we consider the various forms of violence linked to the practice of imprisonment—circuits of violence linked to one another—then we begin to see that the extraordinary has some connection to the ordinary.

Davis's point about torture applies to police killings. By and large, Americans tend to think of police killings of African Americans as aberrant and extraordinary, failing to see their connections to the routine, to the everyday, and to the ordinary. A central aim of this Article is to disrupt that tendency. I do so by highlighting the significant "circuits of violence" through which the ordinary (African Americans' vulnerability to ongoing police surveillance and contact) becomes the extraordinary (serious bodily injury and death). Informing this focus is my view that if the law more tightly restricted police officers' authority to investigate African Americans, this would both increase the social value of our lives and diminish officers' opportunities to kill us. For there is a direct relationship between the scope of ordinary police authority, on the one hand, and African American vulnerability to extraordinary police violence, on the other. This Article focuses on the former—ordinary police authority—to reveal how it can function as a predicate for the latter—extraordinary police violence.

A significant part of the problem is Fourth Amendment law. Few people understand that the Fourth Amendment is one of the most important constitutional provisions for regulating police conduct. More important than the Miranda warnings, more important than the right to counsel, more important than equal protection and due process rights, Fourth Amendment law is ground zero for understanding the constitutional constraints on police investigation practices. It is Fourth Amendment law that determines when the police can engage us, and it is Fourth Amendment law that determines the circumstances under which those engagements are reasonable. Because every encounter police officers have with African Americans is a potential killing field, it is crucial that we understand how Fourth Amendment law effectively "pushes" police officers to target African Americans and "pulls" African Americans into contact with the police. Racial profiling is an important part of the story.

Over the past four decades, the Supreme Court has interpreted the Fourth Amendment to enable and sometimes expressly legalize racial profiling. By racial profiling I mean, borrowing from Randall Kennedy, a process in which police officers use "race as a factor in deciding who to place under suspicion and/or surveillance." As I will show, the Court's legalization of racial profiling exposes African Americans not only to the violence of ongoing police surveillance and contact but also to the violence of serious bodily injury and death. Put another way, the legalization of racial profiling facilitates the precarious line between stopping black people and killing black people.

The claim that the Court enables and sometimes expressly authorizes racial profiling might sound like hyperbole, but it is not. To understand the scope of the problem, it is helpful to distinguish between the de jure legalization of racial profiling (or instances in which it is permissible as a matter of law under Fourth Amendment doctrine for police officers to employ race as a basis for suspicion) and the de facto legalization of racial profiling (or instances in which Fourth Amendment law turns a blind eye to racial profiling or makes it easy for the police to get away with the practice). Throughout this Article I will sometimes speak generally about the legalization of racial profiling. When I do so, I mean to refer to both the de jure and the de facto dimensions of the problem.

The Supreme Court's legalization of racial profiling is embedded in the very structure of Fourth Amendment doctrine. At the core of this doctrine is a prohibition against unreasonable searches and seizures. The Court's inquiry as to whether the government violates this prohibition is twofold. The first, or what I call the "trigger question," is: Does a police officer's conduct constitute a search or seizure under the Fourth Amendment? The second, or what I call the "justification question," asks: Assuming that police conduct constitutes a search or seizure, is that search or seizure reasonable, and hence justified? By persistently answering the former question negatively (the Fourth Amendment was not triggered) and the latter question affirmatively (a search or seizure was justified), the Supreme Court has legalized racial profiling. This legalization of racial profiling has left African Americans less secure in their "persons, papers, houses and effects"—and sometimes dead. Put another way, African Americans often experience the Fourth Amendment as a system of surveillance, social control, and violence, not as a constitutional boundary that protects them from unreasonable searches and seizures.

This Article . . . discusses the cases in which the Supreme Court has ruled that particular police practices fall outside the scope of the Fourth Amendment. The discussion includes immigration enforcement cases and war on terror surveillance practices. My aim is to demonstrate—with some specificity—the broad discretion police officers have to force race-based interactions with African Americans without triggering the Fourth Amendment.

[I also focus] on the Fourth Amendment's "justification" analysis, or the cases in which the Supreme Court decides whether a particular search or seizure is reasonable. My point of departure is traffic stops. That traffic infractions can be a site for racial profiling will surprise no one. Presumably, we are all by now familiar with the pithy if demoralizing expressions "Driving While Black" or "Driving While Brown." [T]he racial profiling problem that traffic stops present transcends the stop itself. Stopping a car is one of a range of legal options Fourth Amendment law empowers the officer to pursue. The existence of these options, including the authority to arrest, renders traffic stops gateway seizures. The options open the door to more intrusive, potentially violence-producing—but constitutionally reasonable—encounters with the police. . . .

Fourth Amendment doctrine expressly authorizes or facilitates the very social practice it ought to prevent: racial profiling. This authorization and facilitation exposes African Americans not only to the violence of frequent police contact but also to the violence of police killings and physical abuse.

15th ed., p. 42; at the end of Note 1, add:

Consider also *United States v. Brown*, 925 F.3d 1150 (9th Cir. 2019) (relying on a 2011 Department of Justice Report that found "a pattern or practice of unnecessary or excessive force" and "serious concerns" about racially discriminatory policing by the Seattle Police Department to emphasize that African Americans and Latinos in Seattle might flee from the police for reasons other than guilt and noting that data about how minorities are treated by the police "can inform the inferences to be drawn from an individual who decides to step away, run, or flee from police without a clear reason to do otherwise"). *But see United States v. Knights*, 989 F.3d 1281 (11th Cir. 2021) (discussed Note 7, Supp. p. 50).

15th ed., p. 43; in Note 3, after the citation to CRIMPRO § 1.5(j), add:

See also North Carolina Task Force for Racial Equity in Criminal Justice, 2020 Report, *available at* https://ncdoj.gov/wp-content/uploads/2020/12/TRECReportFinal_12132020.pdf (discussing possible legislative restrictions on policing that would serve racial justice ends, many of which have been adopted already in other states including, for example, prohibitions on chokeholds, limiting the use of no-knock warrants, and requiring police to wear body cameras).

15th ed., p. 48; change the citation for the Taylor excerpt as follows:

The Atlantic (November 1, 2001).

§ 4. MISDEMEANORS

15th ed., p. 53; add the following to footnote a:

See also Sandra G. Mayson & Megan T. Stevenson, *Misdemeanors by the Numbers,* 61 B.C. L. Rev. 971 (2020); Megan T. Stevenson & Sandra G. Mayson, *The Scale of Misdemeanor Justice*, 98 B.U. L. Rev. 731 (2018).

§ 5. REMEDIES FOR GOVERNMENT MISCONDUCT

15th ed., p. 59; before Section 6, add:

SCOTT CALVERT & DAN FROSCH—POLICE RETHINK POLICIES AS CITIES PAY MILLIONS TO SETTLE MISCONDUCT CLAIMS
The Wall Street Journal (October 22, 2020).

The 20 U.S. cities and counties with the biggest police departments have paid over $2 billion since 2015 for alleged misconduct and civil rights violations, according to a Wall Street Journal analysis.

The payments have settled allegations of excessive force, wrongful detention and other abuses that sometimes stretch back decades and in extreme cases resulted in death or permanent injury.

New York City, the nation's largest police department, has rung up more than $1.1 billion in payouts since 2015, followed by Chicago at about $253 million, according to data gathered by the Journal through public-records requests. Los Angeles County paid out more than $238 million since fiscal year 2015.

Police departments have faced increased scrutiny from politicians and protesters over their funding and treatment of minorities since the killing of George Floyd in Minneapolis police custody in May. Officials in several cities said they now use misconduct claims to guide police reforms, with the goal of reducing incidents that can spur potentially costly lawsuits.

Chicago is using claims data to identify root causes and modify police policies and procedures, said Tamika Puckett, the city's chief risk officer, a position created last year by Mayor Lori Lightfoot, a Democrat.

"We haven't always taken that approach," Ms. Puckett said. "What we're trying to do is prevent what happened in the past from reoccurring." . . .

Houston Police Chief Art Acevedo, who serves as president of the Major Cities Chiefs Association, said chiefs are examining the conduct that leads to settlements—not just in their own departments but nationwide. "There's consequences to these payouts," he said. "Litigation that visits City A today will more than likely visit City B tomorrow." . . .

The number and size of payouts are higher in places that favor plaintiffs because of factors like the attitudes of judges and juries, more expansive state laws and propensity of cities to settle, according to University of California, Los Angeles law professor Joanna Schwartz.

Police officers hardly ever pay personally, and police departments seldom have to sacrifice any part of their funding, according to [Professor] Schwartz's research.

§ 6. POLICE DEPARTMENT HIRING AND TRAINING

15th ed., p. 63; after the Final Report of the President's Task Force on 21st Century Policing, add:

But consider Robin S. Engel, Hannah D. McManus & Gabrielle T. Isaza, Moving Beyond "Best Practice": Experiences in Police Reform and a Call for Evidence to Reduce Officer-Involved Shootings, The Annals of the American Academy (January 2020), available at https://journals.sagepub.com/doi/pdf/10.1177/0002716219889328 (arguing for more evidence-based approaches to police reform and exploring the dearth of available data about the effectiveness of five of the most popular police reforms: (1) deploying body-worn cameras; (2) de-escalation training; (3) implicit bias training; (4) early intervention systems; and (5) civilian oversight boards).

§ 7. THE MOVEMENT TO DEFUND THE POLICE

JESSICA M. EAGLIN—TO "DEFUND" THE POLICE
73 Stanford L. Rev. Online 120 (2021).

Much public debate circles around grassroots activists' demand to "defund the police," raised in public consciousness in the summer of 2020. Yet confusion about the demand is pervasive. [There are] four alternative, substantive policy positions that legal reforms related to police funding can validate. . . . To defund the police can refer to a long-term policy aim to abolish the police, to recalibrate what police do in society, to create accountability measures through conditional funding, or simply to save government resources.

A.   Police Abolition

Abolitionists challenge the idea that imprisonment and policing are a solution for social, political, and economic problems in the United States. They believe that after years of trying to "reform" the police, reform efforts are doomed to fail. Abolitionists emphasize that the police are an institution designed to surveil and control marginalized populations, particularly black people. Accordingly, the aim should be abolishing the police and other arms of the "prison industrial complex" in order to reimagine public safety. The abolitionist project is both pragmatic—for example, reducing police presence should also reduce police killings—and existential—in that it reflects a long-term goal of replacing police with alternative means of ensuring safety. . . .

From the abolitionist perspective, defunding the police is a first step toward abolishing the police. It is a demand to enact "nonreformist reforms" of the police, by beginning to divest from police and from the expanding carceral state. Importantly, abolitionists neither seek to eliminate police tomorrow nor to exist in a world without replacements. Rather, they seek to create ways to connect that are sensitive to the needs of the most marginalized in society, particularly intersectionally vulnerable black people. In the long term, such a world would not include police, in any form or for any function. Defunding the police moves society in that direction.

B.   Police Recalibration

To defund the police can also mean supporting the idea that we need to reprioritize existing public resources to create healthier communities. Significant amounts of public resources to toward police, yet more policing does not always make a community safer, particularly when considering economically disadvantaged black and brown communities. Other forms of public spending could increase safety more effectively while also creating a more equitable society. While abolitionists seek to transform society by ending policing, recalibrationists seek to transform it by altering police responsibilities. Those changes can occur through reductions in funding to police. . . .

Like abolitionists, policymakers urging recalibration-oriented defunding reforms are deeply concerned with structural marginalization. . . . To recalibrationists, the point of reductions in police funding is not the long-term elimination of all police; rather, it is the transformation of their function in society. . . .

Both [abolitionists and recalibrationists] seek to build alternative ways to ensure safety in communities, yet recalibrationists seek to explicitly change police organizations as well. Because abolitionists envision a long-term end to policing, such transformations are, at best, a side effect. For recalibrationists, the effect on policing is the point. From the recalibration perspective, to defund the police can be a first step toward foundationally transforming the police, which can in turn transform society, too.

C.   Police Oversight

Defunding the police could also fit within the managerialist idea that we need to reprioritize allocation of our constrained public resources to better shape the behavior of police departments and individual police officers. That police lack accountability is a well-established problem in legal and policy circles. Managerialists suggest that funding can be the lever to create needed police accountability. By attaching funding to technocratic metrics that measure lawful or effective policing, managerialists aim to "use the power of the purse" to shift policing practices. While incentivizing adherence to such metrics need not lead to reductions in funding to police departments, managerialists suggest that it could. In this sense, the manipulation of success measurements may reduce currently guaranteed funding to state and local police departments while incentivizing different department-wide, system policing practices. . . .

Unlike the first or second interpretations, the managerial or oversight interpretation of "defunding" is oriented around the lawfulness or effectiveness of the police. The point of funding reform is not to change society, but to make police better at the existing panoply of tasks society expects them to do. That is, the central purpose of this kind of defunding would be to control individual officers through systemic reforms. If manipulating funding streams reduces the significance of structural marginalization, that is a welcome side-effect of the reform. But it is not the central purpose. Thus, proponents of the managerialist frame are more likely to speak of individual bias and discretion. And they are more likely to consider structural forces that subordinate racial minorities to be beyond the reach of police reforms. . . .

D.   Fiscal Constraints

Finally, defunding the police could relate to the idea that resources are scarce in the public sector, so all government agencies have a responsibility to tighten their belts. The primary aim is reducing costs, not transforming policing institutions, though fiscal-constraint-type reforms tend to have that effect as well. Under this interpretation, defunding the police is just that—an effort to reduce government spending in the area of criminal administration without any commitment to changes in practices and policies. . . .

The fiscal-constraint interpretation of defunding the police likely conflicts with efforts to address structural marginalization as such reforms tend to entrench the marginalizing structures. . . . For example, a fiscal-constraints orientation can facilitate the expansion of proprietary, data-driven technology to allow police to continue proactive policing at a lower cost while avoiding critical engagement with whether the practice should continue at all. . . .

Like managerialists, cost-reductionists may not consider themselves to be defunding the police. Rather, both envision themselves as embracing principles of good management. Both focus narrowly, emphasizing the allocation of money within police budgets. Both are committed to actively funding police departments rather than intentionally removing funding from their budgets. In this sense, managerialists and cost-reductionists are both a world away from abolitionists and recalibrationists. However, managerialists and cost-reductionists diverge in one very important way. While managerialists are concerned with shaping individual officers' behavior through systematic reforms, cost-reductionists are preoccupied with savings. . . .

* * *

Discursively, the social meaning of "defund the police" emerges from "[o]ne of the most contested planks" of the Black Lives Matter movement: the call to "invest/divest." According to the Movement for Black Lives' policy platform, this means "investments in Black communities, determined by Black communities, and divestment from exploitative forces including prisons, fossil fuels, police, surveillance and exploitative corporations. In recent years, the "invest/divest" demand has morphed into the demand to "defund the police." . . .

That the demand to defund the police challenges our worldview about policing is quite obvious, but bears explaining. Police offer "an interpretive lens through which people make sense of, and give order to, their world." This ontological commitment emerges from a way of thinking that suggests the place where government should exist—the thing it is good for—is first and foremost criminal law enforcement. This worldview has influenced politics and social policy in numerous ways, in part by driving politicians and policymakers to frame social issues as crime issues. That is, we came to see the world through policing. It emerged as the last place to critique and the first place to invest local finances.

The term also challenges our assumptions about defunding and the government. In the United States, we similarly ascribe an interpretive lens to the demand to defund. The concept has deep roots in efforts to transform the welfare state in the United States since the 1970s. By 1982, the term was commonplace in news and media debates about "liberal causes" ranging from abortions, to education, to unionism, and more. In law-and-policy parlance, then, to defund means to destroy, specifically in the public sector. The connotation is negative and exclusionary. It suggests an absence of government resources and, more precisely, an absence of government all together. . . .

As a discourse, to defund the police creates the space to politically and normatively question the status quo. . . . [S]ome argue that protestors should say something different, so that the public may embrace their demands. That critique is flawed. It points the finger at activists for not creating a slogan that fits comfortably within existing worldviews. Others say that precision in the substantive ask is the most important component of the demand in this moment. Such a critique demonstrates willingness to consider substantive distinctions between policies, but also resistance to critical reflection on existing worldviews. But these worldviews—our commitments to the present—also demand change.

BERNARD STARR—THE ALTERNATIVE TO DEFUNDING THE POLICE: INCREASE FUNDING FOR VETTING TO KEEP RACIST AND VIOLENT COPS OUT

Opinion, New York Daily News (June 5, 2021).

As a psychologist, when I saw Derek Chauvin killing George Floyd I wondered: "How the hell did he get on the Minneapolis police force?" The level of out-of-control violence that he displayed almost always has a history. His defiant voice was punctuated by the fact that he knew he was being videoed and as warnings came from bystanders—including a firefighter who pleaded to take Floyd's pulse. Yet Chauvin persisted.

This could not be an isolated incident, I concluded. I later learned that 18 previous complaints had been made against him. Unfortunately, the details have not been made public.

You would think that after the Floyd tragedy, followed by the murder conviction of Chauvin and the indictments of the three other officers for aiding and abetting him, that police throughout the land would be especially restrained in committing acts of violence, particularly against citizens of color. But that's not happening. The rate of police killings and violence a year after George Floyd's murder has remained the same.

And so continues the backlash calling for defunding, and even disbanding, of police departments. But would defunding help prevent or eliminate police racism and violence?

The answer is no. In fact, defunding police departments is more likely to make the problem worse. Furthermore, in response to the spike in crime rates across the country, the public—including all ethnic groups—is crying out for more police protection rather than less. Crime is real and the public needs trained and competent police for the protection of citizens and property.

Consider that defunding translates into downsizing, meaning fewer cops. But downsizing doesn't guarantee that the "bad" cops will be eliminated. In almost all police departments, downsizing would be by seniority, not psychopathology. Chauvin was a 19-year veteran of the Minneapolis police force. Defunding would not have cost him his job. On the contrary, with fewer cops, he would probably have had to work more hours to compensate for dismissals.

Outrage after heinous acts will not stop or prevent the violence. But effective actions at the front end—in the recruiting process—can. If you hire people prone to violence and racism, big surprise: They commit violent and racist acts. And the notion that to right the wrongs, we must just impose better training, modify regulations about applying deadly force and offer seminars and workshops to curtail racism and violence is unrealistic. Discipline after missteps is important, but often too late.

Police departments need to do a better job of hiring people in the first place. The problem is, the number of qualified applicants for police jobs is in free-fall. Some desperate departments, like the Spokane County Sheriff's Office, are offering signing bonuses. It's no surprise that, because of the dearth of qualified applicants, police departments, especially small and rural ones, hire cops who were fired from other police departments.

Rachel Harmon, a leading scholar on policing and laws that regulate police behavior at the University of Virginia Law School, confirmed in an email that indeed, police departments are often willing to look the other way or dismiss the seriousness of the previous firings: "As for officers who have already committed misconduct, departments sometimes hire them because they do not adequately investigate, sometimes because they believe the officer deserves a second chance, and sometimes because small and poorly resourced departments have more limited options and an officer with training and experience can be hard to pass up."

Harmon's comment suggests that publishing a national register of police who have been fired may be useful but still will have limited effectiveness.

Large police departments have extensive vetting procedures on their books but often skip over them because they are too costly to implement. To interview family, friends, teachers and previous employers is time-consuming and expensive. And funds are often lacking for in-depth interviews by expert clinical psychologists and psychiatrists. Harmon notes that "psychological testing before hiring is not designed to or especially good at picking out officers who may use excessive force."

Such tests, though, are primarily pencil and paper tests that can identify personality types and behavioral characteristics but cannot provide comprehensive psychological profiles.

There's a better way. Psychoanalyst Dr. Henry Kellerman author and editor of 40 books including "The Psychoanalysis of Symptoms, and Personality: How it Forms," told me in an interview that "experts can identify the potential for extreme violence... Yet, such diagnostic detection requires a high level of clinical training and experience."

Astute, well-trained diagnostic experts can spot dangerous red flag expressions that laypeople would often overlook. But the level of expertise and intensity of psychological examination described by Kellerman for effective psychological evaluation exceeds the resources of virtually every police department in the United States. . . .

We must "bite the bullet" and invest in procedures that can work. That means more funding, not defunding.

CHAPTER 4

THE RIGHT TO COUNSEL

■ ■ ■

§ 1. THE RIGHT TO APPOINTED COUNSEL AND RELATED PROBLEMS

A. THE RIGHT TO APPOINTED COUNSEL IN CRIMINAL PROCEEDINGS

15th ed., p. 72; at the end of Note 4, add:

Consider also Alexis Hoag, *Black on Black Representation*, 96 N.Y.U. L. Rev. (forthcoming 2021), *available at* https://papers.ssrn.com/sol3/papers.cfm?abstract_id=3785013 (calling for the expansion of the Sixth Amendment right to counsel of choice to indigent defendants and arguing that such an expansion could mitigate anti-Black racism in the criminal legal system).

§ 2. THE RIGHT TO APPOINTED COUNSEL IN PROCEEDINGS OTHER THAN CRIMINAL PROSECUTIONS: THE CONTINUED VITALITY OF THE *BETTS VS. BRADY* APPROACH

A. PROBATION AND PAROLE REVOCATION HEARINGS: JUVENILE COURT PROCEEDINGS; PARENTAL STATUS TERMINATION PROCEEDINGS; CONTEMPT HEARINGS

15th ed., p. 88; after Note 2, add:

2A. *Supervised release.* As discussed Supp. p. 90, the federal courts and some state courts have statutorily prescribed periods of supervised release that convicted defendants must serve following their incarceration. The Supreme Court recently held in *United States v. Haymond*, 139 S.Ct. 2369 (2019), that the Sixth Amendment right to a jury and proof beyond a reasonable doubt applies to a federal supervised-release statute that imposes a mandatory minimum term of five years imprisonment (and up to life imprisonment) when a defendant commits certain listed felonies while on supervised release for certain crimes. *See* Note 11, Supp. p. 90 for a more complete discussion of *Haymond*. If the Sixth Amendment is deemed applicable for purposes of the jury trial right and the right to proof beyond a reasonable doubt, the Sixth Amendment should also require a right to counsel, taking at least this form of supervised release out of the *Gagnon* due process, case-by-case analysis with respect to counsel. Do you think other forms of supervised release should trigger Sixth Amendment counsel protections? *See* Note 6, Supp. pp. 89–90 and Note 11, Supp. p. 90.

CHAPTER 5

THE PERFORMANCE OF COUNSEL

■ ■ ■

§ 6. CLIENT CONTROL

15th ed., p. 206; in Note 5, add a new footnote e after "appeal" in the 6th line of the 2nd paragraph:

[e] As discussed in the Supplement addition, to Ch. 22, § 3, Note 13, *Garza v. Idaho*, Supp. p. 75, held that this position also applied to the failure to follow a defendant's directive to appeal where the defendant had entered a plea agreement that included an appeal waiver. The *Garza* opinion relied upon both this aspect of the *Flores-Ortega* opinion and its discussion (described below) of the application of *Strickland*'s prejudice prong in a lack-of-consultation-case, which looked only to whether defendant would have chosen to appeal, not to whether that appeal would have been successful.

PART 2

POLICE PRACTICES

■ ■ ■

CHAPTER 6

ARREST, SEARCH AND SEIZURE

■ ■ ■

§ 2. PROTECTED AREAS AND INTERESTS

B. PREMISES

15th ed., p. 254; before Note 6, add:

5A. *Surveillance from outside the curtilage—garage door opener.* As described in *United States v. Correa,* 908 F.3d 208 (7th Cir.2018): "Members of a Drug Enforcement Agency task force lawfully found drugs in a traffic stop and seized several garage openers * * * they also found in the car. An agent took the garage openers and drove around downtown Chicago pushing their buttons to look for a suspected stash house. He found the right building when the door of a shared garage opened," which led to identity and search of defendant's condo in that building. The court had no occasion to consider the possible application of *Kyllo,* however, as "the use of the garage door opener was close to the edge but did not violate the Fourth Amendment, at least where it opened a garage shared by many residences of the building." (As the court explained, defendant could not make out a property/curtilage claim, as his unit was on another floor, and he could not make out an expectation-of-privacy claim given the use of the garage by the multiple unit owners.) What would be the proper result if the garage had instead been part of defendant's single-family dwelling? Consider that in *Correa* the court went on to conclude that defendant's *opener* had been searched with each press of the button, which was unobjectionable "because these searches produced only an address, not any meaningful private information about the interior or contents of the garage."

C. MOVEMENTS AND LOCATION

15th ed., p. 260; before *Carpenter*, add:

NOTES AND QUESTIONS

1. *Pushing in on a car tire.* In *United States v. Richmond,* 965 F.3d 352 (5th Cir. 2019), a trooper passing a truck noticed that its tires "were 'shaking,' 'wobbly,' and 'unbalanced,' " so he made a lawful traffic stop and then "pushed on [one] tire with his hand," producing "a 'solid thumping noise' that indicated something besides air was inside." The trooper ultimately had the tires examined, revealing "secret compartments that contained methamphetamine." As for defendant's contention that "touching the tire was a trespass which counts as a search" under *Jones* and *Jardines,* the court agreed. But the defendant did not prevail, as the court went on to conclude that because the officer had "probable cause to believe that the tire posed a safety risk" and "operation of a vehicle in such circumstances is a misdemeanor," there was a sufficient basis for a warrantless search.

2. *Chalking a tire.* In *Taylor v. City of Saginaw,* 922 F.3d 328 (6th Cir. 2019), the city's parking enforcement officer used chalk to mark tires of legally parked cars in a limited-time parking zone so as to later determine how long they had been parked, the purpose of which "is to raise revenue, and not to mitigate a public hazard." The court concluded such action, given the

"intentional physical contact with Taylor's vehicle," constituted a search under *Jones*. The court was not convinced that such action was a reasonable search under the "community caretaking exception" (*see* 15th ed., p. 427, Note 10), but indicated the city would have another opportunity on remand to show that such exception—or some other—was applicable.

3.   *Inserting a key in a lock.* The police sometimes gain possession of a physical key and want to know if it is a match for a particular locked item such as a car or suitcase. If the police insert the key in the lock, without actually opening the lock, is that a search? *See United States v. Dixon*, 984 F.3d 814, 819 (9th Cir. 2020) (ruling that inserting a key in a lock is a search under a *Jones* property-based analysis, even though earlier circuit precedent had held that it was not a search under *Katz*).

15th ed., p. 265; replace Notes 2 and 3 with the following new Notes 2, 3, and 4:

2.   **Carpenter *and Automated License Plate Readers.*** Modern police agencies often use automated license plate readers (ALPRs) that take pictures of the license plates of cars on the road. In some cases, the ALPRs are in fixed locations. In other cases, the ALPRs are mounted on police squad cars. In both cases, the government can use ALPRs to create massive databases of where cars are located on the road at various times. They can use these databases to try to reconstruct where cars were in the past based on license plate "hits" in the database, or else they can try to find out where cars are at present when a plate registers in the database in real time.

Should use of ALPRs constitute a search under *Carpenter*?

In *Commonwealth v. McCarthy*, 142 N.E.3d 1090 (Mass. 2020), the police suspected that McCarthy regularly brought heroin to a co-conspirator on Cape Cod in Massachusetts. Going to Cape Cod by car required passing over one of two bridges, each of which had an ALPR on each end. The police set up an alert on the state ALPR system to tell them when McCarthy's car crossed either bridge.

For two and a half months, the police learned the precise dates, times, directions, and specific lanes that McCarthy's car traveled on the two bridges to or from Cape Cod. The police then used a later ALPR hit to know when McCarthy's car had crossed one of the bridges and that McCarthy was likely meeting with his co-conspirator. Upon seeing that meeting, the police made their arrest.

The Massachusetts Supreme Judicial Court first adopted the "mosaic theory" of the Fourth Amendment, the idea that there is an "an aggregation principle for the technological surveillance of public conduct" under the Fourth Amendment. Under this view, enough collection of ALPR information, for enough time, could constitute a search:

"When collected for a long enough period, the cumulative nature of the information collected implicates a privacy interest on the part of the individual who is the target of the tracking. . . . As the analogy goes, the color of a single stone depicts little, but by stepping back one can see a complete mosaic.

"A detailed account of a person's movements, drawn from electronic surveillance, encroaches upon a person's reasonable expectation of privacy because the whole reveals far more than the sum of the parts. The difference is not one of degree but of kind. Prolonged surveillance reveals types of information not revealed by short-term surveillance, such as what a person does repeatedly, what he does not do, and what he does ensemble. Aggregated location data reveals a highly detailed profile, not simply of where we go, but by easy inference, of our associations—political, religious, amicable and amorous, to name only a few—and of the pattern of our professional and avocational pursuits.

"In determining whether a reasonable expectation of privacy has been invaded, it is not the amount of data that the Commonwealth seeks to admit in evidence that counts, but, rather, the amount of data that the government collects or to which it gains access. . . . For this reason, our constitutional analysis ideally would consider every ALPR record of a defendant's vehicle that had been stored and collected by the government up to the time of the defendant's arrest. That information, however, is not in the record before us.

"With enough cameras in enough locations, the historic location data from an ALPR system in Massachusetts would invade a reasonable expectation of privacy and would constitute a search for constitutional purposes. The one-year retention period indicated in the [state] retention policy certainly is long enough to warrant constitutional protection. Like CSLI data, ALPRs allow the police to reconstruct people's past movements without knowing in advance who police are looking for, thus granting police access to a category of information otherwise [and previously] unknowable. Like both CSLI and GPS data, ALPRs circumvent traditional constraints on police surveillance power by being cheap (relative to human surveillance) and surreptitious.

"The constitutional question is not merely an exercise in counting cameras; the analysis should focus, ultimately, on the extent to which a substantial picture of the defendant's public movements are revealed by the surveillance.

"For that purpose, where the ALPRs are placed matters too. ALPRs near constitutionally sensitive locations—the home, a place of worship, etc.—reveal more of an individual's life and associations than does an ALPR trained on an interstate highway. A network of ALPRs that surveils every residential side street paints a much more nuanced and invasive picture of a driver's life and public movements than one limited to major highways that open into innumerable possible destinations. For while no ALPR network is likely to be as detailed in its surveillance as GPS or CSLI data, one well may be able to make many of the same inferences from ALPR data that implicate expressive and associative rights."

After stating that general principle, the Court then held that the alerts from the ALPR database were not enough to trigger a search in McCarthy's case. Because the surveillance was limited, no Fourth Amendment search had occurred:

"There is no real question that the government, without securing a warrant, may use electronic devices to monitor an individual's movements in public to the extent that the same result could be achieved through visual surveillance. It is an entirely ordinary experience to drive past a police officer in a cruiser observing traffic on the side of the road, and, of course, an officer may read or write down a publicly displayed license plate number. In this way, a single license plate reader is similar to traditional surveillance techniques.

"On the other hand, four factors distinguish ALPRs from an officer parked on the side of the road: (1) the policy of retaining the information for, at a minimum, one year; (2) the ability to record the license plate number of nearly every passing vehicle; (3) the continuous, twenty-four hour nature of the surveillance; and (4) the fact that the recorded license plate number is linked to the location of the observation. These are enhancements of what reasonably might be expected from the police.

"The limited number of cameras and their specific placements, however, also are relevant in determining whether they reveal a mosaic of location information that is sufficiently detailed to invade a reasonable expectation of privacy. The cameras in question here gave police only the ability to determine whether the defendant was passing onto or off of the Cape at a particular moment, and when he had done so previously.

"This limited surveillance does not allow the Commonwealth to monitor the whole of the defendant's public movements, or even his progress on a single journey. These particular cameras make this case perhaps more analogous to CSLI, if there were only two cellular telephone towers collecting data. Such a limited picture does not divulge the whole of the defendant's physical movements, or track enough of his comings and goings so as to reveal the privacies of life.

"While we cannot say precisely how detailed a picture of the defendant's movements must be revealed to invoke constitutional protections, it is not that produced by four cameras at fixed locations on the ends of two bridges."

If you are a police officer trying to comply with the decision in *McCarthy*, when do you think you need a warrant to query your ALPR database?

3. Carpenter *and long-term aerial surveillance.* In *Leaders of a Beautiful Struggle v. Baltimore Police Dept.*, 2 F.4th 330 (4th Cir. 2021) (en banc), a group of community advocates sought to enjoin Baltimore's Aerial Investigation Research (AIR) program. The AIR program, which existed only briefly as a pilot program, consisted of multiple airplanes that flew over the city of Baltimore during daylight hours when weather permitted. The purpose of the program was to allow the Baltimore police to track individuals and vehicles from identified past crime scenes and to otherwise extract information to assist the police department in investigations of serious crimes.

Each airplane in the AIR program was equipped with a camera, and the AIR cameras took photographs of the city that together captured 32 square miles of Baltimore every second. The cameras were set at a resolution so that each pixel of an image was a single person or vehicle, "magnified to a point where people and cars are individually visible, but only as blurred dots or blobs." Camera images were retained for 45 days.

In concluding that a preliminary injunction was justified, the *en banc* Fourth Circuit ruled 8–7 that the plaintiffs were likely to succeed on their claim that use of the AIR program was a search under *Carpenter*:

"*Carpenter* applies squarely to this case. More like the CSLI in *Carpenter* and GPS-data in *Jones* than the radio-beeper in *Knotts*, the AIR program 'tracks every movement' of every person outside in Baltimore. Because the data is retained for 45 days—at least—it is a 'detailed, encyclopedic,' record of where everyone came and went within the city during daylight hours over the prior month-and-a-half. Law enforcement can 'travel back in time' to observe a target's movements, forwards and backwards. Without technology, police can attempt to tail suspects, but AIR data is more like 'attaching an ankle monitor' to every person in the city. Whoever the suspect turns out to be,' they have 'effectively been tailed' for the prior six weeks. Thus, the 'retrospective quality of the data' enables police to 'retrace a person's whereabouts,' granting access to otherwise 'unknowable' information.

"We do not suggest that the AIR program allows perfect tracking of all individuals it captures across all the time it covers. Though data is collected in 12-hour increments, the tracks are often shorter snippets of several hours or less. Still, the program enables photographic, retrospective location tracking in multi-hour blocks, often over consecutive days, with a month and a half of daytimes for analysts to work with. That is enough to yield 'a wealth of detail,' greater than the sum of the individual trips. *See Jones* (Sotomayor, J., concurring) (suggesting people do not expect 'that their movements will be recorded and aggregated in a manner that enables the government to ascertain' details of their private lives). It enables deductions about what a person does repeatedly, what he does not do, and what he does ensemble, which reveals more about a person than does any individual trip viewed in isolation. *Carpenter* held those deductions go to the privacies of life, the epitome of information expected to be beyond the warrantless reach of the government. And here, as there, the government can deduce such information only because it recorded everyone's movements.

"Therefore, because the AIR program opens an intimate window into a person's associations and activities, it violates the reasonable expectation of privacy individuals have in the whole of their movements. The district court reached the opposite conclusion because it believed, as Defendants argue on appeal, that the AIR program is capable of only short-term tracking. It emphasized that AIR images show people only as a series of anonymous dots traversing a map of Baltimore, and the planes do not fly over night, so gaps in the data will prohibit the tracking of individuals over the course of multiple days.

"But those facts don't support the district court's conclusion. The datasets in *Jones* and *Carpenter* had gaps in their coverage, too. The GPS data in *Jones* only tracked driving, in a specific car, precise to within 50 to 100 feet. The raw CSLI in *Carpenter* was a log of thousands of estimated location points from which a cell phone pinged a cell tower. Yet, in both cases, the surveillance still surpassed ordinary expectations of law enforcement's capacity and provided enough information to deduce details from the whole of individuals' movements.

"The same is true here. That Defendants chose to limit data collection to daylight hours and a certain resolution does not make the AIR program equivalent to traditional, short-term surveillance. AIR data is a photographic record of movements, surpassing the precision even of GPS data and CSLI, which record variable location points from which movements can be reconstructed. And while the coverage is not 24/7, most people do most of their moving during the daytime, not overnight. Likewise, many people start and end most days at home, following a relatively habitual pattern in between. These habits, analyzed with other available information, will often be enough for law enforcement to deduce the people behind the pixels. And if a track is interrupted by sunset, police will at least sometimes be able to re-identify the same target over consecutive days. For example, law enforcement could use AIR data to track a person's movements from a crime scene to, eventually, a residential location where the person remains. They could then look through time and track movements from that residence. They could use any number of context clues to distinguish individuals and deduce identity. After all, the AIR program's express goal is to identify suspects and witnesses to help [the police] solve crimes."

Judge Wilkinson dissented:

"The lesson from *Jones* is that *short-term* surveillance of an individual's public movements is less likely to violate a reasonable expectation of privacy. Under that rule, AIR checks out, at least under the factual findings the district court made on our limited record. [District] Judge Bennett reasonably concluded that AIR's built-in limitations meant it could only effectively track short-term public movements. The program's cameras were only able to track outdoor movements. They could not track an individual who enters a building, and analysts could not tell if the person leaving the building was the same person who entered it. And because AIR's surveillance planes could fly only during the daylight hours, AIR surveillance could not be used to track individuals from day-to-day.

"The majority also effectively nullifies the Supreme Court's repeated decisions sanctioning aerial surveillance. If a plane can fly just one thousand feet over a home with cameras able to photograph individual items within the home's curtilage, *Ciraolo*, I fail to see how AIR photographs representing daytime movements on public streets violate a reasonable expectation of privacy. If planes can photograph individual objects on a property as small as one half inch in diameter, *Dow Chemical Co.*, I cannot grasp how AIR photos representing individuals on public streets as mere pixelated dots with no distinguishing features flunks the Fourth Amendment test. Unlike *Riley*, where the Court upheld surveillance by government agents circling four hundred feet above a home in a helicopter to look into a greenhouse partially within the home's curtilage, AIR does not involve the invasion of anyone's home or curtilage. If those precedents do not control this case, the majority should frankly state that it no longer deems them palatable or binding.

"The majority believes that the decision in *Carpenter* requires a different result. But it overreads *Carpenter*. The technology at issue in *Carpenter*, CSLI, was far more invasive of privacy than the limited aerial surveillance in this case. CSLI gave the government 101 location data points for each of the seven days it obtained CSLI data. Because a phone goes wherever its owner goes, CSLI provides a comprehensive record of the person's movements. And CSLI is used by the government to target individuals of interest, whereas AIR was used only to track the public movements of non-preidentified individuals—those who happen to be present at the scene of a violent crime.

"The majority asserts that AIR is at least as intrusive as CSLI. But the majority can only reach this conclusion by tossing out the district court's factual findings and replacing them with 'facts' more convenient to its preferred conclusion. It dramatically declares that AIR was used to track every Baltimorean's movements over a forty-five-day period, just as if the city had attached ankle bracelets to everyone in the city. It also claims that all Baltimoreans were effectively 'tailed' for six weeks because of AIR. But these alternative 'facts' trample upon reality and the record. The district court's actual factual findings reveal substantial differences between AIR and CSLI. Whereas CSLI could be used to reliably track an individual's movement from day to day, the district court found that AIR could only be used to track someone's outdoor movements for twelve hours at most.

"Make no mistake. The majority is not applying *Carpenter*'s narrow holding. It is extending it beyond recognition to bar all warrantless tracking of public movements. This is a breathtaking transformation of the law. Uncorrected, it comes very close to invalidating aerial surveillance and short-term tracking technologies altogether."

Imagine you are in charge of advising the Baltimore police department about how much aerial surveillance can be conducted, and how long records can be retained, without triggering a Fourth Amendment search. Where exactly is the line? And is the line to be drawn for aerial surveillance under the Fourth Circuit's framework similar or different from the line to be drawn for ALPRs in *McCarthy*, *supra* note 2?

4.   *Real-time tracking a cell phone for a few hours.* In *United States v. Hammond*, 996 F.3d 374 (7th Cir. 2021), the government was looking for Hammond, who was a suspect in a string of armed robberies. Investigators asked Hammond's cell phone provider, AT&T, to locate him using his phone's CSLI. AT&T reported Hammond's location to investigators in real-time every fifteen minutes for about six hours. Investigators used that information to locate Hammond in a hotel parking lot. The Seventh Circuit held that this tracking was not a search under *Carpenter*:

"We are persuaded that the unique facts of this case have more in common with *Knotts* than *Carpenter*. . . . Unlike in *Carpenter*, the record of Hammond's (and Knotts') movements for a matter of hours on public roads does not provide a 'window into the person's life, revealing his familial, political, professional, religious, and sexual associations' to the same, intrusive degree as the collection of historical CSLI. Law enforcement used the real-time CSLI to find Hammond's location in public, not to peer into the intricacies of his private life. The records here and in *Knotts* do not suggest that law enforcement used either the real-time CSLI or the beeper to examine the defendants' movements inside of a home or other highly protected area. And, Hammond does not argue that he was in private areas during this time period. In *Carpenter*, law enforcement's surveillance became a "search" because the surveillance followed Carpenter long enough to follow him into, and record, his private life. But here, and in *Knotts*, law enforcement only followed Hammond on public roads, for the duration of one car trip.

"The *Carpenter* majority was particularly concerned with the retrospective quality of the data that law enforcement collected about Carpenter's movements. The real-time CSLI in this case does not have the same retrospective quality of the historical CSLI in *Carpenter* and again, is much more akin to the beeper data in *Knotts*. Real-time CSLI collected over the course of several hours simply does not involve the same level of intrusion as the collection of historical CSLI.

"Furthermore, one of the aggravating considerations in *Carpenter* was that the historical CSLI contravened society's expectations not only of their own privacy, but also of law enforcement's capabilities. Carpenter recognized that 'prior to the digital age, law enforcement might have pursued a suspect for a brief stretch.' The collection of historical CSLI in *Carpenter* was different because it would be too costly and difficult to follow a suspect for over four months. . . . In this case, society is fully aware that officers may follow and track a suspect's movements for several hours. In sum, law enforcement's ability to locate Hammond on public roads for a six-hour period using real-time CSLI is not inconsistent with society's expectations of privacy from law enforcement's prying eyes."

Is *Hammond* consistent with the Fourth Circuit's decision in the Baltimore AIR program case in Note 3? Should the issue be (a) how much information was actually revealed about that person in this one case, (b) how much information could potentially be revealed about that person using the specific surveillance program at issue, or (c) how much the general technology in use is one that could potentially reveal a great deal of information about people? And for any of these approaches, how much information is required to trigger a search?

More broadly, is the mosaic theory, which attempts to distinguish smaller-scale surveillance that is not a search from larger-scale surveillance that is a search, a workable approach to interpreting the Fourth Amendment? *See generally* Orin S. Kerr, *The Mosaic Theory of the Fourth Amendment,* 111 Mich. L. Rev. 311 (2012) (arguing that the mosaic theory reflects a legitimate concern with government power but that it should be rejected because it cannot be implemented coherently).

D. NETWORKS

15th ed., p. 276; after Note 9, add the following new Notes 9A and 9B:

9A. *Applying* **Carpenter** *to IP addresses used by an unknown suspect.* In the pre-*Carpenter* case of *United States v. Forrester*, discussed in Note 9 at p. 275, the Ninth Circuit considered whether it is a search to monitor the IP addresses of the websites that a known suspect visited while surfing the web. Although post-*Carpenter* caselaw has not addressed that question, several courts have answered whether it is a search under *Carpenter* for the government to learn the IP address that an unknown suspect was using to connect to the Internet. The answer, they have ruled so far, is "no."

For example, in *United States v. Hood*, 920 F.3d 87 (1st Cir. 2019), investigators were investigating an unknown person who had committed a crime using an account on the smartphone messaging application Kik. In an effort to learn who had used the Kik account, investigators asked Kik to disclose the IP addresses that had been used to log into the account during a four-day window when the crime occurred. Kik disclosed that the account had been accessed using three different IP addresses during that time. Investigators traced the IP addresses back to a hotel and a residence in a small town in Maine where Hood had stayed, leading to Hood's arrest. The First Circuit rejected Hood's argument that obtaining his IP addresses was a search under *Carpenter*:

"Hood contends that the IP address data that the government acquired from Kik without a warrant—which concerned Hood's internet activity only on Kik and only over a four-day span—is not materially different from the CSLI that was at issue in *Carpenter*. He notes in this regard that this information enabled [the government] to determine Hood's precise location when he logged on to Kik, as well as the date and time of those digital transmissions. For that reason, he contends, *Carpenter* establishes that the government needed a warrant to acquire the information from Kik that he seeks to suppress, because the notion that anytime one accesses the internet from their cell phone, they are effectively providing the police a specific record of their whereabouts, is in direct contrast to society's expectations.

"But, an internet user generates the IP address data that the government acquired from Kik in this case only by making the affirmative decision to access a website or application. By contrast, as the Supreme Court noted in *Carpenter*, every time a cell phone receives a call, text message, or email, the cell phone pings CSLI to the nearest cell site tower without the cell phone user lifting a finger. In fact, those pings are recorded every time a cell phone application updates of its own accord, possibly to refresh a news feed or generate new weather data, such that even a cell phone sitting untouched in a suspect's pocket is continually chronicling that user's movements throughout the day.

"Moreover, the IP address data that the government acquired from Kik does not itself convey any location information. The IP address data is merely a string of numbers associated with a device that had, at one time, accessed a wireless network. By contrast, CSLI itself reveals—without any independent investigation—the (at least approximate) location of the cell phone user who generates that data simply by possessing the phone. Thus, the government's warrantless acquisition from Kik of the IP address data at issue here in no way gives rise to the unusual concern that the Supreme Court identified in *Carpenter* that, if the third-party doctrine were applied to the acquisition of months of Carpenter's CSLI, 'only the few without cell phones could escape tireless and absolute surveillance.' Accordingly, we conclude that Hood did not have a reasonable expectation of privacy in the information that the government acquired from Kik without a warrant."

9B. *Applying* Carpenter *to geofencing warrants.* Many modern cell phones are logged into Google accounts while in use. If a phone is logged in to a Google account, Google by default keeps highly precise records of where the phone is located. If the government wants to know who was in a particular area at a particular time in the past where and when a crime occurred, investigators may seek a "geofencing warrant." A geofencing warrant asks Google to disclose location information about any phones logged into Google accounts in that particular place at that particular time. The government can use that information to generate a list of possible suspects or witnesses.

Geofencing warrants raise many difficult Fourth Amendment issues, but one of them is whether *Carpenter* applies. Is obtaining geofencing information a Fourth Amendment search? Recall that *Carpenter* stressed that a person cannot opt out of generating CSLI. A cell phone generates CSLI whenever it is being used, and a person must use a cell phone to participate in modern life. In contrast, a person need not be logged into a Google account to use a cell phone. Should that make a difference? Is being logged into Google (and sharing precise location information with Google) indispensable to participation in modern society?

E. NON-FOURTH AMENDMENT CONSTITUTIONAL PROTECTIONS

15th ed., p. 282; before Section 3, add a new sub-section 2F, "Seizures":

F. SEIZURES

In addition to limiting "searches," the Fourth Amendment also limits "seizures." As explained in *Soldal v. Cook County*, 506 U.S. 56 (1992), the two concepts are distinct: "seizures of property are subject to Fourth Amendment scrutiny even though no search within the meaning of the Amendment has taken place." Seizures can be broken down into two basic types: (1) seizures of persons, such as arrests or temporary detentions, and (2) seizures of inanimate objects, such as when the government takes property into police custody. The following new case considers the Fourth Amendment standards for seizures of a person.

TORRES V. MADRID

___ U.S. ___, 141 S.Ct. 989, 209 L.Ed.2d 190 (2021).

CHIEF JUSTICE ROBERTS delivered the opinion of the Court.

The Fourth Amendment prohibits unreasonable "seizures" to safeguard "the right of the people to be secure in their persons." Under our cases, an officer seizes a person when he uses force to apprehend her. The question in this case is whether a seizure occurs when an officer shoots someone who temporarily eludes capture after the shooting. The answer is yes: The application of physical force to the body of a person with intent to restrain is a seizure, even if the force does not succeed in subduing the person.

I

At dawn on July 15, 2014, four New Mexico State Police officers arrived at an apartment complex in Albuquerque to execute an arrest warrant for a woman accused of white collar crimes, but also suspected of having been involved in drug trafficking, murder, and other violent crimes. What happened next is hotly contested. We recount the facts in the light most favorable to petitioner Roxanne Torres because the court below granted summary judgment to Officers Janice Madrid and Richard Williamson, the two respondents here.

The officers observed Torres standing with another person near a Toyota FJ Cruiser in the parking lot of the complex. Officer Williamson concluded that neither Torres nor her companion was the target of the warrant. As the officers approached the vehicle, the companion departed, and Torres—at the time experiencing methamphetamine withdrawal—got into the driver's seat. The officers attempted to speak with her, but she did not notice their presence until one of them tried to open the door of her car.

Although the officers wore tactical vests marked with police identification, Torres saw only that they had guns. She thought the officers were carjackers trying to steal her car, and she hit the gas to escape them. Neither Officer Madrid nor Officer Williamson, according to Torres, stood in the path of the vehicle, but both fired their service pistols to stop her. All told, the two officers fired 13 shots at Torres, striking her twice in the back and temporarily paralyzing her left arm.

Steering with her right arm, Torres accelerated through the fusillade of bullets, exited the apartment complex, drove a short distance, and stopped in a parking lot. After asking a bystander to report an attempted carjacking, Torres stole a Kia Soul that happened to be idling nearby and drove 75 miles to Grants, New Mexico. The good news for Torres was that the hospital in Grants was able to airlift her to another hospital where she could receive appropriate care. The bad news was that the hospital was back in Albuquerque, where the police arrested her the next day. She pleaded no contest to aggravated fleeing from a law enforcement officer, assault on a peace officer, and unlawfully taking a motor vehicle.

Torres later sought damages from Officers Madrid and Williamson under 42 U.S.C. § 1983, which provides a cause of action for the deprivation of constitutional rights by persons acting under color of state law. She claimed that the officers applied excessive force, making the shooting an unreasonable seizure under the Fourth Amendment. The District Court granted summary judgment to the officers, and the Court of Appeals for the Tenth Circuit affirmed on the ground that a suspect's continued flight after being shot by police negates a Fourth Amendment excessive-force claim. The court relied on Circuit precedent providing that no seizure can occur unless there is physical touch or a show of authority, and that such physical touch (or force) must terminate the suspect's movement or otherwise give rise to physical control over the suspect.

II

This case concerns the "seizure" of a "person," which can take the form of physical force or a show of authority that in some way restrains the liberty of the person. The question before us is whether the application of physical force is a seizure if the force, despite hitting its target, fails to stop the person.

We largely covered this ground in *California v. Hodari D.*, 499 U.S. 621 (1991). There we interpreted the term "seizure" by consulting the common law of arrest, the quintessential seizure of the person under our Fourth Amendment jurisprudence. As Justice Scalia explained for himself and six other Members of the Court, the common law treated "the mere grasping or application of physical force with lawful authority" as an arrest, "whether or not it succeeded in subduing the arrestee." Put another way, an officer's application of physical force to the body of a person "for the purpose of arresting him" was itself an arrest—not an *attempted* arrest—even if the person did not yield.

The common law distinguished the application of force from a show of authority, such as an order for a suspect to halt. The latter does not become an arrest unless and until the arrestee complies with the demand. As the Court explained in *Hodari D.*, an arrest requires *either* physical force *or*, where that is absent, *submission* to the assertion of authority.

Hodari D. articulates two pertinent principles. First, common law arrests are Fourth Amendment seizures. And second, the common law considered the application of force to the body of a person with intent to restrain to be an arrest, no matter whether the arrestee escaped. We need not decide whether *Hodari D.*, which principally concerned a show of authority, controls the outcome of this case as a matter of *stare decisis*, because we independently reach the same conclusions.

At the adoption of the Fourth Amendment, a "seizure" was the act of taking by warrant. A seizure did not necessarily result in actual control or detention. It is true that, when speaking of property, from the time of the founding to the present, the word 'seizure' has meant a 'taking possession. But the Framers selected a term—seizure—broad enough to apply to all the concerns of the Fourth Amendment: "persons," as well as "houses, papers, and effects." As applied to a person, the word 'seizure' readily bears the meaning of a laying on of hands or application of physical force to restrain movement, even when it is ultimately unsuccessful. Then, as now, an ordinary user of the English language could remark: "She seized the purse-snatcher, but he broke out of her grasp."

The "seizure" of a "person" plainly refers to an arrest. That linkage existed at the founding. Samuel Johnson, for example, defined an "arrest" as "any seizure of the person." 1 A Dictionary of the English Language 108 (1773).

The common law rule identified in *Hodari D.*—that the application of force gives rise to an arrest, even if the officer does not secure control over the arrestee—achieved recognition to such an extent that English lawyers could confidently (and accurately) proclaim that "all the authorities, from the earliest time to the present, establish that a corporal touch is sufficient to constitute an arrest, even though the defendant do not submit." *Nicholl* v. *Darley*, 148 Eng. Rep. 974 (Exch. 1828).

The slightest application of force could satisfy this rule. In *Genner* v. *Sparks*, 87 Eng. Rep. 928 (Q. B. 1704), the defendant did not submit to the authority of an arrest warrant, but the court explained that the bailiff would have made an arrest if he "had but touched the defendant even with the end of his finger." The touching of the person—frequently called a laying of hands—was enough. Only later did English law grow to recognize arrest without touching through a submission to a show of authority. Even so, the traditional rule persisted that all an arrest required was "corporal seising or touching the defendant's body." 3 W. Blackstone, Commentaries on the Laws of England 288 (1768).

Early American courts adopted this mere-touch rule from England, just as they embraced other common law principles of search and seizure. Justice Baldwin, instructing a jury in his capacity as Circuit Justice, defined an arrest to include touching or putting hands upon the arrestee in the execution of process. State courts agreed that any touching, however slight, is enough, provided the officer made his intent to arrest clear. Courts continued to hold that an arrest required only the application of force—not control or custody—through the framing of the Fourteenth Amendment, which incorporated the protections of the Fourth Amendment against the States.

This case, of course, does not involve laying hands, but instead a shooting. Neither the parties nor the United States as *amicus curiae* suggests that the officers' use of bullets to restrain Torres alters the analysis in any way. And we are aware of no common law authority addressing an arrest under such circumstances, or indeed any case involving an application of force from a distance.

The closest decision seems to be *Countess of Rutland's Case*, 77 Eng. Rep. 332 (Star Chamber 1605). In that case, serjeants-at-mace tracked down Isabel Holcroft, Countess of Rutland, to execute a writ for a judgment of debt. They "shewed her their mace, and touching her body with it, said to her, we arrest you, madam." We think the case is best understood as an example of an arrest made by touching with an object, for the serjeants-at-mace announced the arrest at the time they touched the countess with the mace. However one reads *Countess of Rutland*, we see no basis for drawing an artificial line between grasping with a hand and other means of applying physical force to effect an arrest.

We will not carve out this greater intrusion on personal security from the mere-touch rule just because founding-era courts did not confront apprehension by firearm. While firearms have existed for a millennium and were certainly familiar at the founding, we have observed that law enforcement did not carry handguns until the latter half of the 19th century, at which point it became possible to use deadly force from a distance as a means of apprehension. So it should come as no surprise that neither we nor the dissent has located a common law case in which an officer used a gun to apprehend a suspect. But the focus of the Fourth Amendment is the privacy and security of individuals, not the particular manner of arbitrary invasion by governmental officials. There is nothing subtle about a bullet, but the Fourth Amendment preserves personal security with respect to methods of apprehension old and new.

We stress, however, that the application of the common law rule does not transform every physical contact between a government employee and a member of the public into a Fourth Amendment seizure. A seizure requires the use of force *with intent to restrain*. Accidental force will not qualify. See *County of Sacramento v. Lewis*, 523 U.S. 833 (1998). Nor will force intentionally applied for some other purpose satisfy this rule. In this opinion, we consider only force used to apprehend. We do not accept the dissent's invitation to opine on matters not presented here—pepper spray, flash-bang grenades, lasers, and more.

Moreover, the appropriate inquiry is whether the challenged conduct *objectively* manifests an intent to restrain, for we rarely probe the subjective motivations of police officers in the Fourth Amendment context. Only an objective test allows the police to determine in advance whether the conduct contemplated will implicate the Fourth Amendment. While a mere touch can be enough for a seizure, the amount of force remains pertinent in assessing the objective intent to restrain. A tap on the shoulder to get one's attention will rarely exhibit such an intent.

Nor does the seizure depend on the subjective perceptions of the seized person. Here, for example, Torres claims to have perceived the officers' actions as an attempted carjacking. But the conduct of the officers—ordering Torres to stop and then shooting to restrain her movement—

satisfies the objective test for a seizure, regardless whether Torres comprehended the governmental character of their actions.

The rule we announce today is narrow. In addition to the requirement of intent to restrain, a seizure by force—absent submission—lasts only as long as the application of force. That is to say that the Fourth Amendment does not recognize any *continuing* arrest during the period of fugitivity. The fleeting nature of some seizures by force undoubtedly may inform what damages a civil plaintiff may recover, and what evidence a criminal defendant may exclude from trial. But brief seizures are seizures all the same.

Applying these principles to the facts viewed in the light most favorable to Torres, the officers' shooting applied physical force to her body and objectively manifested an intent to restrain her from driving away. We therefore conclude that the officers seized Torres for the instant that the bullets struck her.

The officers and the dissent derive from our cases a different touchstone for the seizure of a person: "an intentional acquisition of physical control." *Brower v. County of Inyo*, 489 U.S. 593, 596 (1989). Under their alternative rule, the use of force becomes a seizure only when there is a governmental termination of freedom of movement through means intentionally applied.

This approach improperly erases the distinction between seizures by *control* and seizures by *force*. In all fairness, we too have not always been attentive to this distinction when a case did not implicate the issue. But each type of seizure enjoys a separate common law pedigree that gives rise to a separate rule.

Unlike a seizure by force, a seizure by acquisition of control involves either voluntary submission to a show of authority or the termination of freedom of movement. A prime example of the latter comes from *Brower*, where the police seized a driver when he crashed into their roadblock. Under the common law rules of arrest, actual control is a necessary element for this type of seizure. Such a seizure requires that a person be stopped by the very instrumentality set in motion or put in place in order to achieve that result. But that requirement of control or submission never extended to seizures by force.

* * *

We hold that the application of physical force to the body of a person with intent to restrain is a seizure even if the person does not submit and is not subdued. Of course, a seizure is just the first step in the analysis. The Fourth Amendment does not forbid all or even most seizures—only unreasonable ones. All we decide today is that the officers seized Torres by shooting her with intent to restrain her movement.

JUSTICE GORSUCH, with whom JUSTICE THOMAS and JUSTICE ALITO join, dissenting.

The majority holds that a criminal suspect can be simultaneously seized and roaming at large. On the majority's account, a Fourth Amendment "seizure" takes place whenever an officer "merely touches" a suspect. It's a seizure even if the suspect refuses to stop, evades capture, and rides off into the sunset never to be seen again. That view is as mistaken as it is novel.

Today's majority . . . accepts that a seizure of the inanimate objects mentioned in the Fourth Amendment (houses, papers, and effects) requires possession. And when it comes to persons, the majority agrees (as *Hodari D.* held) that a seizure in response to a "show of authority" takes place if and when the suspect submits to an officer's possession. The majority insists that a different rule should apply *only* in cases where an officer "touches" the suspect. Here—and here alone— possession is not required. So, under the majority's logic, we are quite literally asked to believe the officers in this case "seized" Ms. Torres's person, but *not* her car, when they shot both and both continued speeding down the highway.

The majority's need to resort to such a schizophrenic reading of the word "seizure" should be a signal that something has gone seriously wrong.

[The majority] scrambles to locate a case—any case—suggesting that common law courts considered "touchings" by weapon enough to effect an arrest in the debt-collection context. Ultimately, the majority asks us to dwell at length on the Countess of Rutland's case. In at least that lone instance, the majority promises, we will find bailiffs who arrested a debtor by touching her with an object (a mace) rather than a laying on of hands. See *ante* (citing *Countess of Rutland's Case*, 77 Eng. Rep. 332 (Star Chamber 1605)). But it turns out the dispute concerned whether a countess could be civilly arrested *at all*, not when or how the arrest was completed. The court had no reason to (and did not) decide whether the bailiffs accomplished their arrest when they "shewed her their mace," "touched" her with the mace, or "compelled the coachman to carry" her to jail. And no one questions that these things together—a show of authority followed by compelled detention—have always been enough to complete an arrest.

The common law offers a vast legal library. Like any other, it must be used thoughtfully. We have no business wandering about and randomly grabbing volumes off the shelf, plucking out passages we like, scratching out bits we don't, all before pasting our own new pastiche into the U.S. Reports. That does not respect legal history; it rewrites it.

If text, history, and precedent cannot explain today's result, what can? The majority seems to offer a clue when it promises its new rule will help us avoid line-drawing problems. Any different standard, the majority worries, would be difficult to apply.

Even within its field of operation, the majority's rule seems destined to underdeliver on its predicted efficiencies. The majority tells us that its new test requires an "objective intent to restrain." But what qualifies is far from clear. The majority assures us that a "tap on the shoulder to get one's attention will rarely exhibit such an intent." Suppose, though, the circumstances "objectively" indicate that the tap was "intended" to secure a person's attention for a minute, a quarter hour, or longer. Would that be enough?

Then there's the question what kind of "touching" will suffice. Imagine that, with an objective intent to detain a suspect, officers deploy pepper spray that enters a suspect's lungs as he sprints away. Does the application of the pepper spray count? Suppose that, intending to capture a fleeing suspect, officers detonate flash-bang grenades that are so loud they damage the suspect's eardrum, even though he manages to run off. Or imagine an officer shines a laser into a suspect's eyes to get him to stop, but the suspect is able to drive away with now-damaged retinas. Are these "touchings"? What about an officer's bullet that shatters the driver's windshield, a piece of which cuts her as she speeds away? Maybe the officer didn't touch the suspect, but he set in motion a series of events that yielded a touching. Does that count? While assuring us that its new rule will prove easy to administer, the majority refuses to confront its certain complications. Lower courts and law enforcement won't have that luxury.

If efficiency cannot explain today's decision, what's left? Maybe it is an impulse that individuals like Ms. Torres *should* be able to sue for damages. Sometimes police shootings are justified, but other times they cry out for a remedy. The majority seems to give voice to this sentiment when it disparages the traditional possession rule as "artificial" and promotes its alternative as more sensitive to "personal security" and "new" policing realities. It takes pains to explain, too, that its new rule will provide greater protection for personal "privacy" interests, which we're told make up the "essence" of the Fourth Amendment.

But tasked only with applying the Constitution's terms, we have no authority to posit penumbras of "privacy" and "personal security" and devise whatever rules we think might best serve the Amendment's "essence." The Fourth Amendment allows this Court to protect against specific governmental actions—unreasonable searches and seizures of persons, houses, papers, and effects—and that is the limit of our license.

NOTES AND QUESTIONS

1. ***Three kinds of seizures of persons.*** *Torres* suggests that there are three types of "seizures" of a person:

(a) *Seizure by control from voluntary submission to a show of authority*, such as when an officer orders a suspect to stop and the suspect complies with the order.

(b) *Seizure by control from termination of freedom of movement*, such as when an officer forces a car the suspect is driving to come to a stop.

(c) *Seizure by physical force to the body of a person with intent to restrain*, regardless of whether the person is brought under control.

Putting aside the historical basis for these categories—upon which the majority and dissent offer different views—do they make sense in practice today?

2. ***The test for seizures of property.*** In *United States v. Jacobsen*, 466 U.S. 109 (1984), the Court stated that "a seizure of property occurs when there is some meaningful interference with an individual's possessory interests in that property." The Court added that "this definition follows from our oft-repeated definition of the 'seizure' of a person within the meaning of the Fourth Amendment—meaningful interference, however brief, with an individual's freedom of movement."

3. ***The duration of Fourth Amendment seizures.*** *Torres* says that the duration of a seizure-by-physical-force "lasts only as long as the application of force." In *Torres*, the seizure lasted only "for the instant that the bullets struck [Torres]." But how long does a seizure last when the government takes control of a person? How about when it takes control of property? The Supreme Court has been less than clear on this, leading to some lower court confusion. *Compare Lee v. City of Chicago*, 330 F.3d 456 (7th Cir. 2003) (a seizure is the single act of initially taking control) *with Brewster v. Beck*, 859 F.3d 1194 (9th Cir. 2017) (a seizure is ongoing during detention). The dispute may be only academic, however, as the duration of any detention often is critical to whether a seizure is reasonable—whether it is considered an ongoing seizure or an initial seizure followed by detention. *See, e.g., United States v. Place*, 462 U.S. 696, 709 (1983) ("The length of the detention of respondent's luggage alone precludes the conclusion that the seizure was reasonable in the absence of probable cause.").

4. ***Is a move-on order directing a person to leave a public place a "seizure"?*** An officer may tell a person to "move on," ordering them to leave a public space. The order requires a person to leave that place but does not limit where else the person can go. If a person is ordered to move on and complies with the order, has that person been seized? Under *Florida v. Bostick*, 501 U.S. 429, 439 (1991), the test for whether a person is seized by voluntary submission to a show of authority depends on whether a reasonable person would believe he was "not free to decline the officers' requests or otherwise terminate the encounter." Courts have divided on how this test applies to move-on orders. *Compare Bennett v. City of Eastpointe*, 410 F.3d 810, 834 (6th Cir. 2005) (person forced to leave town in response to a move-on order was seized) *with Peery v. City of Miami*, 977 F.3d 1061 (11th Cir. 2020) (order to leave does not lead to seizure; under *Bostick*, "the key question is whether a reasonable person can terminate the encounter with police," and "a person who is told to leave one place but remains free to go anywhere else that he wishes can undoubtedly terminate his encounter.")

5. ***Persistent questioning that ripens a consensual encounter into a seizure by show of authority.*** In *United States v. Mabry*, 997 F.3d 1239 (D.C. Cir. 2021), several uniformed

officers approached Mabry, who was standing with two other men on a sidewalk, at night. Officers frisked the two other men, and Mabry lifted his shirt to show the officers he was not carrying a weapon. Officers then began to question Mabry about what was in the satchel he was carrying. The officers repeatedly asked Mabry to see what was in the satchel, and he repeatedly declined. The court ruled that the repeated questioning helped the situation cross the line from a consensual encounter to a seizure:

"This case illustrates how a consensual encounter with the police can, subtly but surely, ripen into a show of authority that triggers the Fourth Amendment. . . . The persistent nature of his questioning—which continued despite Mabry's attempts to end the encounter—communicated that [the officer] was not taking no for an answer. The broader context intensified the coercive nature of the encounter. For example, the entire encounter occurred at night, with uniformed officers shining their flashlights at the three men, while Mabry's avenues of egress were at least partially restricted by the officers, their car, and a fence. Considering all the circumstances, a reasonable person would not have felt free to ignore [the officer] and walk away."

6. ***Seizures of persons in the context of*** Terry ***stops.*** For more on the standard for seizing a person, offered in the context of temporary stops under *Terry v. Ohio, see* main casebook pages 401–10.

§ 4. SEARCH WARRANTS

B. EXECUTION OF THE WARRANT

15th ed., p. 313; add the following new Note 4A before Note 5:

4A. ***Relying on a ruse to trigger*** **Michigan v. Summers.** *United States v. Ramirez,* 976 F.3d 946 (9th Cir. 2020) considers whether the government can use a ruse to cause a suspect to be at a place where a warrant is executed in order to detain them under *Michigan v. Summers* [p. 311]. The government contacted a suspect and pretended that they were investigating a burglary at his home. According to the officer, the suspect needed to come home immediately to tell the officers what had been stolen. When the suspect arrived home, the officers told him the truth: They were executing a warrant at his home and they wanted to interview him about the crime. The officers detained him under *Summers,* and under questioning, he confessed.

Held: Relying on a ruse to get the benefit of the *Summers* detention power violated the Fourth Amendment. "Permitting the agents' conduct would eviscerate the limitations implemented by the *Summers* rule, allowing law enforcement to seize people located away from the premises to be searched. Law enforcement could turn a warrant to search a home into a warrant to search any number of items outside the home, so long as they could trick a resident into bringing those items to the home to be searched before the warrant was executed. The deceit employed in this case opens a loophole that the Fourth Amendment does not condone."

CHAPTER 7

WARRANTLESS AND LESSER-GROUNDS SEARCHES AND SEIZURES

• • •

§ 1. WARRANTLESS ARRESTS AND SEARCHES OF THE PERSON

15th ed., p. 325; end of Note 3, add:

[Editor's Note: The Ninth Circuit later withdrew the *Rosenbaum* opinion as quoted above and replaced it with one that no longer included this *Devenpeck* discussion.]

15th ed., p. 336; end of Note 2, add:

In *State v. Moore*, 839 S.E.2d 882 (S.C.2020), where the *Brown* abandonment theory was deemed a close question, the court instead upheld the warrantless search regarding three cell phones found at a crime scene on a different basis: in each instance, the warrantless search was limited to the phone's SIM card, which "contains limited storage capacity" and "therefore never contains the vast majority of the information available on an unlocked cell phone,"

15th ed., p. 344; add the following new Note 9:

9. ***State constitutional law can offer greater regulation: The Massachusetts example.*** State courts can impose rules on state and local police under state constitutions that go beyond the federal constitution. Efforts by the Massachusetts Supreme Judicial Court to address racially discriminatory traffic stops are particularly notable. First, in *Commonwealth v. Lora*, 886 N.E.2d 688 (Mass. 2008), the court held that the Equal Protection clause of the state constitution provided for suppression of the fruits of a traffic stop that was the product of discriminatory policing:

"Evidence of racial profiling is relevant in determining whether a traffic stop is the product of selective enforcement violative of the equal protection guarantee of the Massachusetts Declaration of Rights; and that evidence seized in the course of a stop violative of equal protection should, ordinarily, be excluded at trial." The court adopted a burden shifting approach. First, the defendant has the burden "to present sufficient evidence of impermissible discrimination," based primarily on "statistical evidence demonstrating disparate treatment of persons based on their race." If the defendant met that standard, the burden shifted to the state "to provide a race-neutral explanation for such a stop."

More recently, in *Commonwealth v. Long*, 152 N.E.3d 725 (Mass. 2020), the court concluded that *Lora* "set the bar too high for defendants attempting to establish a reasonable inference of a discriminatory stop." *Lora* focused on the use of statistical evidence to show discrimination. But in *Long*, the court concluded that *Lora* "has proved infeasible for defendants" because "providing statistical evidence sufficient to raise a reasonable inference that a motor vehicle stop was racially motivated" was too difficult. In its place, *Long* adopted a reasonable person standard based on the facts of each case:

"While a defendant must show more than the fact that he or she was a member of a constitutionally protected class and was stopped for a traffic infraction, the burden must not be so heavy that it makes any remedy illusory. The requirement that a defendant establish a reasonable inference that a traffic stop was motivated by racial bias means simply that the defendant must produce evidence upon which a reasonable person could rely to infer that the officer discriminated on the basis of the defendant's race or membership in another protected class. Conclusive evidence is not needed.

"The burden shifting framework under *Lora* remains the same, even as we elaborate on the ways in which a defendant can present nonstatistical evidence of a race-based pretextual stop. A defendant first should raise a reasonable inference of racial profiling through a motion to suppress. The motion should describe all of the circumstances of the traffic stop that support a reasonable inference that the decision to make the stop was motivated (whether explicitly or implicitly) by race. The defendant need not submit admissible evidence; rather, the motion simply must point to specific facts about the stop that support such an inference.

"These facts, including statements by the defendant and others, may be based on the defendant's personal knowledge, the defendant's own investigation, evidence obtained during discovery, and other relevant sources. If the defendant's motion establishes such an inference, the defendant is entitled to a hearing, at which the Commonwealth would bear the burden of rebutting the inference. Of course, a traffic stop motivated by race is unconstitutional, even if the officer also was motivated by the legitimate purpose of enforcing the traffic laws.

"When examining the totality of the circumstances, judges should consider factors such as: (1) patterns in enforcement actions by the particular police officer; (2) the regular duties of the officer involved in the stop; (3) the sequence of events prior to the stop; (4) the manner of the stop; (5) the safety interests in enforcing the motor vehicle violation; and (6) the specific police department's policies and procedures regarding traffic stops. These factors are not exhaustive; any relevant facts may be raised for the judge's consideration.

"Once a reasonable inference of racial profiling has been established, the Commonwealth would bear the burden of rebutting that inference. To meet its burden, the Commonwealth would have to do more than merely point to the validity of the traffic violation that was the asserted reason for the stop. Rather, it would have to grapple with all of the reasonable inferences and all of the evidence that a defendant presented, and would have to prove that the stop was not racially motivated. If the Commonwealth does not rebut the reasonable inference that the stop was motivated at least in part by race, the defendant would have established that the stop violated the equal protection principles of [the Massachusetts constitution], and therefore was illegal, and any evidence derived from the stop would have to be suppressed."

15th ed., p. 348; before Note 4, add:

Just a few years later, in MITCHELL v. WISCONSIN, 139 S.Ct. 2525 (2019), another "implied consent" statute case, Mitchell was arrested for driving under the influence after a preliminary breath test indicated his blood alcohol concentration (BAC) was well beyond the legal limit. Police transported him to a nearby hospital for a blood test, but Mitchell was unconscious by the time he reached the hospital. His blood was drawn anyway under a state statute (like that found in over half of the states) that presumes a person incapable of withdrawing implied consent has not done so. The blood analysis showed Mitchell's BAC was above the legal limit, so he was charged with violating the drunk-driving laws. His motion to suppress was denied, and he was convicted. Alito, J., in an opinion for four Justices, concluded:

"Today, we consider what police officers may do in a narrow but important category of cases: those in which the driver is unconscious and therefore cannot be given a breath test. In such cases, we hold, the exigent-circumstances rule almost always permits a blood test without a warrant. When a breath test is impossible, enforcement of the drunk-driving laws depends upon the administration of a blood test. And when a police officer encounters an unconscious driver, it is very likely that the driver would be taken to an emergency room and that his blood would be drawn for diagnostic purposes even if the police were not seeking BAC information. In addition, police officers most frequently come upon unconscious drivers when they report to the scene of an accident, and under those circumstances, the officers' many responsibilities—such as attending to other injured drivers or passengers and preventing further accidents—may be incompatible with the procedures that would be required to obtain a warrant. Thus, when a driver is unconscious, the general rule is that a warrant is not needed. * * *

"When police have probable cause to believe a person has committed a drunk-driving offense and the driver's unconsciousness or stupor requires him to be taken to the hospital or similar facility before police have a reasonable opportunity to administer a standard evidentiary breath test, they may almost always order a warrantless blood test to measure the driver's BAC without offending the Fourth Amendment. We do not rule out the possibility that in an unusual case a defendant would be able to show that his blood would not have been drawn if police had not been seeking BAC information, and that police could not have reasonably judged that a warrant application would interfere with other pressing needs or duties. Because Mitchell did not have a chance to attempt to make that showing, a remand for that purpose is necessary."

Thomas, J., concurring in the judgment, objected: "Today, the plurality adopts a difficult-to-administer rule: Exigent circumstances are generally present when police encounter a person suspected of drunk driving—except when they aren't. The plurality's presumption will rarely be rebutted, but it will nevertheless burden both officers and courts who must attempt to apply it. 'The better (and far simpler) way to resolve' this case is to apply 'the per se rule' I proposed [in *McNeely* and *Birchfield*, under which] the natural metabolization of alcohol in the blood stream ' "creates an exigency once police have probable cause to believe the driver is drunk," ' regardless of whether the driver is conscious. Because I am of the view that the Wisconsin Supreme Court should apply that rule on remand, I concur only in the judgment."

Sotomayor, J., for three Justices, dissenting, objected: "The State of Wisconsin conceded in the state courts that it had time to get a warrant to draw Gerald Mitchell's blood, and that should be the end of the matter. Because the plurality needlessly casts aside the established protections of the warrant requirement in favor of a brand new presumption of exigent circumstances that Wisconsin does not urge, that the state courts did not consider, and that contravenes this Court's precedent, I respectfully dissent. * * *

"Rather than simply applying this Court's precedents to address—and reject—Wisconsin's implied-consent theory, the plurality today takes the extraordinary step of relying on an issue, exigency, that Wisconsin has affirmatively waived. Wisconsin has not once, in any of its briefing before this Court or the state courts, argued that exigent circumstances were present here. * * *

"There are good reasons why Wisconsin never asked any court to consider applying any version of the exigency exception here. The Court's precedents foreclose it. According to the plurality, when the police attempt to obtain a blood sample from a person suspected of drunk driving, there will 'almost always' be exigent circumstances if the person falls unconscious. As this case demonstrates, however, the fact that a suspect fell unconscious at some point before the blood draw does not mean that there was insufficient time to get a warrant."

Gorsuch, J., dissenting, objected that "the application of the exigent circumstances doctrine in this area poses complex and difficult questions that neither the parties nor the courts below discussed. Rather than proceeding solely by self-direction, I would have dismissed this case as improvidently granted and waited for a case presenting the exigent circumstances question."

§ 2. WARRANTLESS ENTRIES AND SEARCHES OF PREMISES

15th ed., p. 373; add the following new Note 1A:

1A. *Hot pursuit as a categorical rule or case-by-case test, for misdemeanors or felonies. Lange v. California*, 141 S.Ct. 1263 (2021), establishes that there is no categorical hot pursuit exception when an officer is in hot pursuit of a suspect for a misdemeanor offense: "A great many misdemeanor pursuits involve exigencies allowing warrantless entry. But whether a given one does so turns on the particular facts of the case." The Court explained: "The flight of a suspected misdemeanant does not always justify a warrantless entry into a home. An officer must consider all the circumstances in a pursuit case to determine whether there is a law enforcement emergency. On many occasions, the officer will have good reason to enter—to prevent imminent harms of violence, destruction of evidence, or escape from the home. But when the officer has time to get a warrant, he must do so—even though the misdemeanant fled."

Notably, *Lange* does not directly answer whether the hot pursuit exception is categorical for felony offenses. But does it matter? If hot pursuit is justified for misdemeanors "on many occasions," it may be that felony hot pursuit is so often justified that the differences are slim between a categorial rule and a case-by-case test.

§ 3. WARRANTLESS SEIZURES AND SEARCHES OF VEHICLES AND CONTAINERS

15th ed., p. 382; at the top, add the following new Note 6:

6. *Does the automobile exception apply to other means of transportation?* Courts have considered whether the automobile exception applies to means of transportation other than cars. In general, courts have ruled that the automobile exception applies broadly. For example, the exception applies to searches of the following:

(a) *Commercial buses, see United States v. Pina*, 648 Fed. Appx. 899 (11th Cir. 2016) (probable cause to believe drugs were present on a bus permitted search of "the bus and every piece of luggage" inside it).

(b) *Airplanes, see United States v. Gooch*, 603 F.2d 122 (10th Cir. 1979) ("Although [an airplane] does not travel public thoroughfares where both its occupants and its contents are in plain view, it ordinarily lands at airports open to the public where its occupants and contents are similarly visible. The pervasive regulation of automobiles and their drivers is even exceeded by the regulation of airplanes and their pilots.")

(c) *Bicycles, see People v. Santana*, 212 A.D.2d 404 (N.Y. App. 1995) ("Bicycles and motor vehicles share characteristics of ready mobility, and users of both mechanisms on the public street have a diminished expectation of privacy with respect thereto.") (search of bicycle's handlebar, where drugs were stored inside).

(d) *Trains, see Symes v. United States*, 633 A.2d 51, 55 (D.C. 1993) (concluding that "the mobility of the train and its impending departure provided the requisite exigent circumstances to justify the officers' deviation from the warrant requirement of the Fourth Amendment") (search of a sleeping car of an Amtrak train during a stop-over).

(e)   *Unhitched trailers, see United States v. Navas*, 597 F.3d 492 (2d Cir. 2010) ("Trailers are routinely parked, legs dropped, with the expectation of promptly returning them to the road as soon as they have been loaded or a cab becomes available to haul them. The dropping of the legs in no way suggests that the trailer will not promptly return to service on the highways.")

At the same time, courts have ruled that the automobile exception does not apply to searches of these items:

(a)   *Packages found inside vehicles operated by third-party shipping companies, see Robey v. Superior Court*, 302 P.3d 574 (Cal. 2013) (concluding that "the concerns justifying an immediate warrantless search of a lawfully stopped automobile do not apply to packages consigned for shipment" because the government can remove a shipped package from the shipping company's vehicle under exigent circumstances and then obtain a warrant) (search of a FedEx package discovered while inside a FedEx truck).

(b)   *Wheelchairs, see United States v. Cunningham*, No. 20–cr–104–CJW, April 29, 2021, at 11 (N.D. Iowa 2021) (concluding that the automobile exception does not apply to search of a wheelchair because "while wheelchairs have some mobility, that mobility is limited when compared to automobiles") (lifting up the seat cushion on a person's wheelchair, revealing a gun).

15th ed., p. 388; after first paragraph of Note 4, add:

Compare *United States v. Knapp*, 917 F.3d 1161 (10th Cir. 2019), concluding that "such a rule risks expanding *Robinson*'s limited exception to grant unqualified authority to search an arrestee's grab area. The better formulation, we believe, would be to limit *Robinson* to searches of an arrestee's clothing, including containers concealed under or within her clothing. Accordingly, visible containers in an arrestee's hand such as Ms. Knapp's purse are best considered to be within the area of an arrestee's immediate control—thus governed by *Chimel*—the search of which must be justified in each case." Such justification was deemed lacking in the instant case as "not only were Ms. Knapp's hands cuffed behind her back," but "officers were nearby" and "the purse was closed and three to four feet behind her."

15th ed., p. 391; just before *Gant*, add the following new Note 7:

7.   ***When an occupant removes a container from a car.*** The automobile exception applies to containers found inside cars. But what rule applies if the officer orders a person out of a car and the person takes the container with them? Can the container be searched under the automobile exception because it was in a car before the officer's order, or does the person's removal of the container upon exiting the car mean that a warrant is needed to search it? Courts have held that the automobile exception still applies as long as the officers had probable cause before the container was removed. *See, e.g., State v. Lang*, 942 N.W.2d 388 (Neb. 2020) (where suspect was ordered out of a car and took her purse with her, the purse could be searched under the automobile exception because "the location of the purse at the time it was searched does not change its character as a container that was inside the vehicle when officers developed probable cause to search the vehicle").

15th ed., p. 399; replace Note 4 with the following:

4.   ***What is the "passenger compartment" of an SUV?*** The notion that a search incident to arrest of a car only extends to its "passenger compartment" dates back to *New York v. Belton*, 453 U.S. 454 (1981). In 1981, when *Belton* was decided, most vehicles were sedans with an enclosed

compartment where passengers sat and a separate trunk in the back not reachable from the inside of the car. The passenger compartment thus excluded the trunk. *See id.* at 460 n.4 ("Our holding encompasses only the interior of the passenger compartment of an automobile and does not encompass the trunk.")

How does the "passenger compartment" limit apply to sport utility vehicles (SUVs), which today far outsell sedans? In an SUV, the passenger compartment and the trunk are merged into one enclosed area. Lower courts agree that the "passenger compartment" for an SUV, still relevant under *Arizona v. Gant*, includes its trunk area. Because the rear enclosed area of the SUV could be reached by an occupant, it counts as part of the passenger compartment. *See United States v. Stegall*, 850 F.3d 981, 985 (8th Cir. 2017) (citing cases). *See also United States v. White*, 131 Fed.Appx. 54 (6th Cir. 2005) (holding that the open bed of a pickup truck is not part of the passenger compartment because it is not reachable to seated occupants without exiting the vehicle).

15th ed., p. 401; add the following new Note 10 before the materials on Stop and Frisk:

10. *A community caretaking exception that is limited to cars.* Cady v. Dombrowski, 413 U.S. 433 (1973), holds that it was reasonable for officers to search the trunk of a police officer's personal car without a warrant to recover the officer's service revolver when the car was seriously damaged in an accident and was left outside unguarded. This was justified by a community caretaking rationale, the Court indicated: "Where, as here, the trunk of an automobile, which the officer reasonably believed to contain a gun, was vulnerable to intrusion by vandals, we hold that the search was not unreasonable."

In *Caniglia v. Strom*, 141 S.Ct. 1596 (2021), the Court clarified that the community caretaking exception is limited to cars and does not allow searches of homes. Caniglia had urged his wife to kill him with his handgun, and later he agreed to go to the hospital for a psychiatric evaluation. Officers then entered Caniglia's home and seized his guns out of fear that he would harm himself or others upon his return. Held: Entering the home could not be justified by the community caretaking exception because that exception did not extend to homes: "What is reasonable for vehicles is different from what is reasonable for homes."

§ 4. STOP AND FRISK

A. POLICE ACTION SHORT OF A SEIZURE

15th ed., p. 410; at the bottom, add the following new Note 7:

7. *Recent cases on whether a person's race is relevant to whether a reasonable person in his situation would feel free to leave.* Recent lower-court caselaw has divided on whether the "reasonable person would feel free to leave" test should factor in the subject's race. Some courts have said race should not be considered, and others have said it should be. For the view that race should not be considered, consider *United States v. Knights*, 989 F.3d 1281 (11th Cir. 2021):

"We may not consider race to determine whether a seizure has occurred. True, race can be relevant in other Fourth Amendment contexts. For example, we consider a suspect's personal characteristics to decide whether he gave consent to a search or seizure because that question is subjective. But the existence of a seizure is an objective question. We ask whether a reasonable person would have believed he was not free to leave in the light of the totality of the circumstances. The circumstances of the situation are key to this inquiry—in particular, the police officer's objective behavior. An objective test has important virtues: we can readily apply it, and law enforcement can know ex ante what conduct implicates the Fourth Amendment.

"We consider a suspect's personal characteristics in our seizure analysis only insofar as they have an objectively discernible relationship to a reasonable person's understanding of his freedom of action. For example, we can consider age because both we and the police can draw commonsense conclusions about the effect of age on a person's perception of his freedom to leave that apply broadly to children as a class. By contrast, most personal characteristics, including race, do not lend themselves to objective conclusions.

"Knights argues that an objectively discernible relationship follows from the existence of racial disparities in the frequency of police stops, arrests, and other interactions. But even if empirical research can provide evidence of how individuals of different demographics have interacted with or perceive the police, this research also reinforces that perceptions vary within groups. See, e.g., David K. Kessler, Free to Leave? An Empirical Look at the Fourth Amendment's Seizure Standard, 99 J. Crim. L. & Criminology 51, 77 & n.151 (2009). There is no uniform life experience for persons of color, and there are surely divergent attitudes toward law enforcement officers among members of the population.

"Even if we could derive uniform—or at least predominant—attitudes from a characteristic like race, we have no workable method to translate general attitudes towards the police into rigorous analysis of how a reasonable person would understand his freedom of action in a particular situation. Take the evidence Knights offers that black individuals as a group tend to be wary of the police. How could we consider that tendency, in conjunction with other factors, in a systematic way? In which situations is race a relevant factor? How would we weigh race against countervailing considerations? Would that weight vary with the race of a police officer or a particular police department's history with its community? With so many open questions like these, short of assuming that all interactions between police officers and black individuals are seizures, we would be left to pure speculation.

"And even if we could devise an objective way to consider race, we could not apply a race-conscious reasonable-person test without running afoul of the Equal Protection Clause. Just as the scope of Fourth Amendment protection does not vary with the state of mind of the particular individual being approached, it does not vary with the race of the individual being approached. So we may not consider race in deciding whether a seizure has occurred, and the objective circumstances of Knights's encounter with the police remain dispositive."

Judge Rosenbaum authored a concurring opinion. Judge Rosenbaum agreed that Equal Protection clause caselaw barred explicitly considering race. According to Judge Rosenbaum, however, some legal response was needed because, in reality, race was quite relevant to whether a reasonable person would feel free to leave:

"As a matter of the commonsense reality of police-citizen interactions, Black individuals from every background have long expressed that race can and does affect whether a citizen feels 'free to leave' a police encounter. Of course, we wish race were not relevant. But wishing does not make it so.

"The evidence demonstrates that race can matter during interactions with the police. Black Americans on the whole are 2.5 times more likely to be shot and killed by police officers than white Americans. The pattern is even more pronounced with respect to young Black men between the ages of 15 and 19: in a recent study, they were found to be 21 times more likely than their white counterparts to be killed during police encounters.

"So it is no wonder that Black male teens still report a fear of police and a serious concern for their personal safety and mortality in the presence of police officers. When we consider unarmed individuals, Black Americans are five times more likely than white Americans to be killed by police. And these disproportionate rates of deadly encounters persist, despite findings that, even accounting for threat level, Black Americans who are fatally shot by police are no more likely to be posing an imminent lethal threat to the officers at the moment they are killed than white Americans fatally shot by police.

"Because of these circumstances, Black Americans' lived experiences make them materially less likely than white Americans to believe they have the freedom to leave an interaction with the police. Indeed, the dynamics surrounding an encounter between a police officer and a black citizen are quite different from those that surround an encounter between an officer and the so-called average, reasonable person. For Black citizens, the fear of violence often overlays the entire law-enforcement encounter. Because of these circumstances, commentators have concluded that Black people have 'internalized racial obedience toward, and fear of, the police.' Devon W. Carbado, (E)racing the Fourth Amendment, 100 Mich. L. Rev. 946, 966 (2002).

"Black people often tread more carefully around law enforcement than the Court's hypothetical reasonable person does because of the grave awareness that a misstep or discerned disrespectful word may cause the officer to misperceive a threat and escalate an encounter into a physical one. Black community members have explained that, for them, the 'whole goal' of a police encounter is to 'just kind of stay alive. Just make it to the next day." A Black Mother and Son on 'The Talk': 'When I get Pulled Over by a Police Officer, I Do Not Have Any Rights', KJZZ (June 11, 2020). Towards that end, parents have long found it necessary to have 'The Talk' with their Black children to try to help them keep safe when they encounter the police. When a citizen perceives staying alive as the 'whole goal' of a police interaction, it is difficult to say that an encounter is truly 'consensual.' "

Judge Rosenbaum then invited the Supreme Court to introduce a race-neutral warning requirement before engaging in a consensual interaction. By clarifying whether a person was seized, a warning rule could help put every citizen on the same footing:

"The Supreme Court could require officers who wish to engage in consensual interactions—at the very least with respect to those individuals an officer wants, without reasonable suspicion, to investigate in some way—to, at the outset, inform the approached individual that he or she may decline or end the interaction without penalty. While not perfect, this solution has the benefit of establishing a bright line so both citizens and officers know that any continued interaction is presumed consensual."

In contrast to the Eleventh Circuit, other courts have held that explicit consideration of race is entirely proper in the seizure analysis. Consider *Dozier v. United States*, 220 A.3d 933 (D.C. 2019):

"Being innocent is not the same as being perceived to be innocent. Even the innocent person we posit in our Fourth Amendment analysis might well fear that he is perceived with particular suspicion by hyper-vigilant police officers expecting to find criminal activity in a particular area.

"This fear is particularly justified for persons of color, who are more likely to be subjected to this type of police surveillance. As is known from well-publicized and documented examples, an African-American man facing armed policemen would reasonably be especially apprehensive. The fear of harm and resulting protective conditioning to submit to avoid harm at the hands of police is relevant to whether there was a seizure because feeling 'free' to leave or terminate an encounter with police officers is rooted in an assessment of the consequences of doing so.

"A person who reasonably is apprehensive that walking away, ignoring police presence, or refusing to answer police questions or requests might lead to detention and, possibly, more aggressive police action, is not truly free to exercise a constitutional prerogative—'to be secure in their persons,' even if they do not submit—in the same manner as a person who is not viewed with similar suspicion by police and, as a result, largely unafraid of triggering an aggressive reaction."

B. GROUNDS FOR TEMPORARY SEIZURE
FOR INVESTIGATION

15th ed., p. 411; before Note 1, add:

KANSAS V. GLOVER
___ U.S. ___, 140 S.Ct. 1183, 206 L.Ed.2d 412 (2020).

JUSTICE THOMAS delivered the opinion of the Court.

This case presents the question whether a police officer violates the Fourth Amendment by initiating an investigative traffic stop after running a vehicle's license plate and learning that the registered owner has a revoked driver's license. We hold that when the officer lacks information negating an inference that the owner is the driver of the vehicle, the stop is reasonable. * * *

Under this Court's precedents, the Fourth Amendment permits an officer to initiate a brief investigative traffic stop when he has "a particularized and objective basis for suspecting the particular person stopped of criminal activity." "Although a mere 'hunch' does not create reasonable suspicion, the level of suspicion the standard requires is considerably less than proof of wrongdoing by a preponderance of the evidence, and obviously less than is necessary for probable cause."

Because it is a "less demanding" standard, "reasonable suspicion can be established with information that is different in quantity or content than that required to establish probable cause." The standard "depends on the factual and practical considerations of everyday life on which reasonable and prudent men, not legal technicians, act." Courts "cannot reasonably demand scientific certainty . . . where none exists." Rather, they must permit officers to make "commonsense judgments and inferences about human behavior." * * *

Before initiating the stop, Deputy Mehrer observed an individual operating a 1995 Chevrolet 1500 pickup truck with Kansas plate 295ATJ. He also knew that the registered owner of the truck had a revoked license and that the model of the truck matched the observed vehicle. From these three facts, Deputy Mehrer drew the commonsense inference that Glover was likely the driver of the vehicle, which provided more than reasonable suspicion to initiate the stop.

The fact that the registered owner of a vehicle is not always the driver of the vehicle does not negate the reasonableness of Deputy Mehrer's inference. Such is the case with all reasonable inferences. The reasonable suspicion inquiry "falls considerably short" of 51% accuracy.

Glover's revoked license does not render Deputy Mehrer's inference unreasonable either. Empirical studies demonstrate what common experience readily reveals: Drivers with revoked licenses frequently continue to drive and therefore to pose safety risks to other motorists and pedestrians. * * *

Glover and the dissent respond with two arguments as to why Deputy Mehrer lacked reasonable suspicion. Neither is persuasive.

First, Glover and the dissent argue that Deputy Mehrer's inference was unreasonable because it was not grounded in his law enforcement training or experience. Nothing in our Fourth Amendment precedent supports the notion that, in determining whether reasonable suspicion exists, an officer can draw inferences based on knowledge gained only through law enforcement training and experience. We have repeatedly recognized the opposite. * * * The inference that the driver of a car is its registered owner does not require any specialized training; rather, it is a reasonable inference made by ordinary people on a daily basis. * * *

The dissent's rule would also impose on police the burden of pointing to specific training materials or field experiences justifying reasonable suspicion for the myriad infractions in municipal criminal codes. And by removing common sense as a source of evidence, the dissent would considerably narrow the daylight between the showing required for probable cause and the "less stringent" showing required for reasonable suspicion. Finally, it would impermissibly tie a traffic stop's validity to the officer's length of service. * * *

In reaching this conclusion, we in no way minimize the significant role that specialized training and experience routinely play in law enforcement investigations. We simply hold that such experience is not *required* in every instance.

Glover and the dissent also contend that adopting Kansas' view would eviscerate the need for officers to base reasonable suspicion on "specific and articulable facts" particularized to the individual, because police could instead rely exclusively on probabilities. Their argument carries little force.

As an initial matter, we have previously stated that officers, like jurors, may rely on probabilities in the reasonable suspicion context. Moreover, as explained above, Deputy Mehrer did not rely exclusively on probabilities. He knew that the license plate was linked to a truck matching the observed vehicle and that the registered owner of the vehicle had a revoked license. Based on these minimal facts, he used common sense to form a reasonable suspicion that a specific individual was potentially engaged in specific criminal activity—driving with a revoked license. * * * "The standard takes into account the totality of the circumstances—the whole picture." As a result, the presence of additional facts might dispel reasonable suspicion. For example, if an officer knows that the registered owner of the vehicle is in his mid-sixties but observes that the driver is in her mid-twenties, then the totality of the circumstances would not "raise a suspicion that the particular individual being stopped is engaged in wrongdoing." Here, Deputy Mehrer possessed no exculpatory information—let alone sufficient information to rebut the reasonable inference that Glover was driving his own truck—and thus the stop was justified.[2] * * *

JUSTICE KAGAN, with whom JUSTICE GINSBURG joins, concurring.

When you see a car coming down the street, your common sense tells you that the registered owner may well be behind the wheel. Not always, of course. Families share cars; friends borrow them. Still, a person often buys a vehicle to drive it himself. So your suspicion that the owner is driving would be perfectly reasonable.

Now, though, consider a wrinkle: Suppose you knew that the registered owner of the vehicle no longer had a valid driver's license. That added fact raises a new question. What are the odds that someone who has lost his license would continue to drive? The answer is by no means obvious. You might think that a person told not to drive on pain of criminal penalty would obey the order— so that if his car was on the road, someone else (a family member, a friend) must be doing the driving. Or you might have the opposite intuition—that a person's reasons for driving would overcome his worries about violating the law, no matter the possible punishment. But most likely (let's be honest), you just wouldn't know. Especially if you've not had your own license taken away, your everyday experience has given you little basis to assess the probabilities. Your common sense can therefore no longer guide you.

Even so, Deputy Mark Mehrer had reasonable suspicion to stop the truck in this case, and I join the Court's opinion holding as much. Crucially for me, Mehrer knew yet one more thing about the vehicle's registered owner, and it related to his proclivity for breaking driving laws. As the

---

[2]   The dissent argues that this approach impermissibly places the burden of proof on the individual to negate the inference of reasonable suspicion. Not so. As the above analysis makes clear, it is the information possessed by *the officer* at the time of the stop, not any information offered by the individual after the fact, that can negate the inference.

Court recounts, Mehrer learned from a state database that Charles Glover, the truck's owner, had had his license revoked under Kansas law. And Kansas almost never revokes a license except for serious or repeated driving offenses. Crimes like vehicular homicide and manslaughter, or vehicular flight from a police officer, provoke a license revocation; so too do multiple convictions for moving traffic violations within a short time. In other words, a person with a revoked license has already shown a willingness to flout driving restrictions. That fact, as the Court states, provides a "reason[ ] to infer" that such a person will drive without a license—at least often enough to warrant an investigatory stop.

* * * I would find this a different case if Kansas had barred Glover from driving on a ground that provided no similar evidence of his penchant for ignoring driving laws. Consider, for example, if Kansas had suspended rather than revoked Glover's license. Along with many other States, Kansas suspends licenses for matters having nothing to do with road safety, such as failing to pay parking tickets, court fees, or child support. * * *

JUSTICE SOTOMAYOR, dissenting.

* * * To assess whether an officer had the requisite suspicion to seize a driver, past cases have considered the "totality of the circumstances—the whole picture," and analyzed whether the officer assembled "fact on fact and clue on clue."

The stop at issue here, however, rests on just one key fact: that the vehicle was owned by someone with a revoked license. The majority concludes—erroneously, in my view—that seizing this vehicle was constitutional on the record below because drivers with revoked licenses (as opposed to suspended licenses) in Kansas "have already demonstrated a disregard for the law or are categorically unfit to drive." This analysis breaks from settled doctrine and dramatically alters both the quantum and nature of evidence a State may rely on to prove suspicion.

The State bears the burden of justifying a seizure. This requires the government to articulate factors supporting its reasonable suspicion, usually through a trained agent. While the Court has not dictated precisely what evidence a government must produce, it has stressed that an officer must at least "articulate more than an 'inchoate and unparticularized suspicion or "hunch" ' of criminal activity." That articulation must include both facts and an officer's "rational inferences from those facts." * * *

Additionally, reasonable suspicion eschews judicial common sense, in favor of the perspectives and inferences of a reasonable officer viewing "the facts through the lens of his police experience and expertise." It is the reasonable officer's assessment, not the ordinary person's—or judge's—judgment, that matters.

Finally, a stop must be individualized—that is, based on "a suspicion that the particular [subject] being stopped is engaged in wrongdoing." * * * The inquiry ordinarily involves some observation or report about the target's behavior—not merely the class to which he belongs. * * *

Faithful adherence to these precepts would yield a significantly different analysis and outcome than that offered by the majority.

For starters, the majority flips the burden of proof. It permits Kansas police officers to effectuate roadside stops whenever they lack "information negating an inference" that a vehicle's unlicensed owner is its driver. This has it backwards: The State shoulders the burden to supply the key inference that tethers observation to suspicion. The majority repeatedly attributes such an inference to Deputy Mehrer. But that is an after-the-fact gloss on a seven-paragraph stipulation. Nowhere in his terse submission did Deputy Mehrer indicate that he had any informed belief about the propensity of unlicensed drivers to operate motor vehicles in the area—let alone that he relied on such a belief in seizing Glover.

The consequence of the majority's approach is to absolve officers from any responsibility to investigate the identity of a driver where feasible. But that is precisely what officers ought to do—and are more than capable of doing. Of course, some circumstances may not warrant an officer approaching a car to take a closer look at its occupants. But there are countless other instances where officers have been able to ascertain the identity of a driver from a distance and make out their approximate age and gender. Indeed, our cases are rife with examples of officers who have perceived more than just basic driver demographics. The majority underestimates officers' capabilities and instead gives them free rein to stop a vehicle involved in no suspicious activity simply because it is registered to an unlicensed person. That stop is based merely on a guess or a "hunch" about the driver's identity.

With no basis in the record to presume that unlicensed drivers routinely continue driving, the majority endeavors to fill the gap with its own "common sense." But simply labeling an inference "common sense" does not make it so, no matter how many times the majority repeats it. Whether the driver of a vehicle is likely to be its unlicensed owner is "by no means obvious." And like the concurrence, I "doubt" that our collective judicial common sense could answer that question, even if our Fourth Amendment jurisprudence allowed us to do so.

Contrary to the majority's claims, the reasonable-suspicion inquiry does not accommodate the average person's intuition. Rather, it permits reliance on a particular type of common sense—that of the reasonable officer, developed through her experiences in law enforcement. * * * By relying on judicial inferences instead, the majority promotes broad, inflexible rules that overlook regional differences.

Allowing judges to offer their own brand of common sense where the State's proffered justifications for a search come up short also shifts police work to the judiciary. Our cases—including those the majority cites—have looked to officer sensibility to establish inferences about human behavior, even though they just as easily could have relied on the inferences "made by ordinary people on a daily basis." There is no reason to depart from that practice here. * * *

The majority today has paved the road to finding reasonable suspicion based on nothing more than a demographic profile. Its logic has thus made the State's task all but automatic. That has never been the law, and it never should be.

NOTE

Does *Glover* support the result earlier reached in *Foster v. City of Indio*, 908 F.3d 1294 (9th Cir.2018) (given that "California had issued concealed carry permits to approximately .2% of its adult population," it follows that "a reasonable officer could conclude that there is a high probability that a person identified in a 911 call as carrying a concealed handgun is violating California's gun laws")?

C. PERMISSIBLE EXTENT AND SCOPE OF TEMPORARY SEIZURE

15th ed., p. 425; add the following new Note 7A after the end of Note 7:

7A. *Determining whether a question is part of the "mission" of a traffic stop.* *Rodriguez* [p.423] holds that "the tolerable duration of police inquiries in the traffic-stop context is determined by the seizure's 'mission'—to address the traffic violation that warranted the stop, and attend to related safety concerns." Questions that are related to the mission of the stop are permitted, while questions unrelated to mission of the stop are subject to *Rodriguez*'s time limit. But how can you tell if a particular question is related to the mission of a stop?

In *United States v. Buzzard*, 1 F.4th 198 (4th Cir. 2021), an officer patrolling alone at night in a high-crime area conducted a traffic stop. The officer recognized the passenger in the car, Martin, as a convicted felon who was recently out of jail and had a history of drug addiction. During the stop, the officer asked the occupants of the car if there was "anything illegal" inside the car. The occupants volunteered their drug paraphernalia in response. The Fourth Circuit held that the officer's question was related to the mission of the stop, namely the officer's safety, and was therefore permitted even if it extended the duration of the stop:

"[The officer] was outnumbered, and he asked the question because of the time of night and the high drug area, Mr. Martin's history, and Mr. Martin's behavior. Given the totality of the circumstances, it makes sense that he needed to know more about what Buzzard and Martin had in the car.

"It's true that the question 'Is there anything illegal in the vehicle?' could be interpreted more broadly than one worded slightly differently (for example, 'Is there anything dangerous in the vehicle?' or 'Are there weapons in the vehicle?'). But given the importance of officer safety and the Supreme Court's repeated recognition that traffic stops are especially fraught with danger to police officers, we decline to require such laser-like precision from an officer asking a single question in these circumstances."

Is this realistic? Wouldn't a question about whether there is "something illegal" in a car naturally be interpreted as a question about drugs, especially when directed to a passenger with a known history of drug addiction?

E. PROTECTIVE SEARCH

15th ed., p. 432; add Note 6A after Note 6:

6A. *Can* Terry *frisks begin with a search through pockets?* In *United States v. Brown*, 996 F.3d 998 (9th Cir. 2021), the Ninth Circuit held that an officer exceeded the scope of a permitted *Terry* frisk when he "did not perform any patdown or other initial limited intrusion but instead proceeded directly to extract and examine an item in [the suspect's] pocket." According to Judge Collins, this limit was inherent in *Terry*'s limited authority to search to locate weapons. An officer could begin a frisk with a patdown. If a patdown was inconclusive about whether a felt item was a weapon, the officer could then reach into the suspect's pockets to get a better feel for what was inside. But absent special circumstances, "a pocket search as the initial means of intrusion" exceeded *Terry*'s frisk authority. Thus, in *Brown*, "the officer's immediate action in proceeding to remove and examine an item from Brown's pocket objectively exceeded what was necessary to verify that Brown did not have a weapon" and violated the Fourth Amendment.

§ 6. CONSENT SEARCHES

A. THE NATURE OF "CONSENT"

15th ed., p. 450; replacing "In none of" paragraph:

In none of the three cases collectively decided in *Birchfield* does it appear there was ever an express claim that the implied-consent statute *itself* provides a basis for a warrantless search by, in effect, making the act of driving on the state's highways a sufficient manifestation of such consent. And in the more recent Supreme Court decision on the subject, *Mitchell v. Wisconsin*, p. 46 supra, the plurality opinion relied instead upon the established exigent circumstances exception to the search warrant requirement despite the fact, as the dissent noted, that the state court's "primary argument has always been that Mitchell consented to the blood draw through the

State's 'implied-consent law.'" Indeed, the plurality emphasized that the Court's prior decisions on the subject "have not rested on the idea that these laws do what their popular name might seem to suggest—that is, create actual consent to all the searches they authorize." The dissent, agreeing on that point, "would go further and hold that the state statute, however phrased, cannot itself create the actual and informed consent that the Fourth Amendment requires."

15th ed., p. 450; end of page, add:

   14.   *"Revocation" of consent.* In *State v. Randall*, 930 N.W.2d 223 (Wis.2019), a "police officer arrested Jessica M. Randall for operating a motor vehicle while under the influence of an intoxicant. Ms. Randall gave the officer permission to take a sample of her blood for the purpose of determining its alcohol concentration. But before the Wisconsin State Laboratory of Hygiene could test it, she sent a letter revoking the consent she had previously given. The letter also demanded the immediate return of her blood sample. This, she says, made the subsequent test of her blood sample a violation of her constitutional right to be free of unreasonable (searches and seizures." Should she prevail?

CHAPTER 9

POLICE INTERROGATION AND CONFESSIONS

▪ ▪ ▪

§ 3. APPLYING AND EXPLAINING *MIRANDA*

A. WHEN ARE THE *MIRANDA* RIGHTS TRIGGERED?

15th ed., p. 528; after Note 2, add:

3. *Incorporating race into the custody analysis.* Consider Devon W. Carbado, *From Stopping Black People to Killing Black People: The Fourth Amendment Pathways to Police Violence,* 105 Calif. L. Rev. 125, 141–42 (2017): "According to the Court [in *JDB*]:

> In some circumstances, a child's age 'would have affected how a reasonable person' in the suspect's position 'would perceive his or her freedom to leave.' That is, a reasonable child subjected to police questioning will sometimes feel pressured to submit when a reasonable adult would feel free to go. We think it clear that courts can account for that reality without doing any damage to the objective nature of the custody analysis.

The foregoing reasoning applies to race. To appreciate how, substitute race for age throughout the passage above, focusing specifically on black and white experiences. Under this thought experiment, the quote now reads:

> In some circumstances, a person's race 'would have affected how a reasonable person' in the suspect's position 'would perceive his or her freedom to leave.' That is, a reasonable black person subjected to police questioning will sometimes feel pressured to submit when a reasonable white person would feel free to go. We think it clear that courts can account for that reality without doing any damage to the objective nature of the custody analysis.

I should be clear to note that, in performing the race/age substitution, I do not mean to suggest that blacks are to whites what children are to adults. I am mindful of the racial infantilization of black people under both slavery and Jim Crow. My point in substituting race for age is simply to suggest that even if one thinks that age is more relevant than race in determining whether a person is seized, the claim that race is irrelevant is difficult to sustain.

The Court's elision of race should trouble us. It takes off the table an important factor that could heighten a person's sense of constraint in the context of a police encounter. Because, for example, whites and African Americans are not similarly situated with respect to how their racial identity might affect this sense of constraint, the Court's failure to consider race is not race-neutral. It creates a racial preference in the seizure doctrine for people who are not racially vulnerable to, or who do not experience a sense of racial constraint in the context of, interactions with the police. Black people, across intraracial differences, are likely to feel seized earlier in a police interaction than whites, likely to feel "more" seized in any given moment, and less likely to know or feel empowered to exercise their rights. . . ."

D. INVOKING THE *MIRANDA* RIGHT TO COUNSEL

15th ed., p. 574; modify the first sentence in Note 1 as follows:

1. ***How does* Davis *work in practice?*** Marcy Strauss examined state and federal cases over a twelve year time period and noted that courts only found 19 percent of all suspects' statements to be _un_ambiguous requests for counsel.

§ 5. THE VOLUNTARINESS TEST REVISITED

B. THE DEFINITION OF VOLUNTARINESS POST-*MIRANDA*

15th ed., p. 662; at the end of Note 2 add the following:

See also Michael J. Zydney Mannheimer, *Fraudulently Induced Confessions*, 96 Notre Dame L. Rev. 799, 800 (2021) (arguing that "[a] confession induced by non-coercive police deception should be suppressed if the deception relates to a fact material to the suspect's decision to confess" where materiality is defined to include those facts that "a reasonable person in the suspect's position would have attached importance to . . . in deciding whether to exercise or forgo the right to remain silent").

Christopher Slobogin, *The Legality of Trickery During Interrogation*, INTERROGATION, CONFESSION AND TRUTH: COMPARATIVE STUDIES IN CRIMINAL PROCEDURE (Lutz Eidam, Michael Lindeman & Andreas Ransiek eds., Nomos Press 2020) divides deceptive interrogation practices into four categories: "(1) 'impersonation' (e.g., showing sympathy for the suspect, posing as a friend, using an informant to question the suspect); (2) 'rationalization' (e.g., suggestions to the effect that a confession will make the suspect or the victim feel better, or that the crime was accidental or justified); (3) 'fabrication' (e.g., false statements that a co-defendant or forensic evidence has inculpated the suspect, or bluffing and other means of insisting the suspect is guilty); and (4) 'negotiation' (e.g., erroneously stating that, if the suspect confesses, more lenient punishment or release from detention is likely)." Professor Slobogin proposes an "equivalency test" under which "police deception during interrogation amounts to impermissible coercion when, but only when, the deceptive statements would be impermissibly coercive if true" and suggests that this test would prohibit negotiation tactics but permit most forms of impersonation, rationalization, and fabrication.

15th ed., p. 662; at the end of Note 3 add the following:

See also State v. Matsumoto, 452 P.3d 310, 313 & 324 (Haw. 2019) (noting that, in Hawai'i, "deliberate falsehoods extrinsic to the facts of the alleged offense, which are of a type reasonably likely to procure an untrue statement or to influence an accused to make a confession regardless of guilt, will be regarded as coercive per se" and holding that telling a suspect that he failed a polygraph test when the results were inconclusive falls within that category and is coercive per se).

15th ed., p. 663; at the end of Note 4 add the following:

See also State v. Baker, 465 P.3d 860, 878–79 (Haw. 2020) (noting that, [i]n regard to coerciveness, there is no meaningful difference in the impact to an accused between a forgery . . . and oral misrepresentations" and "that false claims of physical evidence result in an unsettling number of false or involuntary confessions" and holding that "misrepresentations about the existence of uncontrovertible physical evidence that directly implicates the accused is an exceptionally coercive interrogation tactic and its use is a strong indicator that the suspect's statement was involuntary" and that such lies "may, standing alone, render the accused's subsequent confession involuntary").

15th ed., p. 663; after Note 4 add the following:

    4A. *Statutory ban on police deception.* Illinois recently became the first state to ban police officers from lying to minors during interrogation. Any oral, written, or sign language confession made by a minor under 18 years of age as a result of custodial interrogation at a police station is presumptively inadmissible if the statement was made after police knowingly communicated false facts about evidence or made unauthorized statements regarding leniency while interrogating the minor. Similar bills are being considered in New York and Oregon. *See* Derrick Bryson Taylor, *Illinois Bars Police from Lying to Minors During Questioning*, N.Y. Times (July 16, 2021); Michael Levenson, *Illinois Lawmakers Bar Police From Using Deception When Interrogating Minors*, N.Y. Times (May 31, 2021). The Illinois statute permits the State to overcome the presumption of inadmissibility by showing by a preponderance of the evidence that the confession was voluntarily given based on the totality of the circumstances.

15th ed., p. 666; after Note 9 add the following:

    9A. *Incorporating race into the totality of the circumstances.* In *Jamison v. McClendon*, 476 F.Supp.3d 386, 413–16 (S.D. Miss. 2020), Judge Carlton Reeves considered a suspect's race when addressing the question of whether his consent to a search of his vehicle was voluntarily given. After explaining the history of racial violence against Black people in the region and citing statistics about police violence against Black men, Judge Reeves noted that "Jamison's traffic stop cannot be separated from this context . . . . In America where Black people 'are considered dangerous even when they are in their living rooms eating ice cream, asleep in their beds, playing in the park, standing in the pulpit of their church, birdwatching, exercising in public, or walking home from a trip to the store to purchase a bag of Skittles,' who can say that Jamison felt free that night . . . to say no to an armed Officer McClendon?" *Id.* at 414–15. If race is a factor that informs the coercion present in an exchange between a suspect and the police for purposes of giving consent, so too it should inform the coercion present when police question suspects and ask them to make statements.

C. THE ADDITION OF A THRESHOLD INQUIRY

15th ed., p. 670; at the end of Note 1 add the following:

See also State v. Bowe, 881 P.2d 538, 546 (Haw. 1994) (holding under the state constitution that, even when an accused is coerced into making a confession by a private individual, the state participates in that violation by allowing the coerced statement to be admitted as evidence at trial).

15th ed., p. 673; after Note 10 add the following:

    11. *Discriminatory interrogation tactics.* In *State v. Baker*, 465 P.3d 860, 874 (Haw. 2020), an interrogating officer relied on gender stereotypes to induce a confession in a sexual assault case, stating that women are "more promiscuous . . . when they're on alcohol . . . cause they lose their inhibitions" and that "[g]uys are programmed to procreate" in an attempt to minimize the nature of the offense and induce a confession. The Hawai'i Supreme Court noted the "fundamental duty of this court to call attention to those interrogation techniques that are 'so offensive to a civilized system of justice that they must be condemned under principles of due process'" and held "that interrogation techniques that rely on stereotyping protected classes of persons are inherently coercive, and strongly weigh against any subsequent statement being voluntary." *Id.* at 874–75. Importantly, the Court clarified that its holding "applies without regard to the source of the legal protection from discrimination," citing both statutorily- and constitutionally-protected classes. *Id.* at 875 n.19.

D. THE PROBLEM OF FALSE CONFESSIONS

15th ed., p. 679; at the end of Note 5, add the following:

See Illinois Senate Bill 2122, discussed *supra*, making certain forms of police deception during custodial interrogations of juveniles impermissible and creating a presumption that any resulting confessions will be inadmissible.

CHAPTER 11

INVESTIGATION BY SUBPOENA

■ ■ ■

§ 2. CHALLENGES TO THE GROUNDING AND SCOPE OF THE SUBPOENA

C. APPLYING THE OVERBREADTH PROHIBITION

15th ed., p. 739; on 3rd line, substitute for *"Press Enterprise"*:

R. Enterprises

CHAPTER 12

THE SCOPE OF THE EXCLUSIONARY RULES

■ ■ ■

§ 2. THE "FRUIT OF THE POISONOUS TREE"

A. FOURTH AMENDMENT VIOLATIONS

15th ed., p. 818; after Note 4, add:

4A. ***Predatory policing.*** Consider Devon W. Carbado, *From Stopping Black People to Killing Black People: The Fourth Amendment Pathways to Police Violence*, 105 Calif. L. Rev. 125, 135 (2017): "An African American's vulnerability to being subjected to a legal arrest that began as an illegal seizure is quite real given how many jurisdictions have engaged in what I have elsewhere called 'predatory policing'—the utilization of policing as a mechanism to raise revenue for cities generally and police departments specifically. Predatory policing includes issuing citations to people for minor infractions, which, when unpaid, result in the issuance of a warrant. Consider how predatory policing manifested itself in Ferguson, whose population numbers twenty-one thousand. According to a U.S. Department of Justice report, as of 2014, Ferguson had issued ninety thousand summonses and citations; and in 2013 alone, Ferguson issued 9,007 warrants. Against that background, police officers have an incentive not only to follow people and ask them for their identification (which many people will 'voluntarily' turn over on the assumption that they have to), but also to demand their identification (when people refuse to comply or assert their rights). If it turns out that the person the officer stops does not have an outstanding warrant, the officer will simply send that person on her way. At worst for the officer, that person will file a formal complaint. Chances are, she won't even do that. Certainly, she won't file a lawsuit. Would you? If the officer's license check reveals that the person has an outstanding warrant, the officer will be able not only to arrest the person, but also to subject the person to a number of additional intrusions . . . ."

PART 3

THE COMMENCEMENT OF FORMAL PROCEEDINGS

∎ ∎ ∎

CHAPTER 13

PRETRIAL RELEASE

■ ■ ■

§ 1. THE RIGHT TO BAIL; PRETRIAL RELEASE PROCEDURES

A. STATE AND FEDERAL BAIL SYSTEMS

15th ed., p. 844; at end of first paragraph add a new footnote aa:

aa *See* Incarcerated and Infected: How the Virus Tore Through the U.S. Prison System—The New York Times (nytimes.com) (April 2021) (with interactive map of virus outbreaks in jails, stating "Local jails are transitory places. . . . The churn of people has meant that some of the nation's largest virus outbreaks have occurred in county jails.").

15th ed., p. 845; at end of Note 1, add:

The burdens of detention are borne disproportionately by the poor and nonwhite. In 2009, the most recent national data available, at least a third of pretrial detainees were in jail because they were too poor to post money bail. A 2021 report found that Black and brown defendants are less likely to be able to afford money bail, but receive bail amounts that are twice as high as bail set for white defendants. https://www.prisonpolicy.org/research/pretrial_detention/.

Multiple studies have found that reducing the use of money bail saves taxpayer dollars otherwise spent on incarceration, and decreases financial, physical, and psychological harms to defendants and their families, all without affecting criminal activity or crime rates. *See* https://www.safetyandjusticechallenge.org/resource/dollars-and-sense-in-cook-county/ (reporting results of reforms in Chicago, citing studies in New York, New Jersey, and Philadelphia).

B. CONSTITUTIONAL LIMITS ON PRETRIAL RELEASE PROCESS

15th ed., p. 848; replacing "Under the" paragraph, add:

Under the Douglas approach, is it equally objectionable to *grant* a wealthy person freedom on conditions an indigent could not meet? Consider *United States v. Boustani*, 932 F.3d 79 (2d Cir.2019), regarding whether "a court may release a defendant subject to conditions of home confinement in which, among other things, the defendant pays for private armed security guards," holding that the Bail Reform Act does not permit a two-tiered bail system in which defendants of lesser means are detained pending trial while wealthy defendants are released to self-funded private jails."

15th ed., p. 849; at end of Note 4, add:

The court of appeals upheld the district court's application of intermediate scrutiny, concluding that "although [Harris] County had a compelling interest in the assurance of a misdemeanor detainee's future appearance and lawful behavior, its policy was not narrowly tailored to meet that interest." It noted that although "[n]either prisoners nor indigents constitute a suspect class," the Supreme Court has required heightened scrutiny when criminal laws detain poor defendants because of their indigence, citing *Tate v. Short*, 401 U.S. 395, 397–99 (1971) (facially neutral statute that authorized imprisonment for failure to pay fines violated the equal protection rights of indigents). Heightened scrutiny is appropriate for indigents when "because of their impecunity they were completely unable to pay for some desired benefit," and "as a consequence, they sustained an absolute deprivation of a meaningful opportunity to enjoy that benefit." *San Antonio Indep. Sch. Dist. v. Rodriguez*, 411 U.S. 1, 20 (1973). Concluded the court: indigent misdemeanor arrestees "sustain an absolute deprivation of their most basic liberty interests—freedom from incarceration," solely because they cannot afford to pay bail.

The court of appeals did not uphold, however, the district court's order that required the state to incarcerate indigent defendants only as long as it would have incarcerated those who could have posted bond. "[T]he precise 'constitutional defect in the process afforded was the automatic imposition of pretrial detention on indigent misdemeanor arrestees.' " An individualized hearing within 48 hours of arrest with "notice, an opportunity to be heard and submit evidence" followed by a "reasoned decision by an impartial decisionmaker" stating "individualized, case-specific reasons for imposing bail" was a sufficient remedy.

Similar reasoning led a panel of the Eleventh Circuit to reject the equal protection challenge of Walker, who was detained when he was unable to pay the "standard $160 cash bond" for the misdemeanor offense of being a pedestrian under the influence of alcohol. *Walker v. City of Calhoun, Georgia*, 901 F.3d 1245 (11th Cir. 2018). "Walker and other indigents suffer no 'absolute deprivation' of the benefit they seek, namely pretrial release," said the court. Rather, they must merely wait some appropriate amount of time to receive the same benefit as the more affluent. . . . [T]he 48-hour window for a bail determination . . .[does not] run afoul of the Constitution." A dissenting judge argued that the policy failed even rational basis review, as the state did not show that a 48-hour detention of only those who cannot afford to pay bond is "reasonably necessary to the accomplishment of legitimate state objectives."

In California, four months after voters defeated a referendum that would have eliminated cash bail, the California Supreme Court held that it was unconstitutional for a court to impose money bail without an individualized determination whether the defendant "had the financial wherewithal to post bail—and, if not, whether less restrictive alternatives could reasonably have satisfied the government's compelling interest in seeking his detention." *In re Humphrey*, 11 Cal. 5th 135, 482 P.3d 1008, 1020–1022 (2021): "Where the record reflects the risk of flight or a risk to public or victim safety, the court should consider whether nonfinancial conditions of release may reasonably protect the public and the victim or reasonably assure the arrestee's presence at trial. If the court concludes that money bail is reasonably necessary, then the court must consider the individual arrestee's ability to pay, along with the seriousness of the charged offense and the arrestee's criminal record, and—unless there is a valid basis for detention—set bail at a level the arrestee can reasonably afford. . . .The experiences of those jurisdictions that have reduced or eliminated financial conditions of release suggest that releasing arrestees under appropriate nonfinancial conditions—such as electronic monitoring, supervision by pretrial services, community housing or shelter, stay-away orders, and drug and alcohol testing and treatment may often prove sufficient to protect the community."

For a collection of legislation reducing or eliminating reliance on financial conditions of release, *see* Releasing People Pretrial Doesn't Harm Public Safety at https://www.prisonpolicy.org. Illinois eliminated cash bail entirely, effective January 2023. *See* the Illinois Pre-Trial Fairness Act, part of Illinois House Bill 3653.

CHAPTER 14

THE DECISION WHETHER TO PROSECUTE

■ ■ ■

§ 1. THE OFFICE OF PROSECUTOR AND THE NATURE OF THE DECISION WHETHER TO PROSECUTE

15th ed., p. 871; after Note 4, add:

4A. ***"Progressive prosecution."*** The Davis and Fryer readings in Chapter 3, *see* Supp. pp. 6–9, introduce some of the goals and policies of a growing group of prosecutors committed to reducing mass incarceration, mass supervision, and racial disparity in criminal justice today. Those efforts include increasing the use of diversion and treatment instead of prosecution, working to eliminate cash bail, taking into account the cost of incarceration and the collateral consequences of arrest and conviction in bargaining and sentencing, providing broader disclosure during discovery, and limiting the length of terms of supervision. For a helpful summary of reforms and research, visit https://fairandjustprosecution.org/.

PART 4

THE ADVERSARY SYSTEM AND THE DETERMINATION OF GUILT OR INNOCENCE

■ ■ ■

CHAPTER 22

GUILTY PLEAS

∎ ∎ ∎

§ 2. REJECTED, KEPT AND BROKEN BARGAINS; UNREALIZED EXPECTATIONS

15th ed., p. 1166; in Note 4, in the carryover paragraph at the top of the page, delete the citation and parenthetical for *United States v. Erwin*, and add:

The Court in *Garza v. Idaho*, 139 S.Ct. 738 (2019), discussed in Note 13 infra, stated that "all jurisdictions appear to treat at least some claims as unwaivable," including the "right to challenge whether the waiver itself is valid and enforceable—for example, on the grounds that it was unknowing and involuntary." It noted in a footnote: "Lower courts have also applied exceptions for other kinds of claims, including 'claims that a sentence is based on race discrimination, exceeds the statutory maximum authorized, or is the product of ineffective assistance of counsel.' King & O'Neill, Appeal Waivers and the Future of Sentencing Policy, 55 Duke L. J. 209, 224 (2005) (collecting federal cases); *see also, e.g., United States v. Puentes-Hurtado*, 794 F.3d 1278, 1284 (CA11 2015) ('[A]ppellate review is also permitted when a defendant claims that the government breached the very plea agreement which purports to bar him from appealing or collaterally attacking his conviction and sentence'); *State v. Dye*, 291 Neb. 989, 999, 870 N.W.2d 628, 634 (2015) (holding that appeal waivers are subject to a 'miscarriage of justice' exception). We make no statement today on what particular exceptions may be required."

§ 3. THE ROLE AND RESPONSIBILITY OF DEFENSE COUNSEL

15th ed., p. 1203; at end of Note 12, add:

Under what circumstances, if any, is a defense attorney's failure to give *Padilla* warnings excusable because of his lack of awareness of his client's immigration status? Consider *Bobadilla v. State*, 117 N.E.3d 1272 (Ind.2019), where the court (a) emphatically asserted that the "best practice is to never assume a client's citizenship status; always ask"; but (b) ruled in defendant's favor only after rejecting the post-conviction lower court's "conclusion that counsel had 'no reason to suspect' Bobadilla was not a United States citizen," given the showing that defense counsel had received paperwork including within the assertion that his client had been born in Mexico.

15th ed., p. 1203; replacing last paragraph in Note 13:

In GARZA v. IDAHO, 139 S.Ct. 738 (2019), Garza signed two plea agreements, each containing an appeal waiver, but after sentencing told his attorney he wanted to appeal. Counsel told Garza an appeal would be "problematical" given his appeal waiver, and did not file notice of appeal. Garza later sought post-conviction relief without success; the state supreme court concluded the presumption of prejudice recognized when trial counsel fails to file an appeal as instructed does *not* apply when defendant had agreed to an appeal waiver. The Supreme Court, per Sotomayor, J., reversed, holding "that the presumption of prejudice recognized in *Flores-Ortega* applies regardless of whether defendant has signed an appeal waiver."

In support of that conclusion, the Court first considered the nature of "two procedural devices on which the case hinges: appeal waivers and notices of appeal": (i) As to the former, it was emphasized that "no appeal waiver serves as an absolute bar to all appellate claims," as "an appeal waiver does not bar claims outside its scope," "the language of appeal waivers can vary widely," and "even a waived appellate claim can still go forward if the prosecution forfeits or waives the waiver"; moreover, "all jurisdictions appear to treat at least some claims as unwaiveable," and recognize that "defendants maintain the right to challenge whether the waiver itself is valid and enforceable—for example, on the grounds that it was unknowing and involuntary." (ii) As for notices of appeal, the Court asserted that filing such a notice "is a purely ministerial task" that "typically takes place during a compressed window" of time when "claims are, accordingly, likely to be ill defined or unknown," and that such filing (a decision which "is ultimately the defendant's, not counsel's, to make") "does not necessarily breach a plea agreement, given the possibility that the defendant will end up raising claims beyond the waiver's scope." The *Garza* majority then continued:

"We now address the crux of this case: whether *Flores-Ortega*'s presumption of prejudice applies despite an appeal waiver. The holding, principles, and facts of *Flores-Ortega* show why that presumption applies equally here.

"With regard to prejudice, *Flores-Ortega* held that, to succeed in an ineffective-assistance claim in this context, a defendant need make only one showing: 'that, but for counsel's deficient failure to consult with him about an appeal, he would have timely appealed.' * * * Because there is no dispute here that Garza wished to appeal, a direct application of *Flores-Ortega*'s language resolves this case.

"*Flores-Ortega*'s reasoning shows why an appeal waiver does not complicate this straightforward application. That case, like this one, involves a lawyer who forfeited an appellate proceeding by failing to file a notice of appeal. As the Court explained, given that past precedents call for a presumption of prejudice whenever ' "the accused is denied counsel at a critical stage," ' it makes even greater sense to presume prejudice when counsel's deficiency forfeits an 'appellate proceeding altogether.' * * *

"That rationale applies just as well here because Garza retained a right to appeal at least some issues despite the waivers he signed. * * *

"[W]hile the defendant in *Flores-Ortega* did not sign an appeal waiver, he did plead guilty, and—as the Court pointed out—'a guilty plea reduces the scope of potentially appealable issues' on its own. In other words, with regard to the defendant's appellate prospects, *Flores-Ortega* presented at most a difference of degree, not kind, and prescribed a presumption of prejudice regardless of how many appellate claims were foreclosed. We do no different today. * * *

"The more administrable and workable rule * * * is the one compelled by our precedent: When counsel's deficient performance forfeits an appeal that a defendant otherwise would have taken, the defendant gets a new opportunity to appeal. That is the rule already in use in 8 of the 10 Federal Circuits to have considered the question, and neither Idaho nor its amici have pointed us to any evidence that it has proved unmanageable there. That rule does no more than restore the status quo that existed before counsel's deficient performance forfeited the appeal, and it allows an appellate court to consider the appeal as that court otherwise would have done—on direct review, and assisted by counsel's briefing."

Thomas, J., for the three dissenters, disagreed: "As with most ineffective-assistance claims, a defendant seeking to show that counsel was constitutionally ineffective for failing to file an appeal must show deficient performance and prejudice. Relying on *Flores-Ortega*, the majority finds that Garza has satisfied both prongs. In so holding, it adopts a rule whereby a criminal defendant's invocation of the words 'I want to appeal' can undo all sworn attestations to the contrary and resurrect waived statutory rights.

"This rule is neither compelled by precedent nor consistent with the use of appeal waivers in plea bargaining. In my view, a defendant who has executed an appeal waiver cannot show prejudice arising from his counsel's decision not to appeal unless he (1) identifies claims he would have pursued that were outside the appeal waiver; (2) shows that the plea was involuntary or unknowing; or (3) establishes that the government breached the plea agreement. Garza has not made any such showing, so he cannot establish prejudice. Furthermore, because Garza's counsel acted reasonably, Garza also cannot establish deficient performance. I would therefore affirm. * * *

"The Court purports to follow *Flores-Ortega*, but glosses over the important factual and legal differences between that case and this one. The most obvious difference is also the most crucial: There was no appellate waiver in *Flores-Ortega*. The proximate cause of the defendant's failure to appeal in that case was his counsel's failure to file one. Not so here. Garza knowingly waived his appeal rights and never expressed a desire to withdraw his plea. It was thus Garza's agreement to waive his appeal rights, not his attorney's actions, that caused the forfeiture of his appeal. Thus, *Flores-Ortega* is inapposite. * * *

"Counsel's choice not to appeal Garza's sentence—the only issue Garza asked his counsel to challenge—was not only not deficient, it was the only professionally reasonable course of action for counsel under the circumstances. That is because filing an appeal would have been worse than pointless even judging by Garza's own express desires; it would have created serious risks for Garza while having no chance at all of achieving Garza's stated goals for an appeal. Garza had pleaded guilty under Rule 11, expressly waived his right to appeal his sentence, and stated that his desire in appealing was to have his consecutive sentences 'r[u]n concurrent.' But that kind of appeal challenges the defining feature of a Rule 11 plea: the agreed-upon sentence from which the trial court has no discretion to deviate. Here, that sentence includes the consecutive sentences that Garza agreed to, then sought to challenge. Had Garza's counsel reflexively filed an appeal and triggered resentencing, Garza might have faced life in prison, especially in light of the trial court's concern that the agreed-upon sentence (from which it could not deviate under Rule 11) might have been too lenient. And Garza's admissions at the plea hearings and his written plea form could have been (and thus likely would have been) used against him if he had proceeded to trial on any additional charges filed by the State after breaching the plea agreements. * * *

"As for prejudice, Garza cannot benefit from a presumed prejudice finding since he cannot establish that his counsel caused the forfeiture of his appeal, as *Flores-Ortega* requires. Garza knowingly and voluntarily bargained away his right to appeal in exchange for a lower sentence. If any prejudice resulted from that decision, it cannot be attributed to his counsel. It does not matter that certain appellate issues—specifically, (1) the voluntariness of the plea agreement and (2) a breach of the agreement by the State—are not waivable. Garza did not ask his counsel to appeal those issues. In fact, Garza has not identified any nonwaived issue that he would have brought on direct appeal; he simply identified "sentencing review" as his primary objective. Moreover, declining to file an appeal raising these nonwaivable claims is unlikely to be prejudicial; this Court has repeatedly stated that collateral review is a better avenue to address involuntariness and ineffective assistance claims, as these claims often require extra-record materials and present conflicts with counsel."

CHAPTER 23

TRIAL BY JURY

∎ ∎ ∎

§ 1. RIGHT TO JURY TRIAL

15th ed., p. 1234; replace Note 3 with:

In RAMOS v. LOUISIANA, 140 S.Ct. 1390 (2020), the Court held that the Sixth Amendment right to a jury trial—as incorporated against the States by way of the Fourteenth Amendment—requires a unanimous verdict to convict a defendant of a serious offense. The decision overturned *Apodaca v. Louisiana*, 406 U.S. 404 (1972), where the Court had split 4–1–4, with four justices concluding the Sixth Amendment did not include a unanimity requirement, four others concluding that it did and that the requirement was fully applicable to the states, and Justice Powell agreeing that the Sixth Amendment required unanimity, but that requirement did not bind the states. Relying on *Apodaca*, Oregon and Louisiana continued to allow guilty verdicts of 11–1 or 10–2 in felony cases, the only states to do so. Ramos challenged his conviction after only ten members of his Louisiana trial jury concluded he was guilty. Justice GORSUCH's opinion for the Court began by explaining the racist origins of these two states' laws:

"Louisiana first endorsed nonunanimous verdicts for serious crimes at a constitutional convention in 1898. According to one committee chairman, the avowed purpose of that convention was to "establish the supremacy of the white race," and the resulting document included many of the trappings of the Jim Crow era: a poll tax, a combined literacy and property ownership test, and a grandfather clause that in practice exempted white residents from the most onerous of these requirements.

Nor was it only the prospect of African-Americans voting that concerned the delegates. Just a week before the convention, the U.S. Senate passed a resolution calling for an investigation into whether Louisiana was systemically excluding African-Americans from juries. Seeking to avoid unwanted national attention, and aware that this Court would strike down any policy of overt discrimination against African-American jurors as a violation of the Fourteenth Amendment, the delegates sought to undermine African-American participation on juries in another way. With a careful eye on racial demographics, the convention delegates sculpted a "facially race-neutral" rule permitting 10-to-2 verdicts in order "to ensure that African-American juror service would be meaningless."

Adopted in the 1930s, Oregon's rule permitting nonunanimous verdicts can be similarly traced to the rise of the Ku Klux Klan and efforts to dilute "the influence of racial, ethnic, and religious minorities on Oregon juries." In fact, no one before us contests any of this; courts in both Louisiana and Oregon have frankly acknowledged that race was a motivating factor in the adoption of their States' respective nonunanimity rules."

Justice Gorsuch then recounted the evidence supporting the strong historical basis for requiring unanimity, and rejected Louisiana's invitation to "distinguish between the historic features of common law jury trials that (we think) serve 'important enough' functions to migrate silently into the Sixth Amendment and those that don't. And, on the State's account, we should conclude that unanimity isn't worthy enough to make the trip. But to see the dangers of Louisiana's overwise approach, there's no need to look any further than *Apodaca* itself. There, four

Justices, pursuing the functionalist approach Louisiana espouses, began by describing the " 'essential' " benefit of a jury trial as " 'the interposition . . . of the commonsense judgment of a group of laymen' " between the defendant and the possibility of an " 'overzealous prosecutor.' " And measured against that muddy yardstick, they quickly concluded that requiring 12 rather than 10 votes to convict offers no meaningful improvement. Meanwhile, these Justices argued, States have good and important reasons for dispensing with unanimity, such as seeking to reduce the rate of hung juries.

Who can profess confidence in a breezy cost-benefit analysis like that? Lost in the accounting are the racially discriminatory *reasons* that Louisiana and Oregon adopted their peculiar rules in the first place.[44] What's more, the plurality never explained why the promised benefit of abandoning unanimity—reducing the rate of hung juries—always scores as a credit, not a cost. But who can say whether any particular hung jury is a waste, rather than an example of a jury doing exactly what the plurality said it should—deliberating carefully and safeguarding against overzealous prosecutions? And what about the fact, too, that some studies suggest that the elimination of unanimity has only a small effect on the rate of hung juries? Or the fact that others profess to have found that requiring unanimity may provide other possible benefits, including more open-minded and more thorough deliberations? It seems the *Apodaca* plurality never even conceived of such possibilities.

Our real objection here isn't that the *Apodaca* plurality's cost-benefit analysis was too skimpy. The deeper problem is that the plurality subjected the ancient guarantee of a unanimous jury verdict to its own functionalist assessment in the first place. And Louisiana asks us to repeat the error today, just replacing *Apodaca*'s functionalist assessment with our own updated version. All this overlooks the fact that, at the time of the Sixth Amendment's adoption, the right to trial by jury *included* a right to a unanimous verdict. When the American people chose to enshrine that right in the Constitution, they weren't suggesting fruitful topics for future cost-benefit analyses. They were seeking to ensure that their children's children would enjoy the same hard-won liberty they enjoyed. As judges, it is not our role to reassess whether the right to a unanimous jury is "important enough" to retain. With humility, we must accept that this right may serve purposes evading our current notice. We are entrusted to preserve and protect that liberty, not balance it away aided by no more than social statistics.[47]

Justice Gorsuch concluded that each of the traditional stare decisis factors supported abandoning *Apodaca*: "the quality of the decision's reasoning; its consistency with related decisions; legal developments since the decision; and reliance on the decision." On the first point,

---

[44]   The dissent chides us for acknowledging the racist history of Louisiana's and Oregon's laws, and commends the *Apodaca* plurality's decision to disregard these facts. But if the Sixth Amendment calls on judges to assess the functional benefits of jury rules, as the *Apodaca* plurality suggested, how can that analysis proceed to ignore the very functions those rules were adopted to serve? The dissent answers that Louisiana and Oregon eventually recodified their nonunanimous jury laws in new proceedings untainted by racism. But that cannot explain *Apodaca*'s omission: The States' proceedings took place only *after* the Court's decision. Nor can our shared respect for "rational and civil discourse," supply an excuse for leaving an uncomfortable past unexamined. Still, the dissent is right about one thing—a jurisdiction adopting a nonunanimous jury rule even for benign reasons would still violate the Sixth Amendment.

[47]   The dissent seems to suggest that we must abandon the Sixth Amendment's historical meaning in favor of *Apodaca*'s functionalism because a parade of horribles would follow otherwise. In particular, the dissent reminds us that, at points and places in our history, women were not permitted to sit on juries. But we hardly need *Apodaca*'s functionalism to avoid repeating that wrong. Unlike the rule of unanimity, rules about who qualified as a defendant's "peer" varied considerably at common law at the time of the Sixth Amendment's adoption. Reflecting that fact, the Judiciary Act of 1789—adopted by the same Congress that passed the Sixth Amendment—initially pegged the qualifications for federal jury service to the relevant state jury qualification requirements. 1 Stat. 88. As a result, for much of this Nation's early history the composition of federal juries varied both geographically and over time. Ultimately, however, the people themselves adopted further constitutional amendments that prohibit invidious discrimination. So today the Sixth Amendment's promise of a jury of one's peers means a jury selected from a representative cross-section of the entire community.

he said, the *Apodaca* "plurality spent almost no time grappling with the historical meaning of the Sixth Amendment's jury trial right, this Court's long-repeated statements that it demands unanimity, or the racist origins of Louisiana's and Oregon's laws. Instead, the plurality subjected the Constitution's jury trial right to an incomplete functionalist analysis of its own creation for which it spared one paragraph. And, of course, five Justices expressly rejected the plurality's conclusion that the Sixth Amendment does not require unanimity. Meanwhile, Justice Powell refused to follow this Court's incorporation precedents," that have rejected the "dual-track incorporation" theory.

Justice ALITO dissented, joined by Chief Justice Roberts and Justice Kagan. "[I]t is hard to know what to make of the functionalist charge. One Member of the majority explicitly disavows this criticism,[c] and it is most unlikely that all the Justices in the majority are ready to label all functionalist decisions as poorly reasoned. Most of the landmark criminal procedure decisions from roughly Apodaca's time fall into that category. *Mapp, Miranda, Gideon, Furman.* Are they all now up for grabs?

* * * No one questions that the Sixth Amendment incorporated the core of the common-law jury-trial right, but did it incorporate every feature of the right? Did it constitutionalize the requirement that there be 12 jurors even though nobody can say why 12 is the magic number? And did it incorporate features that we now find highly objectionable, such as the exclusion of women from jury service? * * * Unless one is willing to freeze in place late 18th-century practice, it is necessary to find a principle to distinguish between the features that were incorporated and those that were not. To do this, Justice White's opinion for the Court in *Williams* [15th ed. p. 1265] looked to the underlying purpose of the jury-trial right, which it identified as interposing a jury of the defendant's peers to protect against oppression by a " 'corrupt or overzealous prosecutor' " or a " 'compliant, biased, or eccentric judge.' "

The majority decries this "functionalist" approach but provides no alternative. It does not claim that the Sixth Amendment incorporated every feature of common-law practice, but it fails to identify any principle for identifying the features that were absorbed. On the question of jury service by women, the majority's only answer, buried in a footnote, is that the exclusion of women was outlawed by "further constitutional amendments," presumably the Fourteenth Amendment. Does that mean that the majority disagrees with the holding in *Taylor v. Louisiana*, [15th ed. p. 1274]—another opinion by Justice White—that the exclusion of women from jury service violates the Sixth Amendment?[26] * * *

The *Apodaca* plurality's reasoning was based on the same fundamental mode of analysis as that in *Williams*, which had held just two years earlier that the Sixth Amendment did not

---

[c]   In her concurring opinion, Justice SOTOMAYOR emphasized that the reason that "*Apodaca*, was on shaky ground from the start" "was not because of the functionalist analysis of that Court's plurality: Reasonable minds have disagreed over time—and continue to disagree—about the best mode of constitutional interpretation. That the plurality in *Apodaca* used different interpretive tools from the majority here is not a reason on its own to discard precedent. What matters instead is that, as the majority rightly stresses, *Apodaca* is a universe of one—an opinion uniquely irreconcilable with not just one, but two, strands of constitutional precedent well established both before and after the decision."

Justice KAVANAUGH concurred in part, applying a different stare decisis analysis. Justice THOMAS filed an opinion concurring in the judgment, concluding, "I would simply hold that, because all of the opinions in *Apodaca* addressed the Due Process Clause, its Fourteenth Amendment ruling does not bind us because the proper question here is the scope of the Privileges or Immunities Clause."

[26]   * * * Jury practice at the time of the founding differed from current practice in other important respects. Jurors were not selected at random. "[P]ublic officials called selectmen, supervisors, trustees, or 'sheriffs of the parish' exercised what Tocqueville called 'very extensive and very arbitrary' powers in summoning jurors." And "American trial judges . . . routinely summarized the evidence for jurors and often told jurors which witnesses they found most credible, and why." Any attempt to identify the aspects of late 18th-century practice that were incorporated into the Sixth Amendment should take the full picture into account and provide a principle for the distinction.

constitutionalize the common law's requirement that a jury have 12 members. Although only one State, Oregon, now permits non-unanimous verdicts, many more allow six-person juries.[29] Repudiating the reasoning of *Apodaca* will almost certainly prompt calls to overrule *Williams*."

[29] See Ariz. Rev. Stat. Ann. § 21–102 (2013); Conn. Gen. Stat. § 54–82; Fla. Rule Crim. Proc. § 3.270 (2019); Ind. Code § 35–37–1–1(b)(2); Utah Code § 78B–1–104 (2019).

§ 2. JURY SELECTION

B. SELECTING THE JURY FROM THE VENIRE: VOIR DIRE

15th ed., p. 1255; after "discriminatory treatment," in the sixth line of Rehnquist's dissent in *Batson*, add a new footnote aa:

[aa] In *Flowers v. Mississippi*, discussed *infra* Note 4.c., Justice Thomas made a similar argument in dissent, but the Court had this to say: "[T]he *Batson* Court did not accept the argument that race-based peremptories should be permissible because black, white, Asian, and Hispanic defendants and jurors were all 'equally' subject to race-based discrimination. The Court stated that each removal of an individual juror because of his or her race is a constitutional violation. Discrimination against one defendant or juror on account of race is not remedied or cured by discrimination against other defendants or jurors on account of race. As the Court later explained: Some say that there is no equal protection violation if individuals 'of all races are subject to like treatment, which is to say that white jurors are subject to the same risk of peremptory challenges based on race as are all other jurors. The suggestion that racial classifications may survive when visited upon all persons is no more authoritative today than the case which advanced the theorem, *Plessy* v. *Ferguson*, 163 U.S. 537 (1896). This idea has no place in our modern equal protection jurisprudence. It is axiomatic that racial classifications do not become legitimate on the assumption that all persons suffer them in equal degree.' *Powers*."

15th ed., p. 1256; at the end of Note 3.a., add:

In his dissent in *Flowers*, infra Note 4.c., Justice Thomas critiqued *Batson* and the *Powers* rationale. He stated that Flowers "does not dispute that the jury that convicted him was impartial," and "therefore suffered no legally cognizable injury. The only other plausible reason a defendant could suffer an injury from a *Batson* violation is if the Court thinks that he has a better chance of winning if more members of his race are on the jury. But that thinking relies on the very assumption that *Batson* rejects: that jurors might ' "be partial to the defendant because of their shared race." ' " Justice Thomas continued, " "In the ordinary case, the defendant has no relation whatsoever to the struck jurors," and suffers no injury. Nor do defendant defendants and struck jurors share a "common interest," he said. Flowers' interest, Justice Thomas reasoned, is in "avoiding prison (or execution). A struck juror, by contrast, is unlikely to feel better about being excluded from jury service simply because a convicted criminal may go free." Even if the struck juror suffered a cognizable injury, that injury certainly is not redressed by undoing the valid conviction of another, he noted. The Court has never explained "why a violation of a third party's right to serve on a jury should be grounds for reversal when other violations of third-party rights, such as obtaining evidence against the defendant in violation of another person's Fourth or Fifth Amendment rights, are not."

15th ed., p. 1259; in Note 4.a., substitute for text after "all-white jury" the following:

When even a single instance of race or gender discrimination against a prospective juror is impermissible, does every challenge create a prima facie case? Justice Thomas, dissenting in *Flowers*, Note 4.c. infra, thought so: "Now that we have followed *Batson* to its logical conclusion and applied it to race-and sex-based strikes without regard to the race or sex of the defendant, it is impossible to exercise a peremptory strike that cannot be challenged by the opposing party, thereby requiring a "neutral" explanation for the strike."

15th ed., p. 1260; in Note 4.c., after *Davis* citation, add, followed by a paragraph break:

"[T]he best evidence of discriminatory intent often will be the demeanor of the attorney who exercises the challenge," noted the Court in *Flowers*, infra. "The trial judge must determine whether the prosecutor's proffered reasons are the actual reasons, or whether the proffered reasons are pretextual and the prosecutor instead exercised peremptory strikes on the basis of race. The ultimate inquiry is whether the State was 'motivated in substantial part by discriminatory intent.' "

15th ed., p. 1261; at end of Note 4.c., add two new paragraphs:

Summarizing the evidence that defendants may present to support a claim of discriminatory intent, the Court in *Flowers v. Mississippi*, 139 S.Ct. 2228 (2019), listed the following: "[1] statistical evidence about the prosecutor's use of peremptory strikes against black prospective jurors as compared to white prospective jurors in the case; [2] evidence of a prosecutor's disparate questioning and investigation of black and white prospective jurors in the case; [3] side-by-side comparisons of black prospective jurors who were struck and white prospective jurors who were not struck in the case; [4] a prosecutor's misrepresentations of the record when defending the strikes during the *Batson* hearing; [5] relevant history of the State's peremptory strikes in past cases; [and 6] other relevant circumstances that bear upon the issue of racial discrimination."

In *Flowers*, the Court reviewed the defendant's conviction and death sentence for a quadruple murder after he had been tried for the sixth time. Of the five earlier attempts, all by the same lead prosecutor, the Mississippi Supreme Court reversed twice for prosecutorial misconduct and once for *Batson* error. Two trials ended in hung juries. In a fact-intensive decision applying the *Batson* framework to the "extraordinary facts" of the case, the Court held that at Flowers' sixth trial, the judge committed clear error in concluding that the State's peremptory strike of black prospective juror Carolyn Wright was not motivated in substantial part by discriminatory intent. The Court explained, "We must examine the Wright strike in light of the history of the State's use of peremptory strikes in the prior trials, the State's decision to strike five out of six black prospective jurors at Flowers' sixth trial, and the State's vastly disparate questioning of black and white prospective jurors during jury selection at the sixth trial. * * * In the six trials combined, the State struck 41 of the 42 black prospective jurors it could have struck." In dissent, Justice Thomas, joined by Justice Gorsuch, concluded the state courts' findings that these strikes were not based on race were clearly correct and accused the Court of vacating four murder convictions "because the State struck a juror who would have been stricken by any competent attorney."

CHAPTER 25

THE CRIMINAL TRIAL

■ ■ ■

§ 2. CONFRONTATION AND TESTIMONIAL HEARSAY

15th ed., p. 1321; at the end of Note 3, add:

The widespread use of videoconferencing during the pandemic has produced conflicting authority on which pretrial proceedings carry a right to confrontation and when, if ever, presenting witness testimony by video violates that right. Most courts have continued to find that presenting witness testimony by videoconference is constitutional under *Craig,* although they have differed over what showing of necessity is required. At least one court has held that *Craig* must be limited to its facts, as "*Crawford* did not specifically overrule *Craig,* but it took out its legs." *People v. Jemison,* 505 Mich. 352 (2020). For an evaluation of the drawbacks of videoconferencing and existing research on its effects, *see Diaz v. Commonwealth,* 487 Mass. 336 (2021) (Kafker, J., concurring) (cataloguing ways in which virtual hearings alter evaluation of demeanor evidence, diminish the solemnity of the legal process, and influence the assessments of witnesses and other participants).

CHAPTER 26

REPROSECUTION AND DOUBLE JEOPARDY

■ ■ ■

§ 4. REPROSECUTION BY A DIFFERENT SOVEREIGN

15th ed., p. 1367; after Note 2, add:

3. The Court rejected a challenge to the validity of the dual sovereignty rule in GAMBLE v. UNITED STATES, 139 S.Ct. 1960 (2019). Gamble sought to dismiss a federal indictment for possessing a firearm as a convicted felon, after he had pled guilty to what the parties agreed was the same crime in state court. The Court, in an opinion by Justice Alito, held that the dual sovereignty rule should not be disturbed. The decision reviewed at length the historical evidence concerning prosecutions by different sovereigns, including treatise discussions and case law before and after ratification of the Fifth Amendment. It concluded that the evidence on original meaning was at best muddled, and did not establish that "those who ratified the Fifth Amendment took it to bar successive prosecutions under different sovereigns' laws—much less do so with enough force to break a chain of precedent linking dozens of cases over 170 years." The decision also warned that abandoning the rule would mean that "no American court—state or federal—could prosecute conduct already tried in a foreign court," and described "the foundation laid in our antebellum cases: that a crime against two sovereigns constitutes two offenses because each sovereign has an interest to vindicate."

The Court rejected the argument that incorporation of the Double Jeopardy Clause had invalidated the separate sovereigns doctrine, just as incorporation of the Fourth Amendment had undermined a practice known as the "silver platter doctrine" allowing federal prosecutors to introduce evidence obtained by state authorities using means denied to the federal government. The "silver-platter doctrine," Justice Alito wrote, "was based on the fact that the state searches to which it applied did not at that time violate federal law. Once the Fourth Amendment was incorporated against the States, the status of those state searches changed. Now they did violate federal law, so the basis for the silver-platter doctrine was gone. *See Elkins*, 364 U. S., at 213 ("The foundation upon which the admissibility of state-seized evidence in a federal trial originally rested—that unreasonable state searches did not violate the Federal Constitution— thus disappeared [with incorporation]"). By contrast, the premises of the dual-sovereignty doctrine have survived incorporation intact. Incorporation meant that the States were now required to abide by this Court's interpretation of the Double Jeopardy Clause. But that interpretation has long included the dual-sovereignty doctrine, and there is no logical reason why incorporation should change it. * * * [T]he fact that only same-sovereign successive prosecutions are prosecutions for the "same offense," * * * is just as true after incorporation as before."

Justice Ginsburg argued in dissent, "In our 'compound republic,' the division of authority between the United States and the States was meant to operate as 'a double security [for] the rights of the people.' * * * The separate-sovereigns doctrine, however, scarcely shores up people's rights. Instead, it invokes federalism to withhold liberty." As for the concern that the state and federal governments must have the ability to pursue their separate interests, she stated that when federal-state tension exists, successive prosecutions may escape double-jeopardy blockage under the test prescribed in *Blockburger*. "The Court regards incorporation as immaterial," she continued, "because application of the Double Jeopardy Clause to the States did not affect comprehension of the word 'offence' to mean the violation of one sovereign's law. But the Court attributed a separate-sovereigns meaning to 'offence' at least in part because the Double Jeopardy Clause did not apply to the States. Incorporation of the Clause should prompt the Court to consider the protection against double jeopardy from the defendant's perspective and to ask why each of two governments within the United States should be permitted to try a defendant once for the same offense when neither could try him or her twice." She also noted that the "expansion of federal criminal law has exacerbated the problems created by the separate-sovereigns doctrine."

Justice Gorsuch was the only other Justice to dissent.[b] He disputed the Court's analysis of original intent, concluding that the " 'separate sovereigns exception' to the bar against double jeopardy finds no meaningful support in the text of the Constitution, its original public meaning, structure, or history." "Under our Constitution, the federal and state governments are but two expressions of a single and sovereign people." He also accused the Court of invoking federalism "not to protect individual liberty but to threaten it, allowing two governments to achieve together an objective denied to each. * * * As Justice Black understood * * * "it is just as much an affront to . . . human freedom for a man to be punished twice for the same offense" by two parts of the people's government "as it would be for one . . . to throw him in prison twice for the offense."

   [b]   Concurring in the Court's decision to uphold the separate sovereigns rule, Justice Thomas stated that "the historical record does not bear out my initial skepticism." He went on to explain why he disagreed with the Court's approach to *stare decisis,* noting that it "does not comport with our judicial duty under Article III because it elevates demonstrably erroneous decisions—meaning decisions outside the realm of permissible interpretation—over the text of the Constitution and other duly enacted federal law."

CHAPTER 27

SENTENCING

■ ■ ■

§ 1. INTRODUCTION TO SENTENCING

B. TYPES OF SENTENCES

15th ed., p. 1372; in Note 6 after the first sentence, add:

As the Court recognized in *Timbs v. Indiana,* 139 S.Ct. 682 (2019), Supp. p. 3, "Even absent a political motive, fines may be employed 'in a measure out of accord with the penal goals of retribution and deterrence,' for 'fines are a source of revenue,' while other forms of punishment 'cost a State money.' * * * This concern is scarcely hypothetical. *See* Brief for American Civil Liberties Union et al. as *Amici Curiae* 7 ('Perhaps because they are politically easier to impose than generally applicable taxes, state and local governments nationwide increasingly depend heavily on fines and fees as a source of general revenue.').".

§ 2. ALLOCATING AND CONTROLLING SENTENCING DISCRETION

C. APPELLATE REVIEW

15th ed., p. 1377; at end of Note 3, add:

See also Timbs v. Indiana, 139 S.Ct. 682 (2019), holding that the Fourteenth Amendment's limitation on states incorporates the Excessive Fines Clause of the Eighth Amendment, including its regulation of civil in rem forfeitures when they are at least partially punitive.

§ 3. CONSTITUTIONAL LIMITS ON SENTENCING PROCEDURE

D. JURY TRIAL AND BURDEN OF PROOF

15th ed., p. 1399; at the end of Note 6, add:

And consider the situation, as in *Haymond,* Note 11, Supp. p. 90, where a fact carrying the right to jury and proof beyond a reasonable doubt is found at a proceeding to determine whether to revoke defendant's supervised release, parole, or probation. At a typical revocation proceeding, the judge has the discretion to revoke release upon a preponderance of evidence and to incarcerate the defendant, but only to a term that does not exceed the total sentence imposed for the original offense of conviction. Ordinarily, at such a proceeding, there would be no Sixth Amendment right to counsel, *Gagnon,* 15th ed., p. 86, no Fifth Amendment right to testify or not to take the stand, *Salinas,* 15th ed., p. 586, and no right to confront witnesses, *Williams,* 15th ed., pp. 1378 and 1386. But if the law *requires* the judge to impose years of incarceration once a particular fact is found, eliminating the option of non-incarceration alternatives, that finding might, under *Haymond,* trigger the Sixth Amendment right to a jury and proof beyond a reasonable doubt, just like the mandatory minimum sentencing statute in *Alleyne*. Does that mean that defendants at such a revocation proceeding would have all the other Fifth and Sixth Amendment rights afforded defendants at trial?

15th ed., p. 1400; after Note 10, add:

11. *Revocation proceedings.* Traditionally, probation has operated as a suspension of the term of incarceration set at the initial sentencing for the offense. *See Alabama v. Shelton*, 15th ed., p. 78. If a judge finds that the defendant violated the conditions of release, the judge can revoke release and incarcerate the defendant, but the constitutional requirements for trial are not required at revocation proceedings. *See* 15th ed., p. 1371, Note 4. Parole revocation is similar to probation revocation. A violation of a term of conditional release from prison can lead to revocation of release, ordinarily for the remainder of the term of incarceration set at the initial sentencing. Instead of a judge, however, in most states, a hearing officer will determine at a revocation proceeding whether the parolee violated a term of parole.

In the federal courts and states where *discretionary* release on parole is not available, to provide for transition from prison, the sentencing judge may (or for some crimes, must) impose term of conditional, "supervised release" following a defendant's sentence of incarceration as part of the defendant's sentence. The maximum period of supervised release is set by statute depending on the offense. If a judge finds that the defendant violated a condition of that release, the judge may revoke the defendant's release and sentence the defendant to incarceration for the remaining period of release. For example, say a defendant in convicted in federal court of a Class A felony carrying a potential 5-year term of supervised release. If he is sentenced initially to 10 years' imprisonment plus 3 years' supervised release, and violates the conditions of his release two years into his 3-year term, typically the judge has the option, after finding a violation, to decline revoke his release, to extend his period of supervised release from 3 years to the maximum authorized 5 years, or to revoke his release and require the defendant to serve in prison all or part of the authorized 5 year term of supervised release without credit for time previously served on postrelease supervision. *See* 18 U.S.C. §§ 3583(e)(3); 3583(h).

In UNITED STATES v. HAYMOND, 139 S.Ct. 2369 (2019), the Court invalidated 18 U.S.C. § 3583(k), providing that for defendants convicted of designated crimes, upon a judge's finding by a preponderance that the defendant had committed certain felonies while on release, including possessing child pornography, the judge must revoke the defendant's release and return the defendant to prison for at least five years. Haymond was convicted of possessing child pornography, carrying a potential prison sentence of up to 10 years and a term of supervised release up to life. The judge sentenced him to a prison term of 38 months, followed by 10 years of supervised release. After finding that Haymond knowingly possessed 13 images of child pornography on his cell phone while on supervised release, the court revoked his release and sentenced him to the mandatory five years as § 3583(k) required.

A majority of justices agreed that in authorizing a judge to find by a preponderance the facts that mandated a post-revocation 5-year term of incarceration, subsection (k) violated *Alleyne*. The decision was split 4–1–4, with Justice Breyer casting the deciding vote to strike down the provision as unconstitutional but on narrower grounds than the four-justice plurality.

The plurality opinion, written by Justice Gorsuch and joined by Justices Ginsburg, Sotomayor, and Kagan, explained: "Based on the facts reflected in the jury's verdict, Mr. Haymond faced a lawful prison term of between zero and 10 years * * *. But then a judge—acting without a jury and based only on a preponderance of the evidence—found that Mr. Haymond had engaged in additional conduct in violation of the terms of his supervised release. Under § 3583(k), that judicial factfinding triggered a new punishment in the form of a prison term of at least five years and up to life. So just like the facts the judge found at the defendant's sentencing hearing in *Alleyne*, the facts the judge found here increased 'the legally prescribed range of allowable sentences' in violation of the Fifth and Sixth Amendments. In this case, that meant Mr. Haymond faced a minimum of five years in prison instead of as little as none." Without subsection (k), the judge "would have been free to sentence Mr. Haymond to between zero and two additional years in prison," the plurality emphasized. This "does not mean a jury must find every fact in a revocation hearing that may affect the judge's exercise of discretion within the range of punishments authorized by the jury's verdict. But it does mean that a jury must find any facts that trigger a new mandatory minimum prison term," the plurality explained. The plurality did note "Because we hold that this mandatory minimum rendered Mr. Haymond's sentence unconstitutional in violation of *Alleyne*, we need not address the constitutionality of the statute's effect on his maximum sentence under *Apprendi*," and it declined to consider the constitutionality of other sections of the statute.

The expansive reasoning of the plurality opinion implicates other federal statutes that affect a far greater number of cases, not to mention various state provisions on the revocation of probation, parole, and supervised release. But the narrow reasoning of Justice Breyer's controlling concurring opinion constrained the decision's immediate impact. He said that he "would not transplant the *Apprendi* line of cases to the supervised-release context," which Congress intended to serve a role no different from traditional parole. "Nevertheless, I agree with the plurality that this specific provision of the supervised-release statute, § 3583(k), is unconstitutional." "[T]he consequences for violation of conditions of supervised release under § 3583(e), which governs most revocations, are limited by the severity of the original crime of conviction, not the conduct that results in revocation. * * * Section 3583(k) is difficult to reconcile with this understanding of supervised release. In particular, three aspects of this provision, considered in combination, lead me to think it is less like ordinary revocation and more like punishment for a new offense, to which the jury right would typically attach. First, § 3583(k) applies only when a defendant commits a discrete set of federal criminal offenses specified in the statute. Second, § 3583(k) takes away the judge's discretion to decide whether violation of a condition of supervised release should result in imprisonment and for how long. Third, § 3583(k) limits the judge's discretion in a particular manner: by imposing a mandatory minimum term of imprisonment of "not less than 5 years" upon a judge's finding that a defendant has "commit[ted] any" listed "criminal offense." Taken together, these features of § 3583(k) more closely resemble the punishment of new criminal offenses, but without granting a defendant the rights, including the jury right, that attend a new criminal prosecution. And in an ordinary criminal prosecution, a jury must find facts that trigger a mandatory minimum prison term. *Alleyne*."

Justice Alito authored a dissent, joined by the Chief Justice, and Justices Thomas and Kavanaugh, arguing that the plurality opinion was "not based on the original meaning of the Sixth Amendment, is irreconcilable with precedent, and sports rhetoric with potentially revolutionary implications."

CHAPTER 28

APPEALS

• • •

§ 1. THE DEFENDANT'S RIGHT TO APPEAL

15th ed., p. 1402; at end of Note 2, add:

As for misdemeanors, with "only one conviction or sentence out of every ten thousand misdemeanor judgments actually disturbed on appeal," appellate review "cannot function as a serious remedy or deterrent for error," concluded one study of misdemeanor appeals in the states. Nancy J. King & Michael Heise, *Misdemeanor Appeals*, 99 B.U. L. Rev. 1933 (2019). The systemwide problems plaguing misdemeanor adjudication "do not present claims a convicted defendant could raise on direct appeal," and "afflict the innocent and guilty alike." Direct appeal "is unlikely to end policies and practices by police and lower courts designed to generate revenue rather than to improve public safety; realign bail practices so that nondangerous, indigent defendants are not detained pretrial when they cannot afford money bail; direct resources to overworked appointed counsel and prosecutors who barely have enough time to negotiate a plea, much less investigate the facts; manage cases to reduce the number of times that lawyers and clients must be present in court, only to have a proceeding adjourned; or curb the counterproductive collateral consequences that follow a misdemeanor arrest or charge, even when ultimately dismissed." The authors suggest "[l]awsuits and class actions seeking injunctive relief and targeting oppressive sanctioning, fee, and detention policies" would do more to ensure the legality of misdemeanor procedures than an expansion of access to appeal.

15th ed., p. 1402; before last sentence at end of Note 3, add:

"[N]o appeal waiver serves as an absolute bar to all appellate claims," explained the Court in *Garza v. Idaho*, 139 S.Ct. 738 (2019), Note 13, Supp. p. 75. "[A]ll jurisdictions appear to treat at least some claims as unwaivable," including "the right to challenge whether the waiver itself is valid and enforceable."

§ 4. REVIEW FOR CLAIMS NOT RAISED ON TIME

15th ed., p. 1415; after Note 3.d., add:

GREER v. UNITED STATES; UNITED STATES v. GARY
___ U.S. ___, 141 S.Ct. 2090 (2021).

[The Court held in *Rehaif v. United States*, 588 U.S. ___, 139 S.Ct. 2191 (2019), that to convict a person of being a felon in possession of a firearm, the Government must prove not only that the defendant knew he possessed a firearm, but also that he knew he was a felon when he possessed the firearm. Prior to the *Rehaif* decision, defendants Greer and Gary were separately convicted of being felons in possession of firearms. At Greer's trial, he did not request, nor did the judge deliver, an instruction to the jury requiring a finding that Greer knew he was a felon when he possessed the firearm. Gary pled guilty, and at his plea proceeding the judge did not advise him that if he went to trial, a jury would have to find that he knew he was a felon when he possessed the firearms. Each raised his *Rehaif* claim on direct appeal.]

* * * Rule 52(b) provides: "A plain error that affects substantial rights may be considered even though it was not brought to the court's attention." "Rule 52(b) is permissive, not mandatory." To establish eligibility for plain-error relief, a defendant must satisfy three threshold requirements. *First*, there must be an error. *Second*, the error must be plain. *Third*, the error must affect "substantial rights," which generally means that there must be "a reasonable probability that, but for the error, the outcome of the proceeding would have been different." If those three requirements are met, an appellate court may grant relief if it concludes that the error had a serious effect on "the fairness, integrity or public reputation of judicial proceedings." The defendant has "the burden of establishing entitlement to relief for plain error." That means that the defendant has the burden of establishing each of the four requirements for plain-error relief. Satisfying all four prongs of the plain-error test "is difficult." *Puckett*.

In the two cases before us, all agree that *Rehaif* errors occurred during both defendants' district court proceedings and that the errors were plain, thus satisfying the first two prongs of the plain-error test. We address the third prong: whether the *Rehaif* errors affected the defendants' "substantial rights." Greer has the burden of showing that, if the District Court had correctly instructed the jury on the *mens rea* element of a felon-in-possession offense, there is a "reasonable probability" that he would have been acquitted. And Gary has the burden of showing that, if the District Court had correctly advised him of the *mens rea* element of the offense, there is a "reasonable probability" that he would not have pled guilty.

In a felon-in-possession case where the defendant was in fact a felon when he possessed firearms, the defendant faces an uphill climb in trying to satisfy the substantial-rights prong of the plain-error test based on an argument that he did not know he was a felon. The reason is simple: If a person is a felon, he ordinarily knows he is a felon. * * * That simple truth is not lost upon juries. Thus, absent a reason to conclude otherwise, a jury will usually find that a defendant *knew* he was a felon based on the fact that he *was* a felon. A defendant considering whether to plead guilty would recognize as much and would likely factor that reality into the decision to plead guilty. In short, if a defendant was in fact a felon, it will be difficult for him to carry the burden on plain-error review of showing a "reasonable probability" that, but for the *Rehaif* error, the outcome of the district court proceedings would have been different.

Of course, there may be cases in which a defendant who is a felon can make an adequate showing on appeal that he would have presented evidence in the district court that he did not in fact know he was a felon when he possessed firearms. Indeed, at oral argument, the Government conceded that there are circumstances in which a defendant might make such a showing. But if a defendant does not make such an argument or representation on appeal, the appellate court will have no reason to believe that the defendant would have presented such evidence to a jury, and thus no basis to conclude that there is a "reasonable probability" that the outcome would have been different absent the *Rehaif* error.

* * * Neither defendant has ever disputed the fact of their prior convictions. At trial, Greer stipulated to the fact that he was a felon. And Gary admitted that he was a felon when he pled guilty. Importantly, on appeal, neither Greer nor Gary has argued or made a representation that they would have presented evidence at trial that they did not in fact know they were felons when they possessed firearms. Therefore, Greer cannot show that, but for the *Rehaif* error in the jury instructions, there is a reasonable probability that a jury would have acquitted him. And Gary likewise cannot show that, but for the *Rehaif* error during the plea colloquy, there is a reasonable probability that he would have gone to trial rather than plead guilty. * * *

In response, Greer and Gary advance several arguments, none of which is persuasive. Greer's primary argument is that an appellate court conducting plain-error review of a *Rehaif* instructional error may examine only the trial record, [and] that an appellate court may not consider information about a defendant's prior convictions contained in a pre-sentence report. [Because Greer's stipulation to his status as a felon was part of the trial record, we] need not look to the pre-sentence report to resolve the plain-error question in this case. In any event, * * * [t]his Court has repeatedly stated that an appellate court conducting plain-error review may consider the *entire* record—not just the record from the *particular proceeding* where the error occurred. Therefore, when an appellate court conducts plain-error review of a *Rehaif* instructional error, the court can examine relevant and reliable information from the entire record—including information contained in a pre-sentence report. To be sure, if a defendant believes that particular information in the record is irrelevant or unreliable, she may urge the appellate court to discount that information. But concerns about relevance and reliability should be addressed through case-by-case adjudication rather than through a categorical bar against considering evidence outside the trial record.

For his part, Gary argues that he is exempt from ordinary plain-error review for one of two alternative reasons.

First, Gary contends that his unpreserved *Rehaif* claim is not subject to ordinary plain-error review because his claim falls within a narrow "futility" exception to Rule 52(b). Gary notes that, at the time of his guilty plea, every Court of Appeals to consider the issue had held that knowledge of one's felon status was not an element of a felon-in-possession offense. Given that uniform wall of precedent, he says that it would have been futile for him to contemporaneously object to the omission of that element from his plea colloquy. For that reason, he argues that his claim should be governed by the more lenient harmless-error standard of Rule 52(a) rather than the more exacting plain-error standard of Rule 52(b).

The problem for Gary is that his proposed futility exception lacks any support in the text of the Federal Rules of Criminal Procedure or in this Court's precedents.* * * Rule 52(b) specifically addresses unpreserved errors, while Rule 52(a) makes no mention of such errors. Thus, Rule 52(a) and Rule 52(b) together indicate that unpreserved errors must be analyzed for plain error under Rule 52(b). Consider also Rule 51, which provides that a party's failure to make a contemporaneous objection does not prejudice the party if he did "not have an opportunity" to raise the objection. Rule 51's focus on a party's *opportunity* to object—rather than a party's likelihood of *prevailing* on the objection—also undercuts Gary's proposed futility exception.

Consistent with the text of Rules 51 and 52, this Court's precedents have long drawn a bright line between harmless-error and plain-error review based on preservation. In *Johnson*, for example, the Court applied plain-error review to a claim that was the subject of an 11 to 1 split in authority among the Circuits, with only one Court of Appeals accepting the defendant's position. The "near-uniform precedent both from this Court and from the Courts of Appeals," did not affect the application of Rule 52(b). All that mattered was that the defendant had failed to raise a contemporaneous objection. * * *

Second, Gary asserts that *Rehaif* errors (at least when they occur during a plea proceeding) are "structural" and require automatic vacatur in *every* case without regard to whether a defendant can otherwise satisfy the plain-error test. As this Court has repeatedly made clear, however, the "general rule" is that "a constitutional error does not automatically require reversal of a conviction." *Arizona v. Fulminante*, [15th ed. p. 1417 n.8]. Only in a "very limited class of cases" has the Court concluded that an error is structural, and "thus subject to automatic reversal" on appeal. *Neder v. United States*, [15th ed. p. 1420].

Structural errors are errors that affect the "entire conduct of the [proceeding] from beginning to end." The "highly exceptional" category of structural errors includes, for example, the "denial of counsel of choice, denial of self-representation, denial of a public trial, and failure to convey to a jury that guilt must be proved beyond a reasonable doubt." *United States v. Davila*, [15th ed. p. 1173]. By contrast, discrete defects in the criminal process—such as the omission of a single element from jury instructions or the omission of a required warning from a Rule 11 plea colloquy—are not structural because they do not "*necessarily* render a criminal trial fundamentally unfair or an unreliable vehicle for determining guilt or innocence."

As the Court's precedents make clear, the omission of a single element from jury instructions is not structural. See, *e.g.*, *Neder*. A *Rehaif* error in jury instructions is therefore not structural. And it follows that a *Rehaif* error in a plea colloquy is likewise not structural. The omission of that *mens rea* element from a plea colloquy—like the omission of that *mens rea* element from jury instructions—does not affect the entire framework within which the proceeding occurs. And unlike the errors that this Court has found structural, the omission of a single element from a plea colloquy does not "deprive defendants of basic protections without which a criminal [proceeding] cannot reliably serve its function as a vehicle for determination of guilt or innocence." In short, *Rehaif* errors fit comfortably within the "general rule" that "a constitutional error does not automatically require reversal of a conviction." Rather, a defendant such as Gary must satisfy the ordinary plain-error test. * * *

§ 5. THE HARMLESS ERROR RULE

B. CONSTITUTIONAL ERROR

15th ed., p. 1423; at end of Note 2, add:

In *Greer*, Supp. p. 93, the Court explained that unlike structural defects, which "affect the 'entire conduct of the [proceeding] from beginning to end,'" "discrete defects in the criminal process—such as the omission of a single element from jury instructions or the omission of a required warning from a Rule 11 plea colloquy—are not structural because they do not 'necessarily render a criminal trial fundamentally unfair or an unreliable vehicle for determining guilt or innocence.'" How is this characterization of structural error different from that in *Weaver*?

CHAPTER 29

POST-CONVICTION REVIEW: FEDERAL HABEAS CORPUS

■ ■ ■

§ 5. RETROACTIVITY—WHICH LAW APPLIES?

15th ed., p. 1449; replace Note 1.c. with the following:

c. *Step 3:* **Teague's** *two "exceptions."* *Teague* recognized two categories of new constitutional rules that do require retroactive application on federal collateral review.

The first category consists of new constitutional rules that are "substantive" not "procedural." A rule is procedural, and will not apply retroactively on collateral review, if it regulates "only the manner of determining the defendant's culpability." A substantive rule, by contrast, "alters the range of conduct or the class of persons that the law punishes," and will apply retroactively. For example, decisions that "decriminalize a class of conduct," or that narrow the scope of a criminal statute, fall within this category. *Bousley v. United States*, [15th ed., p. 1442]; *Welch v. United States*, 578 U.S. 120 (2016) (applying retroactively earlier ruling that held a federal sentencing provision was unconstitutionally vague). Also substantive are constitutional rules that prohibit "a certain category of punishment for a class of defendants because of their status or offense," including rulings that the Eighth Amendment prohibits the execution of those who are insane, *Ford v. Wainwright*, 477 U.S. 399 (1986), were under 18 at the time of their offense, *Roper v. Simmons*, 543 U.S. 551 (2005), or were convicted of rape where death did not result and was not intended, *Kennedy v. Louisiana*, 554 U.S. 407 (2008).

Applying this distinction between substantive and procedural rules in *Edwards v. Vannoy*, 141 S.Ct. 1547 (2021), the Court concluded that *Ramos v. Louisiana*, 140 S.Ct. 1390 (2020) [Supp. p. 79], requiring unanimous verdicts for state convictions, announced a procedural rule that affects "only the manner of determining the defendant's culpability." The Court had more difficulty classifying the rule announced in *Miller v. Alabama*, 567 U.S. 460 (2012) [15th ed., p. 1377], barring mandatory sentences of life without parole for defendants convicted of committing homicide as minors. In *Montgomery v. Louisiana*, 577 U.S. 190 (2016), the Court held that *Miller* "announced a substantive rule of constitutional law" because it "rendered life without parole an unconstitutional penalty for 'a class of defendants because of their status'—that is, juvenile offenders whose crimes reflect the transient immaturity of youth." Indeed, Justice Kennedy's opinion for the Court in *Montgomery* held "the Constitution requires state collateral review courts," as well as federal courts, "to give retroactive effect" to the rule in *Miller*. Just five years later, *Montgomery's* authority was undercut by Justice Kavanaugh's opinion for the Court in *Jones v. Mississippi*, 141 S.Ct. 1307 (2021), joined by Justice Barrett and the dissenters in *Montgomery*. Although purporting not to "disturb *Montgomery's* holding that *Miller* applies retroactively on collateral review," the Court stated in *Jones*, "[T]o the extent that *Montgomery's* application of the *Teague* standard is in tension with the Court's retroactivity precedents that both pre-date and postdate *Montgomery*, those retroactivity precedents—and not *Montgomery*—must guide the determination of whether rules other than *Miller* are substantive."

Teague also defined a narrow exception for unique procedural rulings that would qualify for retroactive application, exemplified by the rule in *Gideon*, and described as "watershed rules of criminal procedure" that are necessary to prevent "an impermissibly large risk of an inaccurate conviction" and that alter "our understanding of the bedrock procedural elements essential to the fairness of a proceeding." But after 32 years without finding a single additional rule that fits this description, the Court eventually abandoned this exception in *Edwards v. Vannoy,* 141 S.Ct. 1547 (2021). "Continuing to articulate a theoretical exception that never actually applies in practice offers false hope to defendants, distorts the law, misleads judges, and wastes the resources of defense counsel, prosecutors, and courts," the Court held. "Moreover, no one can reasonably rely on an exception that is non-existent in practice, so no reliance interests can be affected by forthrightly acknowledging reality." "New procedural rules do not apply retroactively on federal collateral review," concluded the Court.

APPENDIX A

SELECTED PROVISIONS OF THE UNITED STATES CONSTITUTION

■ ■ ■

Section 9. * * *

[2] The privilege of the Writ of Habeas Corpus shall not be suspended, unless when in Cases of Rebellion or Invasion the public Safety may require it.

[3] No Bill of Attainder or ex post facto Law shall be passed.

ARTICLE III

Section 1. The judicial Power of the United States, shall be vested in one supreme Court, and in such inferior Courts as the Congress may from time to time ordain and establish. The Judges, both of the supreme and inferior Courts, shall hold their Offices during good Behaviour, and shall, at stated Times, receive for their Services a Compensation, which shall not be diminished during their Continuance in Office.

Section 2. [1] The judicial Power shall extend to all Cases, in Law and Equity, arising under this Constitution, the Laws of the United States, and Treaties made, or which shall be made, under their Authority;—to all Cases affecting Ambassadors, other public Ministers and Consuls;—to all Cases of admiralty and maritime Jurisdiction;—to Controversies to which the United States shall be a Party;—to Controversies between two or more States;—between a State and Citizens of another State;—between Citizens of different States;—between Citizens of the same State claiming Lands under the Grants of different States, and between a State, or the Citizens thereof, and foreign States, Citizens or Subjects.

[3] The trial of all Crimes, except in Cases of Impeachment, shall be by Jury; and such Trial shall be held in the State where the said Crimes shall have been committed; but when not committed within any State, the Trial shall be at such Place or Places as the Congress may by Law have directed.

Section 3. [1] Treason against the United States, shall consist only in levying War against them, or, in adhering to their Enemies, giving them Aid and Comfort. No Person shall be convicted of Treason unless on the Testimony of two Witnesses to the same overt Act, or on Confession in open Court.

[2] The Congress shall have Power to declare the Punishment of Treason, but no Attainder of Treason shall work Corruption of Blood, or Forfeiture except during the Life of the Person attainted.

ARTICLE IV

Section 2. [1] The Citizens of each State shall be entitled to all Privileges and Immunities of Citizens in the several States.

[2] A Person charged in any State with Treason, Felony, or other Crime, who shall flee from Justice, and be found in another State, shall on demand of the executive Authority of the State from which he fled, be delivered up, to be removed to the State having Jurisdiction of the Crime.

ARTICLE VI

[2] This Constitution, and the Laws of the United States which shall be made in Pursuance thereof; and all Treaties made, or which shall be made, under the Authority of the United States, shall be the supreme Law.

AMENDMENT I [1791]

Congress shall make no law respecting an establishment of religion, or prohibiting the free exercise thereof; or abridging the freedom of speech, or of the press; or the right of the people peaceably to assemble, and to petition the Government for a redress of grievances.

AMENDMENT II [1791]

A well regulated Militia, being necessary to the security of a free State, the right of the people to keep and bear Arms, shall not be infringed.

AMENDMENT III [1791]

No Soldier shall, in time of peace be quartered in any house, without the consent of the Owner, nor in time of war, but in a manner to be prescribed by law.

AMENDMENT IV [1791]

The right of the people to be secure in their persons, houses, papers, and effects, against unreasonable searches and seizures, shall not be violated, and no Warrants shall issue, but upon probable cause, supported by Oath or affirmation, and particularly describing the place to be searched, and the persons or things to be seized.

AMENDMENT V [1791]

No person shall be held to answer for a capital, or otherwise infamous crime, unless on a presentment or indictment of a Grand Jury, except in cases arising in the land or naval forces, or in the Militia, when in actual service in time of War or public danger; nor shall any person be subject for the same offence to be twice put in jeopardy of life or limb; nor shall be compelled in any criminal case to be a witness against himself, nor be deprived of life, liberty, or property, without due process of law; nor shall private property be taken for public use, without just compensation.

AMENDMENT VI [1791]

In all criminal prosecutions, the accused shall enjoy the right to a speedy and public trial, by an impartial jury of the State and district wherein the crime shall have been committed, which district shall have been previously ascertained by law, and to be informed of the nature and cause of the accusation; to be confronted with the witnesses against him; to have compulsory process for obtaining witnesses in his favor, and to have the Assistance of Counsel for his defence.

AMENDMENT VII [1791]

In Suits at common law, where the value in controversy shall exceed twenty dollars, the right of trial by jury shall be preserved, and no fact tried by jury, shall be otherwise re-examined in any Court of the United States, than according to the rules of the common law.

AMENDMENT VIII [1791]

Excessive bail shall not be required, nor excessive fines imposed, nor cruel and unusual punishments inflicted.

AMENDMENT IX [1791]

The enumeration in the Constitution, of certain rights, shall not be construed to deny or disparage others retained by the people.

AMENDMENT X [1791]

The powers not delegated to the United States by the Constitution, nor prohibited by it to the States, are reserved to the States respectively, or to the people.

AMENDMENT XIII [1865]

Section 1. Neither slavery nor involuntary servitude, except as a punishment for crime whereof the party shall have been duly convicted, shall exist within the United States, or any place subject to their jurisdiction.

Section 2. Congress shall have power to enforce this article by appropriate legislation.

AMENDMENT XIV [1868]

Section 1. All persons born or naturalized in the United States, and subject to the jurisdiction thereof, are citizens of the United States and of the State wherein they reside. No State shall make or enforce any law which shall abridge the privileges or immunities of citizens of the United States; nor shall any State deprive any person of life, liberty, or property, without due process of law; nor deny to any person within its jurisdiction the equal protection of the laws.

Section 5. The Congress shall have power to enforce, by appropriate legislation, the provisions of the article.

AMENDMENT XV [1870]

Section 1. The right of citizens of the United States to vote shall not be denied or abridged by the United States or by any State on account of race, color, or previous condition of servitude.

Section 2. The Congress shall have power to enforce this article by appropriate legislation.

APPENDIX B

SELECTED FEDERAL STATUTORY PROVISIONS

■ ■ ■

Analysis

Statute	Page
Wire and Electronic Communications Interception and Interception of Oral Communications (18 U.S.C. §§ 2510–2511, 2515–2518, 2520–2521)	103
Stored Wire and Electronic Communications and Transactional Records Access (18 U.S.C. §§ 2702, 2703, 2707, 2708, 2713)	121
Searches and Seizures (18 U.S.C. §§ 3103a, 3105, 3109)	128
Bail Reform Act of 1984 (18 U.S.C. §§ 3141–3150)	130
Speedy Trial Act of 1974 (As Amended) (18 U.S.C. §§ 3161–3162, 3164)	139
Jencks Act (18 U.S.C. § 3500)	144
Litigation Concerning Sources of Evidence (18 U.S.C. § 3504)	145
Criminal Appeals Act of 1970 (As Amended) (18 U.S.C. § 3731)	146
Crime Victims' Rights (18 U.S.C. § 3771)	146
Jury Selection and Service Act of 1968 (As Amended) (28 U.S.C. §§ 1861–1863, 1865–1867)	149
Habeas Corpus (28 U.S.C. §§ 2241–2244, 2253–2255, 2261–2266)	155
Privacy Protection Act of 1980 (42 U.S.C. §§ 2000aa–2000aa–12)	165
Guidelines (28 C.F.R. § 59.4)	169
Foreign Intelligence Surveillance Act (50 U.S.C. § 1861)	172

WIRE AND ELECTRONIC COMMUNICATIONS INTERCEPTION AND INTERCEPTION OF ORAL COMMUNICATIONS

(18 U.S.C. §§ 2510–2511, 2515–2518, 2520–2521).

§ 2510. Definitions

As used in this chapter

(1) "wire communication means any aural transfer made in whole or in part through the use of facilities for the transmission of communications by the aid of wire, cable, or other like connection between the point of origin and the point of reception (including the use of

such connection in a switching station) furnished or operated by any person engaged in providing or operating such facilities for the transmission of interstate or foreign communications or communications affecting interstate or foreign commerce;

(2) "oral communication" means any oral communication uttered by a person exhibiting an expectation that such communication is not subject to interception under circumstances justifying such expectation, but such term does not include any electronic communication;

(3) "State" means any State of the United States, the District of Columbia, the Commonwealth of Puerto Rico, and any territory or possession of the United States;

(4) "intercept" means the aural or other acquisition of the contents of any wire, electronic, or oral communication through the use of any electronic, mechanical, or other device.

(5) "electronic, mechanical, or other device" means any device or apparatus which can be used to intercept a wire, oral, or electronic communication other than—

(a) any telephone or telegraph instrument, equipment or facility, or any component thereof, (i) furnished to the subscriber or user by a provider of wire or electronic communication service in the ordinary course of its business and being used by the subscriber or user in the ordinary course of its business or furnished by such subscriber or user for connection to the facilities of such service and used in the ordinary course of its business; or (ii) being used by a provider of wire or electronic communication service in the ordinary course of its business, or by an investigative or law enforcement officer in the ordinary course of his duties;

(b) a hearing aid or similar device being used to correct subnormal hearing to not better than normal;

(6) "person" means any employee, or agent of the United States or any State or political subdivision thereof, and any individual, partnership, association, joint stock company, trust, or corporation;

(7) "Investigative or law enforcement officer" means any officer of the United States or of a State or political subdivision thereof, who is empowered by law to conduct investigations of or to make arrests for offenses enumerated in this chapter, and any attorney authorized by law to prosecute or participate in the prosecution of such offenses;

(8) "contents", when used with respect to any wire, oral, or electronic communication, includes any information concerning the substance, purport, or meaning of that communication;

(9) "Judge of competent jurisdiction" means—

(a) a judge of a United States district court or a United States court of appeals; and

(b) a judge of any court of general criminal jurisdiction of a State who is authorized by a statute of that State to enter orders authorizing interceptions of wire, oral, or electronic communications;

(10) "communication common carrier" has the meaning given that term in section 3 of the Communications Act of 1934;

(11) "aggrieved person" means a person who was a party to any intercepted wire, oral, or electronic communication or a person against whom the interception was directed;

(12) "electronic communication" means any transfer of signs, signals, writing, images, sounds, data, or intelligence of any nature transmitted in whole or in part by a wire, radio, electromagnetic, photoelectronic or photooptical system that affects interstate or foreign commerce, but does not include—

(A) any wire or oral communication;

(B) any communication made through a tone-only paging device;

(C) any communication from a tracking device (as defined in section 3117 of this title); or

(D) electronic funds transfer information stored by a financial institution in a communications system used for the electronic storage and transfer of funds;

(13) "user" means any person or entity who—

(A) uses an electronic communication service; and

(B) is duly authorized by the provider of such service to engage in such use;

(14) "electronic communications system" means any wire, radio, electromagnetic, photooptical or photoelectronic facilities for the transmission of wire or electronic communications, and any computer facilities or related electronic equipment for the electronic storage of such communications;

(15) "electronic communication service" means any service which provides to users thereof the ability to send or receive wire or electronic communications;

(16) "readily accessible to the general public" means, with respect to a radio communication, that such communication is not—

(A) scrambled or encrypted;

(B) transmitted using modulation techniques whose essential parameters have been withheld from the public with the intention of preserving the privacy of such communication;

(C) carried on a subcarrier or other signal subsidiary to a radio transmission;

(D) transmitted over a communication system provided by a common carrier, unless the communication is a tone only paging system communication; or

(E) transmitted on frequencies allocated under part 25, subpart D, E, or F of part 74, or part 94 of the Rules of the Federal Communications Commission, unless, in the case of a communication transmitted on a frequency allocated under part 74 that is not exclusively allocated to broadcast auxiliary services, the communication is a two-way voice communication by radio;

(17) "electronic storage" means—

(A) any temporary, intermediate storage of a wire or electronic communication incidental to the electronic transmission thereof; and

(B) any storage of such communication by an electronic communication service for purposes of backup protection of such communication;

(18) "aural transfer" means a transfer containing the human voice at any point between and including the point of origin and the point of reception;

(19) "foreign intelligence information", for purposes of section 2517(6) of this title, means—

    (A)   information, whether or not concerning a United States person, that relates to the ability of the United States to protect against—

        (i)   actual or potential attack or other grave hostile acts of a foreign power or an agent of a foreign power;

        (ii)   sabotage or international terrorism by a foreign power or an agent of a foreign power; or

        (iii)   clandestine intelligence activities by an intelligence service or network of a foreign power or by an agent of a foreign power; or

    (B)   information, whether or not concerning a United States person, with respect to a foreign power or foreign territory that relates to—

        (i)   the national defense or the security of the United States; or

        (ii)   the conduct of the foreign affairs of the United States;

(20)   "protected computer" has the meaning set forth in section 1030; and

(21)   "computer trespasser"—

    (A)   means a person who accesses a protected computer without authorization and thus has no reasonable expectation of privacy in any communication transmitted to, through, or from the protected computer; and

    (B)   does not include a person known by the owner or operator of the protected computer to have an existing contractual relationship with the owner or operator of the protected computer for access to all or part of the protected computer.

§ 2511. Interception and disclosure of wire, oral, or electronic communications prohibited

(1)   Except as otherwise specifically provided in this chapter any person who—

    (a)   intentionally intercepts, endeavors to intercept, or procures any other person to intercept or endeavor to intercept, any wire, oral, or electronic communication;

    (b)   intentionally uses, endeavors to use, or procures any other person to use or endeavor to use any electronic, mechanical, or other device to intercept any oral communication when—

        (i)   such device is affixed to, or otherwise transmits a signal through, a wire, cable, or other like connection used in wire communication; or

        (ii)   such device transmits communications by radio, or interferes with the transmission of such communication; or

        (iii)   such person knows, or has reason to know, that such device or any component thereof has been sent through the mail or transported in interstate or foreign commerce; or

        (iv)   such use or endeavor to use (A) takes place on the premises of any business or other commercial establishment the operations of which affect interstate or foreign commerce; or (B) obtains or is for the purpose of obtaining information relating to the operations of any business or other commercial establishment the operations of which affect interstate or foreign commerce; or

        (v)   such person acts in the District of Columbia, the Commonwealth of Puerto Rico, or any territory or possession of the United States;

(c)   intentionally discloses, or endeavors to disclose, to any other person the contents of any wire, oral, or electronic communication, knowing or having reason to know that the information was obtained through the interception of a wire, oral, or electronic communication in violation of this subsection;

(d)   intentionally uses, or endeavors to use, the contents of any wire, oral, or electronic communication, knowing or having reason to know that the information was obtained through the interception of a wire, oral, or electronic communication in violation of this subsection; or

(e)(i) intentionally discloses, or endeavors to disclose, to any other person the contents of any wire, oral, or electronic communication, intercepted by means authorized by sections 2511(2)(a)(ii), 2511(2)(b)–(c), 2511(2)(e), 2516, and 2518 of this chapter, (ii) knowing or having reason to know that the information was obtained through the interception of such a communication in connection with a criminal investigation, (iii) having obtained or received the information in connection with a criminal investigation, and (iv) with intent to improperly obstruct, impede, or interfere with a duly authorized criminal investigation,

shall be punished as provided in subsection (4) or shall be subject to suit as provided in subsection (5).

(2)(a)(i)   It shall not be unlawful under this chapter for an operator of a switchboard, or an officer, employee, or agent of a provider of wire or electronic communication service, whose facilities are used in the transmission of a wire or electronic communication, to intercept, disclose, or use that communication in the normal course of his employment while engaged in any activity which is a necessary incident to the rendition of his service or to the protection of the rights or property of the provider of that service, except that a provider of wire communication service to the public shall not utilize service observing or random monitoring except for mechanical or service quality control checks.

(ii)   Notwithstanding any other law, providers of wire or electronic communication service, their officers, employees, and agents, landlords, custodians, or other persons, are authorized to provide information, facilities, or technical assistance to persons authorized by law to intercept wire, oral, or electronic communications or to conduct electronic surveillance, as defined in section 101 of the Foreign Intelligence Surveillance Act of 1978, if such provider, its officers, employees, or agents, landlord, custodian, or other specified person, has been provided with—

(A)   a court order directing such assistance or a court order pursuant to section 704 of the Foreign Intelligence Surveillance Act of 1978 signed by the authorizing judge, or

(B)   a certification in writing by a person specified in section 2518(7) of this title or the Attorney General of the United States that no warrant or court order is required by law, that all statutory requirements have been met, and that the specified assistance is required,

setting forth the period of time during which the provision of the information, facilities, or technical assistance is authorized and specifying the information, facilities, or technical assistance required. No provider of wire or electronic communication service, officer, employee, or agent thereof, or landlord, custodian, or other specified person shall disclose the existence of any interception or surveillance or the device used to accomplish the interception or surveillance with respect to which the person has been furnished a court order or certification under this chapter, except as may otherwise be required by legal process and then only after prior notification to the Attorney General or to the principal prosecuting attorney of a State or any political subdivision of a State, as may be appropriate. Any such disclosure, shall render such person liable for the civil damages provided for in section 2520. No cause of action shall lie in any court against any provider of wire or electronic communication service, its officers, employees, or agents, landlord, custodian, or other specified person for providing information, facilities, or assistance in accordance with the terms of a court order, statutory authorization, or certification under this chapter.

(iii) If a certification under subparagraph (ii)(B) for assistance to obtain foreign intelligence information is based on statutory authority, the certification shall identify the specific statutory provision and shall certify that the statutory requirements have been met.

(b) It shall not be unlawful under this chapter for an officer, employee, or agent of the Federal Communications Commission, in the normal course of his employment and in discharge of the monitoring responsibilities exercised by the Commission in the enforcement of chapter 5 of title 47 of the United States Code, to intercept a wire or electronic communication, or oral communication transmitted by radio, or to disclose or use the information thereby obtained.

(c) It shall not be unlawful under this chapter for a person acting under color of law to intercept a wire, oral, or electronic communication, where such person is a party to the communication or one of the parties to the communication has given prior consent to such interception.

(d) It shall not be unlawful under this chapter for a person not acting under color of law to intercept a wire, oral, or electronic communication where such person is a party to the communication or where one of the parties to the communication has given prior consent to such interception unless such communication is intercepted for the purpose of committing any criminal or tortious act in violation of the Constitution or laws of the United States or of any State.

(e) Notwithstanding any other provision of this title or section 705 or 706 of the Communications Act of 1934, it shall not be unlawful for an officer, employee, or agent of the United States in the normal course of his official duty to conduct electronic surveillance, as defined in section 101 of the Foreign Intelligence Surveillance Act of 1978, as authorized by that Act.

(f) Nothing contained in this chapter or chapter 121 or 206 of this title, or section 705 of the Communications Act of 1934, shall be deemed to affect the acquisition by the United States Government of foreign intelligence information from international or foreign communications, or foreign intelligence activities conducted in accordance with otherwise applicable Federal law involving a foreign electronic communications system, utilizing a means other than electronic surveillance as defined in section 101 of the Foreign Intelligence Surveillance Act of 1978, and procedures in this chapter or chapter 121 and the Foreign Intelligence Surveillance Act of 1978 shall be the exclusive means by which electronic surveillance, as defined in section 101 of such Act, and the interception of domestic wire, oral, and electronic communications may be conducted.

(g) It shall not be unlawful under this chapter or chapter 121 of this title for any person—

(i) to intercept or access an electronic communication made through an electronic communication system that is configured so that such electronic communication is readily accessible to the general public;

(ii) to intercept any radio communication which is transmitted—

(I) by any station for the use of the general public, or that relates to ships, aircraft, vehicles, or persons in distress;

(II) by any governmental, law enforcement, civil defense, private land mobile, or public safety communications system, including police and fire, readily accessible to the general public;

(III) by a station operating on an authorized frequency within the bands allocated to the amateur, citizens band, or general mobile radio services; or

(IV) by any marine or aeronautical communications system;

    (iii) to engage in any conduct which—

        (I)   is prohibited by section 633 of the Communications Act of 1934; or

        (II) is excepted from the application of section 705(a) of the Communications Act of 1934 by section 705(b) of that Act;

    (iv) to intercept any wire or electronic communication the transmission of which is causing harmful interference to any lawfully operating station or consumer electronic equipment, to the extent necessary to identify the source of such interference; or

    (v) for other users of the same frequency to intercept any radio communication made through a system that utilizes frequencies monitored by individuals engaged in the provision or the use of such system, if such communication is not scrambled or encrypted.

(h)   It shall not be unlawful under this chapter—

    (i)   to use a pen register or a trap and trace device (as those terms are defined for the purposes of chapter 206 (relating to pen registers and trap and trace devices) of this title); or

    (ii) for a provider of electronic communication service to record the fact that a wire or electronic communication was initiated or completed in order to protect such provider, another provider furnishing service toward the completion of the wire or electronic communication, or a user of that service, from fraudulent, unlawful or abusive use of such service.

(i)   It shall not be unlawful under this chapter for a person acting under color of law to intercept the wire or electronic communications of a computer trespasser transmitted to, through, or from the protected computer, if—

    (I)   the owner or operator of the protected computer authorizes the interception of the computer trespasser's communications on the protected computer;

    (II) the person acting under color of law is lawfully engaged in an investigation;

    (III) the person acting under color of law has reasonable grounds to believe that the contents of the computer trespasser's communications will be relevant to the investigation; and

    (IV) such interception does not acquire communications other than those transmitted to or from the computer trespasser.

(j)   It shall not be unlawful under this chapter for a provider of electronic communication service to the public or remote computing service to intercept or disclose the contents of a wire or electronic communication in response to an order from a foreign government that is subject to an executive agreement that the Attorney General has determined and certified to Congress satisfies section 2523.

(3)(a) Except as provided in paragraph (b) of this subsection, a person or entity providing an electronic communication service to the public shall not intentionally divulge the contents of any communication (other than one to such person or entity, or an agent thereof) while in transmission on that service to any person or entity other than an addressee or intended recipient of such communication or an agent of such addressee or intended recipient.

(b)   A person or entity providing electronic communication service to the public may divulge the contents of any such communication—

    (i)   as otherwise authorized in section 2511(2)(a) or 2517 of this title;

    (ii) with the lawful consent of the originator or any addressee or intended recipient of such communication;

(iii) to a person employed or authorized, or whose facilities are used, to forward such communication to its destination; or

(iv) which were inadvertently obtained by the service provider and which appear to pertain to the commission of a crime, if such divulgence is made to a law enforcement agency.

(4)(a) Except as provided in paragraph (b) of this subsection or in subsection (5), whoever violates subsection (1) of this section shall be fined under this title or imprisoned not more than five years, or both.

(b) Conduct otherwise an offense under this subsection that consists of or relates to the interception of a satellite transmission that is not encrypted or scrambled and that is transmitted—

(i) to a broadcasting station for purposes of retransmission to the general public; or

(ii) as an audio subcarrier intended for redistribution to facilities open to the public, but not including data transmissions or telephone calls,

is not an offense under this subsection unless the conduct is for the purposes of direct or indirect commercial advantage or private financial gain.

[(c) Redesignated (b)]

(5)(a)(i) If the communication is—

(A) a private satellite video communication that is not scrambled or encrypted and the conduct in violation of this chapter is the private viewing of that communication and is not for a tortious or illegal purpose or for purposes of direct or indirect commercial advantage or private commercial gain; or

(B) a radio communication that is transmitted on frequencies allocated under subpart D of part 74 of the rules of the Federal Communications Commission that is not scrambled or encrypted and the conduct in violation of this chapter is not for a tortious or illegal purpose or for purposes of direct or indirect commercial advantage or private commercial gain,

then the person who engages in such conduct shall be subject to suit by the Federal Government in a court of competent jurisdiction.

(ii) In an action under this subsection—

(A) if the violation of this chapter is a first offense for the person under paragraph (a) of subsection (4) and such person has not been found liable in a civil action under section 2520 of this title, the Federal Government shall be entitled to appropriate injunctive relief; and

(B) if the violation of this chapter is a second or subsequent offense under paragraph (a) of subsection (4) or such person has been found liable in any prior civil action under section 2520, the person shall be subject to a mandatory $500 civil fine.

(b) The court may use any means within its authority to enforce an injunction issued under paragraph (ii)(A), and shall impose a civil fine of not less than $500 for each violation of such an injunction.

§ 2515. Prohibition of use as evidence of intercepted wire or oral communications

Whenever any wire or oral communication has been intercepted, no part of the contents of such communication and no evidence derived therefrom may be received in evidence in any trial, hearing, or other proceeding in or before any court, grand jury, department, officer, agency, regulatory body, legislative committee, or other authority of the United States, a State, or a political subdivision thereof if the disclosure of that information would be in violation of this chapter.

§ 2516. Authorization for interception of wire, oral, or electronic communications

(1)   The Attorney General, Deputy Attorney General, Associate Attorney General, or any Assistant Attorney General, any acting Assistant Attorney General, or any Deputy Assistant Attorney General or acting Deputy Assistant Attorney General in the Criminal Division or National Security Division specially designated by the Attorney General, may authorize an application to a Federal judge of competent jurisdiction for, and such judge may grant in conformity with section 2518 of this chapter an order authorizing or approving the interception of wire or oral communications by the Federal Bureau of Investigation, or a Federal agency having responsibility for the investigation of the offense as to which the application is made, when such interception may provide or has provided evidence of—

(a)   any offense punishable by death or by imprisonment for more than one year under sections 2122 and 2274 through 2277 of title 42 of the United States Code (relating to the enforcement of the Atomic Energy Act of 1954), section 2284 of title 42 of the United States Code (relating to sabotage of nuclear facilities or fuel), or under the following chapters of this title: chapter 10 (relating to biological weapons), chapter 37 (relating to espionage), chapter 55 (relating to kidnapping), chapter 90 (relating to protection of trade secrets), chapter 105 (relating to sabotage), chapter 115 (relating to treason), chapter 102 (relating to riots), chapter 65 (relating to malicious mischief), chapter 111 (relating to destruction of vessels), or chapter 81 (relating to piracy);

(b)   a violation of section 186 or section 501(c) of title 29, United States Code (dealing with restrictions on payments and loans to labor organizations), or any offense which involves murder, kidnapping, robbery, or extortion, and which is punishable under this title;

(c)   any offense which is punishable under the following sections of this title: section 37 (relating to violence at international airports), section 43 (relating to animal enterprise terrorism), section 81 (arson within special maritime and territorial jurisdiction), section 201 (bribery of public officials and witnesses), section 215 (relating to bribery of bank officials), section 224 (bribery in sporting contests), subsection (d), (e), (f), (g), (h), or (i) of section 844 (unlawful use of explosives), section 1032 (relating to concealment of assets), section 1084 (transmission of wagering information), section 751 (relating to escape), section 832 (relating to nuclear and weapons of mass destruction threats), section 842 (relating to explosive materials), section 930 (relating to possession of weapons in Federal facilities), section 1014 (relating to loans and credit applications generally; renewals and discounts), section 1114 (relating to officers and employees of the United States), section 1116 (relating to protection of foreign officials), sections 1503, 1512, and 1513 (influencing or injuring an officer, juror, or witness generally), section 1510 (obstruction of criminal investigations), section 1511 (obstruction of State or local law enforcement), section 1581 (peonage), section 1582 (vessels for slave trade), section 1583 (enticement into slavery), section 1584 (involuntary servitude), section 1585 (seizure, detention, transportation or sale of slaves), section 1586 (service on vessels in slave trade), section 1587 (possession of slaves aboard vessel), section 1588 (transportation of slaves from United States), section 1589 (forced labor), section 1590 (trafficking with respect to peonage, slavery, involuntary servitude, or forced labor), section 1591 (sex trafficking of children by force, fraud, or coercion), section 1592 (unlawful conduct with respect to documents in furtherance of trafficking, peonage, slavery, involuntary servitude, or forced labor), section 1751 (Presidential and Presidential staff assassination, kidnapping, and assault), section 1951 (interference with commerce by threats or violence), section 1952 (interstate and foreign travel or transportation in aid of racketeering enterprises), section 1958 (relating to use of interstate commerce facilities in the commission of murder for hire), section 1959 (relating to violent crimes in aid of racketeering activity), section 1954 (offer, acceptance, or solicitation to influence operations of employee benefit plan), section 1955 (prohibition of business enterprises of gambling), section 1956 (laundering of monetary instruments), section 1957 (relating to engaging in monetary transactions in property derived from specified unlawful activity), section 659 (theft from interstate shipment), section 664 (embezzlement from pension and welfare funds), section 1343 (fraud by wire, radio, or television), section 1344 (relating to bank fraud), section 1992 (relating to terrorist attacks against mass transportation), sections 2251 and 2252 (sexual exploitation of children), section 2251A (selling or buying of children), section 2252A (relating to material constituting or containing child pornography), section 1466A (relating to child obscenity), section 2260 (production of sexually explicit depictions of a minor for importation into the United States), sections 2421, 2422, 2423, and 2425 (relating to transportation for illegal sexual activity and related crimes), sections 2312, 2313, 2314, and 2315 (interstate transportation of stolen property), section 2321 (relating to trafficking in certain motor vehicles or motor vehicle parts), section 2340A (relating to torture), section 1203 (relating to hostage taking), section 1029 (relating to fraud and related activity in connection with access devices), section 3146 (relating to penalty for failure to appear), section 3521(b)(3) (relating to witness relocation and assistance), section 32 (relating to destruction of aircraft or aircraft facilities), section 38 (relating to aircraft parts fraud), section 1963 (violations with respect to racketeer influenced and corrupt organizations), section 115 (relating to threatening or retaliating against a Federal official), section 1341 (relating to mail fraud), a felony violation of section 1030 (relating to computer fraud and abuse), section 351 (violations with respect to congressional, Cabinet, or Supreme Court assassinations, kidnapping, and assault), section 831 (relating to prohibited transactions involving nuclear materials), section 33 (relating to destruction of motor vehicles or motor vehicle facilities), section 175 (relating to biological weapons), section 175c (relating to variola virus), section 956 (conspiracy to harm persons or property overseas), a felony violation of section 1028 (relating to production of false identification documentation), section 1425 (relating to the procurement of citizenship or nationalization unlawfully), section 1426 (relating to the reproduction of naturalization or citizenship papers), section 1427 (relating to the sale of naturalization or citizenship papers), section 1541 (relating to passport issuance without authority), section 1542 (relating to false statements in passport applications), section 1543 (relating to forgery or false use of passports), section 1544 (relating to misuse of passports), section 1546 (relating to fraud and misuse of visas, permits, and other documents), or section 555 (relating to construction or use of international border tunnels);

(d)   any offense involving counterfeiting punishable under section 471, 472, or 473 of this title;

(e)   any offense involving fraud connected with a case under title 11 or the manufacture, importation, receiving, concealment, buying, selling, or otherwise dealing in narcotic drugs, marihuana, or other dangerous drugs, punishable under any law of the United States;

(f)   any offense including extortionate credit transactions under sections 892, 893, or 894 of this title;

(g)   a violation of section 5322 of title 31, United States Code (dealing with the reporting of currency transactions), or section 5324 of title 31, United States Code (relating to structuring transactions to evade reporting requirement prohibited);

(h)   any felony violation of sections 2511 and 2512 (relating to interception and disclosure of certain communications and to certain intercepting devices) of this title;

(i)   any felony violation of chapter 71 (relating to obscenity) of this title;

(j)   any violation of section 60123(b) (relating to destruction of a natural gas pipeline), section 46502 (relating to aircraft piracy), the second sentence of section 46504 (relating to assault on a flight crew with dangerous weapon), or section 46505(b)(3) or (c) (relating to explosive or incendiary devices, or endangerment of human life, by means of weapons on aircraft) of title 49;

(k)   any criminal violation of section 2778 of title 22 (relating to the Arms Export Control Act);

(l)   the location of any fugitive from justice from an offense described in this section;

(m)   a violation of section 274, 277, or 278 of the Immigration and Nationality Act (8 U.S.C. 1324, 1327, or 1328) (relating to the smuggling of aliens);

(n)   any felony violation of sections 922 and 924 of title 18, United States Code (relating to firearms);

(o)   any violation of section 5861 of the Internal Revenue Code of 1986 (relating to firearms);

(p)   a felony violation of section 1028 (relating to production of false identification documents), section 1542 (relating to false statements in passport applications), section 1546 (relating to fraud and misuse of visas, permits, and other documents), section 1028A (relating to aggravated identity theft) of this title or a violation of section 274, 277, or 278 of the Immigration and Nationality Act (relating to the smuggling of aliens);

(q)   any criminal violation of section 229 (relating to chemical weapons) or section 2332, 2332a, 2332b, 2332d, 2332f, 2332g, 2332h, 2339, 2339A, 2339B, 2339C, or 2339D of this title (related to terrorism);

(r)   any criminal violation of section 1 (relating to illegal restraints of trade or commerce), 2 (relating to illegal monopolizing of trade or commerce), or 3 (relating to illegal restraints of trade or commerce in territories or the District of Columbia) of the Sherman Act (15 U.S.C. 1, 2, 3);

(s)   any violation of section 670 (relating to theft of medical products); or

(t)   any conspiracy to commit any offense described in any subparagraph of this paragraph.

(2)   The principal prosecuting attorney of any State, or the principal prosecuting attorney of any political subdivision thereof, if such attorney is authorized by a statute of that State to make application to a State court judge of competent jurisdiction for an order authorizing or approving the interception of wire, oral, or electronic communications, may apply to such judge for, and such judge may grant in conformity with section 2518 of this chapter and with the applicable State statute an order authorizing, or approving the interception of wire, oral, or electronic communications by investigative or law enforcement officers having responsibility for the investigation of the offense as to which the application is made, when such interception may provide or has provided evidence of the commission of the offense of murder, kidnapping, human trafficking, child sexual exploitation, child pornography production, prostitution, gambling, robbery, bribery, extortion, or dealing in narcotic drugs, marihuana or other dangerous drugs, or other crime dangerous to life, limb, or property, and punishable by imprisonment for more than one year, designated in any applicable State statute authorizing such interception, or any conspiracy to commit any of the foregoing offenses.

(3)   Any attorney for the Government (as such term is defined for the purposes of the Federal Rules of Criminal Procedure) may authorize an application to a Federal judge of competent jurisdiction for, and such judge may grant, in conformity with section 2518 of this title, an order authorizing or approving the interception of electronic communications by an investigative or law enforcement officer having responsibility for the investigation of the offense as to which the application is made, when such interception may provide or has provided evidence of any Federal felony.

§ 2517.   Authorization for disclosure and use of intercepted wire, oral, or electronic communications

(1)   Any investigative or law enforcement officer who, by any means authorized by this chapter, has obtained knowledge of the contents of any wire, oral, or electronic communication, or evidence derived therefrom, may disclose such contents to another investigative or law enforcement officer to the extent that such disclosure is appropriate to the proper performance of the official duties of the officer making or receiving the disclosure.

(2)   Any investigative or law enforcement officer who, by any means authorized by this chapter, has obtained knowledge of the contents of any wire, oral, or electronic communication or evidence derived therefrom may use such contents to the extent such use is appropriate to the proper performance of his official duties.

(3)   Any person who has received, by any means authorized by this chapter, any information concerning a wire, oral, or electronic communication, or evidence derived therefrom intercepted in accordance with the provisions of this chapter may disclose the contents of that communication or such derivative evidence while giving testimony under oath or affirmation in any proceeding held under the authority of the United States or of any State or political subdivision thereof.

(4)   No otherwise privileged wire, oral, or electronic communication intercepted in accordance with, or in violation of, the provisions of this chapter shall lose its privileged character.

(5)   When an investigative or law enforcement officer, while engaged in intercepting wire, oral, or electronic communications in the manner authorized herein, intercepts wire, oral, or electronic communications relating to offenses other than those specified in the order of authorization or approval, the contents thereof, and evidence derived therefrom, may be disclosed or used as provided in subsections (1) and (2) of this section. Such contents and any evidence derived therefrom may be used under subsection (3) of this section when authorized or approved by a judge of competent jurisdiction where such judge finds on subsequent application that the contents were otherwise intercepted in accordance with the provisions of this chapter. Such application shall be made as soon as practicable.

(6)   Any investigative or law enforcement officer, or attorney for the Government, who by any means authorized by this chapter, has obtained knowledge of the contents of any wire, oral, or electronic communication, or evidence derived therefrom, may disclose such contents to any other Federal law enforcement, intelligence, protective, immigration, national defense, or national security official to the extent that such contents include foreign intelligence or counterintelligence (as defined in section 3 of the National Security Act of 1947 (50 U.S.C. 401a)), or foreign intelligence information (as defined in subsection (19) of section 2510 of this title), to assist the official who is to receive that information in the performance of his official duties. Any Federal official who receives information pursuant to this provision may use that information only as necessary in the conduct of that person's official duties subject to any limitations on the unauthorized disclosure of such information.

(7)   Any investigative or law enforcement officer, or other Federal official in carrying out official duties as such Federal official, who by any means authorized by this chapter, has obtained knowledge of the contents of any wire, oral, or electronic communication, or evidence derived

therefrom, may disclose such contents or derivative evidence to a foreign investigative or law enforcement officer to the extent that such disclosure is appropriate to the proper performance of the official duties of the officer making or receiving the disclosure, and foreign investigative or law enforcement officers may use or disclose such contents or derivative evidence to the extent such use or disclosure is appropriate to the proper performance of their official duties.

(8) Any investigative or law enforcement officer, or other Federal official in carrying out official duties as such Federal official, who by any means authorized by this chapter, has obtained knowledge of the contents of any wire, oral, or electronic communication, or evidence derived therefrom, may disclose such contents or derivative evidence to any appropriate Federal, State, local, or foreign government official to the extent that such contents or derivative evidence reveals a threat of actual or potential attack or other grave hostile acts of a foreign power or an agent of a foreign power, domestic or international sabotage, domestic or international terrorism, or clandestine intelligence gathering activities by an intelligence service or network of a foreign power or by an agent of a foreign power, within the United States or elsewhere, for the purpose of preventing or responding to such a threat. Any official who receives information pursuant to this provision may use that information only as necessary in the conduct of that person's official duties subject to any limitations on the unauthorized disclosure of such information, and any State, local, or foreign official who receives information pursuant to this provision may use that information only consistent with such guidelines as the Attorney General and Director of Central Intelligence shall jointly issue.

§ 2518.   Procedure for interception of wire, oral, or electronic communications

(1) Each application for an order authorizing or approving the interception of a wire, oral, or electronic communication under this chapter shall be made in writing upon oath or affirmation to a judge of competent jurisdiction and shall state the applicant's authority to make such application. Each application shall include the following information:

(a)   the identity of the investigative or law enforcement officer making the application, and the officer authorizing the application;

(b)   a full and complete statement of the facts and circumstances relied upon by the applicant, to justify his belief that an order should be issued, including (i) details as to the particular offense that has been, is being, or is about to be committed, (ii) except as provided in subsection (11), a particular description of the nature and location of the facilities from which or the place where the communication is to be intercepted, (iii) a particular description of the type of communications sought to be intercepted, (iv) the identity of the person, if known, committing the offense and whose communications are to be intercepted;

(c)   a full and complete statement as to whether or not other investigative procedures have been tried and failed or why they reasonably appear to be unlikely to succeed if tried or to be too dangerous;

(d)   a statement of the period of time for which the interception is required to be maintained. If the nature of the investigation is such that the authorization for interception should not automatically terminate when the described type of communication has been first obtained, a particular description of facts establishing probable cause to believe that additional communications of the same type will occur thereafter;

(e)   a full and complete statement of the facts concerning all previous applications known to the individual authorizing and making the application, made to any judge for authorization to intercept, or for approval of interceptions of, wire, oral, or electronic communications involving any of the same persons, facilities or places specified in the application, and the action taken by the judge on each such application; and (f)　where the application is for the extension of an order, a statement setting forth the results thus far obtained from the interception, or a reasonable explanation of the failure to obtain such results.

(2)　The judge may require the applicant to furnish additional testimony or documentary evidence in support of the application.

(3)　Upon such application the judge may enter an ex parte order, as requested or as modified, authorizing or approving interception of wire, oral, or electronic communications within the territorial jurisdiction of the court in which the judge is sitting (and outside that jurisdiction but within the United States in the case of a mobile interception device authorized by a Federal court within such jurisdiction), if the judge determines on the basis of the facts submitted by the applicant that—

(a)　there is probable cause for belief that an individual is committing, has committed, or is about to commit a particular offense enumerated in section 2516 of this chapter;

(b)　there is probable cause for belief that particular communications concerning that offense will be obtained through such interception;

(c)　normal investigative procedures have been tried and have failed or reasonably appear to be unlikely to succeed if tried or to be too dangerous;

(d)　except as provided in subsection (11), there is probable cause for belief that the facilities from which, or the place where, the wire, oral, or electronic communications are to be intercepted are being used, or are about to be used, in connection with the commission of such offense, or are leased to, listed in the name of, or commonly used by such person.

(4)　Each order authorizing or approving the interception of any wire, oral, or electronic communication under this chapter shall specify—

(a)　the identity of the person, if known, whose communications are to be intercepted;

(b)　the nature and location of the communications facilities as to which, or the place where, authority to intercept is granted;

(c)　a particular description of the type of communication sought to be intercepted, and a statement of the particular offense to which it relates;

(d)　the identity of the agency authorized to intercept the communications, and of the person authorizing the application; and

(e)　the period of time during which such interception is authorized, including a statement as to whether or not the interception shall automatically terminate when the described communication has been first obtained.

An order authorizing the interception of a wire, oral, or electronic communication under this chapter shall, upon request of the applicant, direct that a provider of wire or electronic communication service, landlord, custodian or other person shall furnish the applicant forthwith all information, facilities, and technical assistance necessary to accomplish the interception unobtrusively and with a minimum of interference with the services that such service provider, landlord, custodian, or person is according the person whose communications are to be intercepted. Any provider of wire or electronic communication service, landlord, custodian or other person furnishing such facilities or technical assistance shall be compensated therefor by the applicant for reasonable expenses incurred in providing such facilities or assistance. Pursuant to section 2522 of this chapter, an order may also be issued to enforce the assistance capability and capacity requirements under the Communications Assistance for Law Enforcement Act.

(5) No order entered under this section may authorize or approve the interception of any wire, oral, or electronic communication for any period longer than is necessary to achieve the objective of the authorization, nor in any event longer than thirty days. Such thirty-day period begins on the earlier of the day on which the investigative or law enforcement officer first begins to conduct an interception under the order or ten days after the order is entered. Extensions of an order may be granted, but only upon application for an extension made in accordance with subsection (1) of this section and the court making the findings required by subsection (3) of this section. The period of extension shall be no longer than the authorizing judge deems necessary to achieve the purposes for which it was granted and in no event for longer than thirty days. Every order and extension thereof shall contain a provision that the authorization to intercept shall be executed as soon as practicable, shall be conducted in such a way as to minimize the interception of communications not otherwise subject to interception under this chapter, and must terminate upon attainment of the authorized objective, or in any event in thirty days. In the event the intercepted communication is in a code or foreign language, and an expert in that foreign language or code is not reasonably available during the interception period, minimization may be accomplished as soon as practicable after such interception. An interception under this chapter may be conducted in whole or in part by Government personnel, or by an individual operating under a contract with the Government, acting under the supervision of an investigative or law enforcement officer authorized to conduct the interception.

(6) Whenever an order authorizing interception is entered pursuant to this chapter, the order may require reports to be made to the judge who issued the order showing what progress has been made toward achievement of the authorized objective and the need for continued interception. Such reports shall be made at such intervals as the judge may require.

(7) Notwithstanding any other provision of this chapter, any investigative or law enforcement officer, specially designated by the Attorney General, the Deputy Attorney General, the Associate Attorney General, or by the principal prosecuting attorney of any State or subdivision thereof acting pursuant to a statute of that State, who reasonably determines that—

    (a) an emergency situation exists that involves—

        (i) immediate danger of death or serious physical injury to any person,

        (ii) conspiratorial activities threatening the national security interest, or

        (iii) conspiratorial activities characteristic of organized crime,

that requires a wire, oral, or electronic communication to be intercepted before an order authorizing such interception can, with due diligence, be obtained, and

    (b) there are grounds upon which an order could be entered under this chapter to authorize such interception,

may intercept such wire, oral, or electronic communication if an application for an order approving the interception is made in accordance with this section within forty-eight hours after the interception has occurred, or begins to occur. In the absence of an order, such interception shall immediately terminate when the communication sought is obtained or when the application for the order is denied, whichever is earlier. In the event such application for approval is denied, or in any other case where the interception is terminated without an order having been issued, the contents of any wire, oral, or electronic communication intercepted shall be treated as having been obtained in violation of this chapter, and an inventory shall be served as provided for in subsection (d) of this section on the person named in the application.

(8)(a) The contents of any wire, oral, or electronic communication intercepted by any means authorized by this chapter shall, if possible, be recorded on tape or wire or other comparable device. The recording of the contents of any wire, oral, or electronic communication under this subsection shall be done in such a way as will protect the recording from editing or other alterations. Immediately upon the expiration of the period of the order, or extensions thereof, such recordings shall be made available to the judge issuing such order and sealed under his directions. Custody of the recordings shall be wherever the judge orders. They shall not be destroyed except upon an order of the issuing or denying judge and in any event shall be kept for ten years. Duplicate recordings may be made for use or disclosure pursuant to the provisions of subsections (1) and (2) of section 2517 of this chapter for investigations. The presence of the seal provided for by this subsection, or a satisfactory explanation for the absence thereof, shall be a prerequisite for the use or disclosure of the contents of any wire, oral, or electronic communication or evidence derived therefrom under subsection (3) of section 2517.

(b)   Applications made and orders granted under this chapter shall be sealed by the judge. Custody of the applications and orders shall be wherever the judge directs. Such applications and orders shall be disclosed only upon a showing of good cause before a judge of competent jurisdiction and shall not be destroyed except on order of the issuing or denying judge, and in any event shall be kept for ten years.

(c)   Any violation of the provisions of this subsection may be punished as contempt of the issuing or denying judge.

(d)   Within a reasonable time but not later than ninety days after the filing of an application for an order of approval under section 2518(7)(b) which is denied or the termination of the period of an order or extensions thereof, the issuing or denying judge shall cause to be served, on the persons named in the order or the application, and such other parties to intercepted communications as the judge may determine in his discretion that is in the interest of justice, an inventory which shall include notice of—

(1)   the fact of the entry of the order or the application;

(2)   the date of the entry and the period of authorized, approved or disapproved interception, or the denial of the application; and

(3)   the fact that during the period wire, oral, or electronic communications were or were not intercepted.

The judge, upon the filing of a motion, may in his discretion make available to such person or his counsel for inspection such portions of the intercepted communications, applications and orders as the judge determines to be in the interest of justice. On an ex parte showing of good cause to a judge of competent jurisdiction the serving of the inventory required by this subsection may be postponed.

(9)   The contents of any wire, oral, or electronic communication intercepted pursuant to this chapter or evidence derived therefrom shall not be received in evidence or otherwise disclosed in any trial, hearing, or other proceeding in a Federal or State court unless each party, not less than ten days before the trial, hearing, or proceeding, has been furnished with a copy of the court order, and accompanying application, under which the interception was authorized or approved. This ten-day period may be waived by the judge if he finds that it was not possible to furnish the party with the above information ten days before the trial, hearing, or proceeding and that the party will not be prejudiced by the delay in receiving such information.

(10)(a)   Any aggrieved person in any trial, hearing, or proceeding in or before any court, department, officer, agency, regulatory body, or other authority of the United States, a State, or a political subdivision thereof, may move to suppress the contents of any wire or oral communication intercepted pursuant to this chapter, or evidence derived therefrom, on the grounds that—

(i)   the communication was unlawfully intercepted;

(ii)   the order of authorization or approval under which it was intercepted is insufficient on its face; or

(iii)   the interception was not made in conformity with the order of authorization or approval.

Such motion shall be made before the trial, hearing, or proceeding unless there was no opportunity to make such motion or the person was not aware of the grounds of the motion. If the motion is granted, the contents of the intercepted wire or oral communication, or evidence derived therefrom, shall be treated as having been obtained in violation of this chapter. The judge, upon the filing of such motion by the aggrieved person, may in his discretion make available to the aggrieved person or his counsel for inspection such portions of the intercepted communication or evidence derived therefrom as the judge determines to be in the interests of justice.

(b)   In addition to any other right to appeal, the United States shall have the right to appeal from an order granting a motion to suppress made under paragraph (a) of this subsection, or the denial of an application for an order of approval, if the United States attorney shall certify to the judge or other official granting such motion or denying such application that the appeal is not taken for purposes of delay. Such appeal shall be taken within thirty days after the date the order was entered and shall be diligently prosecuted.

(c)   The remedies and sanctions described in this chapter with respect to the interception of electronic communications are the only judicial remedies and sanctions for nonconstitutional violations of this chapter involving such communications.

(11) The requirements of subsections (1)(b)(ii) and (3)(d) of this section relating to the specification of the facilities from which, or the place where, the communication is to be intercepted do not apply if—

(a)   in the case of an application with respect to the interception of an oral communication—

(i)   the application is by a Federal investigative or law enforcement officer and is approved by the Attorney General, the Deputy Attorney General, the Associate Attorney General, an Assistant Attorney General, or an acting Assistant Attorney General;

(ii)   the application contains a full and complete statement as to why such specification is not practical and identifies the person committing the offense and whose communications are to be intercepted; and

(iii)   the judge finds that such specification is not practical; and

(b)   in the case of an application with respect to a wire or electronic communication—

(i)   the application is by a Federal investigative or law enforcement officer and is approved by the Attorney General, the Deputy Attorney General, the Associate Attorney General, an Assistant Attorney General, or an acting Assistant Attorney General;

(ii)   the application identifies the person believed to be committing the offense and whose communications are to be intercepted and the applicant makes a showing that there is probable cause to believe that the person's actions could have the effect of thwarting interception from a specified facility;

(iii)   the judge finds that such showing has been adequately made; and

(iv)   the order authorizing or approving the interception is limited to interception only for such time as it is reasonable to presume that the person identified in the application is or was reasonably proximate to the instrument through which such communication will be or was transmitted.

(12) An interception of a communication under an order with respect to which the requirements of subsections (1)(b)(ii) and (3)(d) of this section do not apply by reason of subsection (11)(a) shall not begin until the place where the communication is to be intercepted is ascertained by the person implementing the interception order. A provider of wire or electronic communications service that has received an order as provided for in subsection (11)(b) may move the court to modify or quash the order on the ground that its assistance with respect to the interception cannot be performed in a timely or reasonable fashion. The court, upon notice to the government, shall decide such a motion expeditiously.

§ 2520. Recovery of civil damages authorized

(a) In general.—Except as provided in section 2511(2)(a)(ii), any person whose wire, oral, or electronic communication is intercepted, disclosed, or intentionally used in violation of this chapter may in a civil action recover from the person or entity, other than the United States, which engaged in that violation such relief as may be appropriate.

(b) Relief.—In an action under this section, appropriate relief includes—

(1) such preliminary and other equitable or declaratory relief as may be appropriate;

(2) damages under subsection (c) and punitive damages in appropriate cases; and

(3) a reasonable attorney's fee and other litigation costs reasonably incurred.

(c) Computation of damages.—(1) In an action under this section, if the conduct in violation of this chapter is the private viewing of a private satellite video communication that is not scrambled or encrypted or if the communication is a radio communication that is transmitted on frequencies allocated under subpart D of part 74 of the rules of the Federal Communications Commission that is not scrambled or encrypted and the conduct is not for a tortious or illegal purpose or for purposes of direct or indirect commercial advantage or private commercial gain, then the court shall assess damages as follows:

(A) If the person who engaged in that conduct has not previously been enjoined under section 2511(5) and has not been found liable in a prior civil action under this section, the court shall assess the greater of the sum of actual damages suffered by the plaintiff, or statutory damages of not less than $50 and not more than $500.

(B) If, on one prior occasion, the person who engaged in that conduct has been enjoined under section 2511(5) or has been found liable in a civil action under this section, the court shall assess the greater of the sum of actual damages suffered by the plaintiff, or statutory damages of not less than $100 and not more than $1000.

(2) In any other action under this section, the court may assess as damages whichever is the greater of—

(A) the sum of the actual damages suffered by the plaintiff and any profits made by the violator as a result of the violation; or

(B) statutory damages of whichever is the greater of $100 a day for each day of violation or $10,000.

(d) Defense.—A good faith reliance on—

(1) a court warrant or order, a grand jury subpoena, a legislative authorization, or a statutory authorization;

(2) a request of an investigative or law enforcement officer under section 2518(7) of this title; or

(3)   a good faith determination that section 2511(3) 2511(2)(i), or 2511(2)(j) of this title permitted the conduct complained of;

is a complete defense against any civil or criminal action brought under this chapter or any other law.

(e)   Limitation.—A civil action under this section may not be commenced later than two years after the date upon which the claimant first has a reasonable opportunity to discover the violation.

(f)   Administrative discipline.—If a court or appropriate department or agency determines that the United States or any of its departments or agencies has violated any provision of this chapter, and the court or appropriate department or agency finds that the circumstances surrounding the violation raise serious questions about whether or not an officer or employee of the United States acted willfully or intentionally with respect to the violation, the department or agency shall, upon receipt of a true and correct copy of the decision and findings of the court or appropriate department or agency promptly initiate a proceeding to determine whether disciplinary action against the officer or employee is warranted. If the head of the department or agency involved determines that disciplinary action is not warranted, he or she shall notify the Inspector General with jurisdiction over the department or agency concerned and shall provide the Inspector General with the reasons for such determination.

(g)   Improper disclosure is violation.—Any willful disclosure or use by an investigative or law enforcement officer or governmental entity of information beyond the extent permitted by section 2517 is a violation of this chapter for purposes of section 2520(a).

§ 2521.   Injunction against illegal interception

Whenever it shall appear that any person is engaged or is about to engage in any act which constitutes or will constitute a felony violation of this chapter, the Attorney General may initiate a civil action in a district court of the United States to enjoin such violation. The court shall proceed as soon as practicable to the hearing and determination of such an action, and may, at any time before final determination, enter such a restraining order or prohibition, or take such other action, as is warranted to prevent a continuing and substantial injury to the United States or to any person or class of persons for whose protection the action is brought. A proceeding under this section is governed by the Federal Rules of Civil Procedure, except that, if an indictment has been returned against the respondent, discovery is governed by the Federal Rules of Criminal Procedure.

STORED WIRE AND ELECTRONIC COMMUNICATIONS AND TRANSACTIONAL RECORDS ACCESS

§ 2702.   Voluntary disclosure of customer communications or records

(a)   Prohibitions.—Except as provided in subsection (b) or (c)—

(1)   a person or entity providing an electronic communication service to the public shall not knowingly divulge to any person or entity the contents of a communication while in electronic storage by that service; and

(2)   a person or entity providing remote computing service to the public shall not knowingly divulge to any person or entity the contents of any communication which is carried or maintained on that service—

(A)   on behalf of, and received by means of electronic transmission from (or created by means of computer processing of communications received by means of electronic transmission from), a subscriber or customer of such service;

(B) solely for the purpose of providing storage or computer processing services to such subscriber or customer, if the provider is not authorized to access the contents of any such communications for purposes of providing any services other than storage or computer processing; and

(3) a provider of remote computing service or electronic communication service to the public shall not knowingly divulge a record or other information pertaining to a subscriber to or customer of such service (not including the contents of communications covered by paragraph (1) or (2)) to any governmental entity.

(b) Exceptions for disclosure of communications.—A provider described in subsection (a) may divulge the contents of a communication—

(1) to an addressee or intended recipient of such communication or an agent of such addressee or intended recipient;

(2) as otherwise authorized in section 2517, 2511(2)(a), or 2703 of this title;

(3) with the lawful consent of the originator or an addressee or intended recipient of such communication, or the subscriber in the case of remote computing service;

(4) to a person employed or authorized or whose facilities are used to forward such communication to its destination;

(5) as may be necessarily incident to the rendition of the service or to the protection of the rights or property of the provider of that service;

(6) to the National Center for Missing and Exploited Children, in connection with a report submitted thereto under section 2258A;

(7) to a law enforcement agency—

(A) if the contents—

(i) were inadvertently obtained by the service provider; and

(ii) appear to pertain to the commission of a crime; or

[(B) Repealed. Pub.L. 108–21, Title V, § 508(b)(1)(A), Apr. 30, 2003, 117 Stat. 684]

[(C) Repealed. Pub.L. 107–296, Title II, § 225(d)(1)(C), Nov. 25, 2002, 116 Stat. 2157]

(8) to a governmental entity, if the provider, in good faith, believes that an emergency involving danger of death or serious physical injury to any person requires disclosure without delay of communications relating to the emergency;

(9) to a foreign government pursuant to an order from a foreign government that is subject to an executive agreement that the Attorney General has determined and certified to Congress satisfies section 2523.

(c) Exceptions for disclosure of customer records.—A provider described in subsection (a) may divulge a record or other information pertaining to a subscriber to or customer of such service (not including the contents of communications covered by subsection (a)(1) or (a)(2))—

(1) as otherwise authorized in section 2703;

(2) with the lawful consent of the customer or subscriber;

(3) as may be necessarily incident to the rendition of the service or to the protection of the rights or property of the provider of that service;

(4)   to a governmental entity, if the provider, in good faith, believes that an emergency involving danger of death or serious physical injury to any person requires disclosure without delay of information relating to the emergency;

(5)   to the National Center for Missing and Exploited Children, in connection with a report submitted thereto under section 2258A;

(6)   to any person other than a governmental entity; or

(7)   to a foreign government pursuant to an order from a foreign government that is subject to an executive agreement that the Attorney General has determined and certified to Congress satisfies section 2523.

(d)   Reporting of emergency disclosures.—On an annual basis, the Attorney General shall submit to the Committee on the Judiciary of the House of Representatives and the Committee on the Judiciary of the Senate a report containing—

(1)   the number of accounts from which the Department of Justice has received voluntary disclosures under subsection (b)(8); and

(2)   a summary of the basis for disclosure in those instances where—

(A)   voluntary disclosures under subsection (b)(8) were made to the Department of Justice; and

(B)   the investigation pertaining to those disclosures was closed without the filing of criminal charges.

§ 2703.   Required disclosure of customer communications or records

(a)   Contents of wire or electronic communications in electronic storage.—A governmental entity may require the disclosure by a provider of electronic communication service of the contents of a wire or electronic communication, that is in electronic storage in an electronic communications system for one hundred and eighty days or less, only pursuant to a warrant issued using the procedures described in the Federal Rules of Criminal Procedure (or, in the case of a State court, issued using State warrant procedures) by a court of competent jurisdiction. A governmental entity may require the disclosure by a provider of electronic communications services of the contents of a wire or electronic communication that has been in electronic storage in an electronic communications system for more than one hundred and eighty days by the means available under subsection (b) of this section.

(b)   Contents of wire or electronic communications in a remote computing service.—

(1)   A governmental entity may require a provider of remote computing service to disclose the contents of any wire or electronic communication to which this paragraph is made applicable by paragraph (2) of this subsection—

(A)   without required notice to the subscriber or customer, if the governmental entity obtains a warrant issued using the procedures described in the Federal Rules of Criminal Procedure (or, in the case of a State court, issued using State warrant procedures) by a court of competent jurisdiction; or

(B)   with prior notice from the governmental entity to the subscriber or customer if the governmental entity—

(i)   uses an administrative subpoena authorized by a Federal or State statute or a Federal or State grand jury or trial subpoena; or

(ii)   obtains a court order for such disclosure under subsection (d) of this section; except that delayed notice may be given pursuant to section 2705 of this title.

(2)   Paragraph (1) is applicable with respect to any wire or electronic communication that is held or maintained on that service—

(A)   on behalf of, and received by means of electronic transmission from (or created by means of computer processing of communications received by means of electronic transmission from), a subscriber or customer of such remote computing service; and

(B)   solely for the purpose of providing storage or computer processing services to such subscriber or customer, if the provider is not authorized to access the contents of any such communications for purposes of providing any services other than storage or computer processing.

(c)   Records concerning electronic communication service or remote computing service.—

(1)   A governmental entity may require a provider of electronic communication service or remote computing service to disclose a record or other information pertaining to a subscriber to or customer of such service (not including the contents of communications) only when the governmental entity—

(A)   obtains a warrant issued using the procedures described in the Federal Rules of Criminal Procedure (or, in the case of a State court, issued using State warrant procedures) by a court of competent jurisdiction;

(B)   obtains a court order for such disclosure under subsection (d) of this section;

(C)   has the consent of the subscriber or customer to such disclosure;

(D)   submits a formal written request relevant to a law enforcement investigation concerning telemarketing fraud for the name, address, and place of business of a subscriber or customer of such provider, which subscriber or customer is engaged in telemarketing (as such term is defined in section 2325 of this title); or

(E)   seeks information under paragraph (2).

(2)   A provider of electronic communication service or remote computing service shall disclose to a governmental entity the—

(A)   name;

(B)   address;

(C)   local and long distance telephone connection records, or records of session times and durations;

(D)   length of service (including start date) and types of service utilized;

(E)   telephone or instrument number or other subscriber number or identity, including any temporarily assigned network address; and

(F)   means and source of payment for such service (including any credit card or bank account number),

of a subscriber to or customer of such service when the governmental entity uses an administrative subpoena authorized by a Federal or State statute or a Federal or State grand jury or trial subpoena or any means available under paragraph (1).

(3)   A governmental entity receiving records or information under this subsection is not required to provide notice to a subscriber or customer.

(d)   Requirements for court order.—A court order for disclosure under subsection (b) or (c) may be issued by any court that is a court of competent jurisdiction and shall issue only if the governmental entity offers specific and articulable facts showing that there are reasonable grounds to believe that the contents of a wire or electronic communication, or the records or other information sought, are relevant and material to an ongoing criminal investigation. In the case of a State governmental authority, such a court order shall not issue if prohibited by the law of such State. A court issuing an order pursuant to this section, on a motion made promptly by the service provider, may quash or modify such order, if the information or records requested are unusually voluminous in nature or compliance with such order otherwise would cause an undue burden on such provider.

(e)   No cause of action against a provider disclosing information under this chapter.—No cause of action shall lie in any court against any provider of wire or electronic communication service, its officers, employees, agents, or other specified persons for providing information, facilities, or assistance in accordance with the terms of a court order, warrant, subpoena, statutory authorization, or certification under this chapter.

(f)   Requirement to preserve evidence.—

(1)   In general.—A provider of wire or electronic communication services or a remote computing service, upon the request of a governmental entity, shall take all necessary steps to preserve records and other evidence in its possession pending the issuance of a court order or other process.

(2)   Period of retention.—Records referred to in paragraph (1) shall be retained for a period of 90 days, which shall be extended for an additional 90-day period upon a renewed request by the governmental entity.

(g)   Presence of officer not required.—Notwithstanding section 3105 of this title, the presence of an officer shall not be required for service or execution of a search warrant issued in accordance with this chapter requiring disclosure by a provider of electronic communications service or remote computing service of the contents of communications or records or other information pertaining to a subscriber to or customer of such service.

(h)   Comity analysis and disclosure of information regarding legal process seeking contents of fire or electronic communication.

(1)   Definitions. In this subsection

(A)   the term 'qualifying foreign government' means a foreign government

(i)   with which the United States has an executive agreement that has entered into force under section 2523; and

(ii)   the laws of which provide to electronic communication service providers and remote computing service providers substantive and procedural opportunities similar to those provided under paragraphs (2) and (5); and

(B)   the term 'United States person' has the meaning given the term in section 2523.

(2)   Motions to quash or modify.

(A)   A provider of electronic communication service to the public or remote computing service, including a foreign electronic communication service or remote computing service, that is being required to disclose pursuant to legal process issued under this section the contents of a wire or electronic communication of a subscriber or customer, may file a motion to modify or quash the legal process where the provider reasonably believes

   (i)   that the customer or subscriber is not a United States person and does not reside in the United States; and

   (ii)   that the required disclosure would create a material risk that the provider would violate the laws of a qualifying foreign government.

Such a motion shall be filed not later than 14 days after the date on which the provider was served with the legal process, absent agreement with the government or permission from the court to extend the deadline based on an application made within the 14 days. The right to move to quash is without prejudice to any other grounds to move to quash or defenses thereto, but it shall be the sole basis for moving to quash on the grounds of a conflict of law related to a qualifying foreign government.

   (B)   Upon receipt of a motion filed pursuant to subparagraph (A), the court shall afford the governmental entity that applied for or issued the legal process under this section the opportunity to respond. The court may modify or quash the legal process, as appropriate, only if the court finds that—

   (i)   the required disclosure would cause the provider to violate the laws of a qualifying foreign government;

   (ii)   based on the totality of the circumstances, the interests of justice dictate that the legal process should be modified or quashed; and

   (iii)   the customer or subscriber is not a United States person and does not reside in the United States.

(3)   Comity Analysis. For purposes of making a determination under paragraph (2)(B)(ii), the court shall take into account, as appropriate

   (A)   the interests of the United States, including the investigative interests of the governmental entity seeking to require the disclosure;

   (B)   the interests of the qualifying foreign government in preventing any prohibited disclosure;

   (C)   the likelihood, extent, and nature of penalties to the provider or any employees of the provider as a result of inconsistent legal requirements imposed on the provider;

   (D)   the location and nationality of the subscriber or customer whose communications are being sought, if known, and the nature and extent of the subscriber or customer's connection to the United States, or if the legal process has been sought on behalf of a foreign authority pursuant to section 3512, the nature and extent of the subscriber or customer's connection to the foreign authority's country;

   (E)   the nature and extent of the provider's ties to and presence in the United States;

   (F)   the importance to the investigation of the information required to be disclosed;

   (G)   the likelihood of timely and effective access to the information required to disclosed through means that would cause less serious negative consequences; and

   (H)   if the legal process has been sought on behalf of a foreign authority pursuant to section 3512, the investigative interests of the foreign authority making the request for assistance.

(4)   Disclosure obligations during pendency of challenge. A service provider shall preserve, but not be obligated to produce, information sought during the pendency of a motion brought under this subsection, unless the court finds that immediate production is necessary to prevent an adverse result identified in section 705(a)(2).

(5)   Disclosure to qualifying foreign government.

(A)   It shall not constitute a violation of a protective order issued under section 2705 for a provider of electronic communication service to the public or remote computing service to disclose to the entity within a qualifying foreign government, designated in an executive agreement under section 2523, the fact of the existence of legal process issued under this section seeking the contents of a wire or electronic communication of a customer or subscriber who is a national or resident of the qualifying foreign government.

(B)   Nothing in this paragraph shall be construed to modify or otherwise affect any other authority to make a motion to modify or quash a protective order issued under section 2705.

§ 2707.   Civil action

(a)   Cause of action.—Except as provided in section 2703(e), any provider of electronic communication service, subscriber, or other person aggrieved by any violation of this chapter in which the conduct constituting the violation is engaged in with a knowing or intentional state of mind may, in a civil action, recover from the person or entity, other than the United States, which engaged in that violation such relief as may be appropriate.

(b)   Relief.—In a civil action under this section, appropriate relief includes—

(1)   such preliminary and other equitable or declaratory relief as may be appropriate;

(2)   damages under subsection (c); and

(3)   a reasonable attorney's fee and other litigation costs reasonably incurred.

(c)   Damages.—The court may assess as damages in a civil action under this section the sum of the actual damages suffered by the plaintiff and any profits made by the violator as a result of the violation, but in no case shall a person entitled to recover receive less than the sum of $1,000. If the violation is willful or intentional, the court may assess punitive damages. In the case of a successful action to enforce liability under this section, the court may assess the costs of the action, together with reasonable attorney fees determined by the court.

(d)   Administrative discipline.—If a court or appropriate department or agency determines that the United States or any of its departments or agencies has violated any provision of this chapter, and the court or appropriate department or agency finds that the circumstances surrounding the violation raise serious questions about whether or not an officer or employee of the United States acted willfully or intentionally with respect to the violation, the department or agency shall, upon receipt of a true and correct copy of the decision and findings of the court or appropriate department or agency promptly initiate a proceeding to determine whether disciplinary action against the officer or employee is warranted. If the head of the department or agency involved determines that disciplinary action is not warranted, he or she shall notify the Inspector General with jurisdiction over the department or agency concerned and shall provide the Inspector General with the reasons for such determination.

(e)   Defense.—A good faith reliance on—

(1)   a court warrant or order, a grand jury subpoena, a legislative authorization, or a statutory authorization (including a request of a governmental entity under section 2703(f) of this title);

(2)   a request of an investigative or law enforcement officer under section 2518(7) of this title; or

(3)   a good faith determination that section 2511(3), section 2702(b)(9), or section 2702(c)(7) of this title permitted the conduct complained of.

(f)   Limitation.—A civil action under this section may not be commenced later than two years after the date upon which the claimant first discovered or had a reasonable opportunity to discover the violation.

(g)   Improper disclosure.—Any willful disclosure of a "record", as that term is defined in section 552a(a) of title 5, United States Code, obtained by an investigative or law enforcement officer, or a governmental entity, pursuant to section 2703 of this title, or from a device installed pursuant to section 3123 or 3125 of this title, that is not a disclosure made in the proper performance of the official functions of the officer or governmental entity making the disclosure, is a violation of this chapter. This provision shall not apply to information previously lawfully disclosed (prior to the commencement of any civil or administrative proceeding under this chapter) to the public by a Federal, State, or local governmental entity or by the plaintiff in a civil action under this chapter.

§ 2708.   Exclusivity of remedies

The remedies and sanctions described in this chapter are the only judicial remedies and sanctions for nonconstitutional violations of this chapter.

§ 2713.   Required preservation and disclosure of communications and records

A provider of electronic communication service or remote computing service shall comply with the obligations of this chapter to preserve, backup, or disclose the contents of a wire or electronic communication and any record or other information pertaining to a customer or subscriber within such provider's possession, custody, or control, regardless of whether such communication, record, or other information is located within or outside of the United States.

SEARCHES AND SEIZURES

(18 U.S.C. §§ 3103a, 3105, 3109).

§ 3103a.   Additional grounds for issuing warrant

(a)   In general.—In addition to the grounds for issuing a warrant in section 3103 of this title, a warrant may be issued to search for and seize any property that constitutes evidence of a criminal offense in violation of the laws of the United States.

(b)   Delay.—With respect to the issuance of any warrant or court order under this section, or any other rule of law, to search for and seize any property or material that constitutes evidence of a criminal offense in violation of the laws of the United States, any notice required, or that may be required, to be given may be delayed if—

(1)   the court finds reasonable cause to believe that providing immediate notification of the execution of the warrant may have an adverse result (as defined in section 2705, except if the adverse results consist only of unduly delaying a trial);

(2)   the warrant prohibits the seizure of any tangible property, any wire or electronic communication (as defined in section 2510), or, except as expressly provided in chapter 121,

any stored wire or electronic information, except where the court finds reasonable necessity for the seizure; and

(3)   the warrant provides for the giving of such notice within a reasonable period not to exceed 30 days after the date of its execution, or on a later date certain if the facts of the case justify a longer period of delay.

(c)   Extensions of delay.—Any period of delay authorized by this section may be extended by the court for good cause shown, subject to the condition that extensions should only be granted upon an updated showing of the need for further delay and that each additional delay should be limited to periods of 90 days or less, unless the facts of the case justify a longer period of delay.

(d)   Reports.—

(1)   Report by judge.—Not later than 30 days after the expiration of a warrant authorizing delayed notice (including any extension thereof) entered under this section, or the denial of such warrant (or request for extension), the issuing or denying judge shall report to the Administrative Office of the United States Courts—

(A)   the fact that a warrant was applied for;

(B)   the fact that the warrant or any extension thereof was granted as applied for, was modified, or was denied;

(C)   the period of delay in the giving of notice authorized by the warrant, and the number and duration of any extensions; and

(D)   the offense specified in the warrant or application.

(2)   Report by administrative office of the United States courts.—Beginning with the fiscal year ending September 30, 2007, the Director of the Administrative Office of the United States Courts shall transmit to Congress annually a full and complete report summarizing the data required to be filed with the Administrative Office by paragraph (1), including the number of applications for warrants and extensions of warrants authorizing delayed notice, and the number of such warrants and extensions granted or denied during the preceding fiscal year.

(3)   Regulations.—The Director of the Administrative Office of the United States Courts, in consultation with the Attorney General, is authorized to issue binding regulations dealing with the content and form of the reports required to be filed under paragraph (1).

§ 3105.   Persons authorized to serve search warrant

A search warrant may in all cases be served by any of the officers mentioned in its direction or by an officer authorized by law to serve such warrant, but by no other person, except in aid of the officer on his requiring it, he being present and acting in its execution.

§ 3109.   Breaking doors or windows for entry or exit

The officer may break open any outer or inner door or window of a house, or any part of a house, or anything therein, to execute a search warrant, if, after notice of his authority and purpose, he is refused admittance or when necessary to liberate himself or a person aiding him in the execution of the warrant.

BAIL REFORM ACT OF 1984

(18 U.S.C. §§ 3141–3150).

§ 3141. Release and detention authority generally

(a) Pending trial.—A judicial officer authorized to order the arrest of a person under section 3041 of this title before whom an arrested person is brought shall order that such person be released or detained, pending judicial proceedings, under this chapter.

(b) Pending sentence or appeal.—A judicial officer of a court of original jurisdiction over an offense, or a judicial officer of a Federal appellate court, shall order that, pending imposition or execution of sentence, or pending appeal of conviction or sentence, a person be released or detained under this chapter.

§ 3142. Release or detention of a defendant pending trial

(a) In general.—Upon the appearance before a judicial officer of a person charged with an offense, the judicial officer shall issue an order that, pending trial, the person be—

(1) released on personal recognizance or upon execution of an unsecured appearance bond, under subsection (b) of this section;

(2) released on a condition or combination of conditions under subsection (c) of this section;

(3) temporarily detained to permit revocation of conditional release, deportation, or exclusion under subsection (d) of this section; or

(4) detained under subsection (e) of this section.

(b) Release on personal recognizance or unsecured appearance bond.—The judicial officer shall order the pretrial release of the person on personal recognizance, or upon execution of an unsecured appearance bond in an amount specified by the court, subject to the condition that the person not commit a Federal, State, or local crime during the period of release and subject to the condition that the person cooperate in the collection of a DNA sample from the person if the collection of such a sample is authorized pursuant to section 3 of the DNA Analysis Backlog Elimination Act of 2000 (42 U.S.C. 14135a), unless the judicial officer determines that such release will not reasonably assure the appearance of the person as required or will endanger the safety of any other person or the community.

(c) Release on conditions.—

(1) If the judicial officer determines that the release described in subsection (b) of this section will not reasonably assure the appearance of the person as required or will endanger the safety of any other person or the community, such judicial officer shall order the pretrial release of the person—

(A) subject to the condition that the person not commit a Federal, State, or local crime during the period of release and subject to the condition that the person cooperate in the collection of a DNA sample from the person if the collection of such a sample is authorized pursuant to section 3 of the DNA Analysis Backlog Elimination Act of 2000 (42 U.S.C. 14135a); and

(B) subject to the least restrictive further condition, or combination of conditions, that such judicial officer determines will reasonably assure the appearance of the person as required and the safety of any other person and the community, which may include the condition that the person—

(i)   remain in the custody of a designated person, who agrees to assume supervision and to report any violation of a release condition to the court, if the designated person is able reasonably to assure the judicial officer that the person will appear as required and will not pose a danger to the safety of any other person or the community;

(ii)   maintain employment, or, if unemployed, actively seek employment;

(iii) maintain or commence an educational program;

(iv)   abide by specified restrictions on personal associations, place of abode, or travel;

(v)   avoid all contact with an alleged victim of the crime and with a potential witness who may testify concerning the offense;

(vi)   report on a regular basis to a designated law enforcement agency, pretrial services agency, or other agency;

(vii) comply with a specified curfew;

(viii) refrain from possessing a firearm, destructive device, or other dangerous weapon;

(ix)   refrain from excessive use of alcohol, or any use of a narcotic drug or other controlled substance, as defined in section 102 of the Controlled Substances Act (21 U.S.C. 802), without a prescription by a licensed medical practitioner;

(x)   undergo available medical, psychological, or psychiatric treatment, including treatment for drug or alcohol dependency, and remain in a specified institution if required for that purpose;

(xi)   execute an agreement to forfeit upon failing to appear as required, property of a sufficient unencumbered value, including money, as is reasonably necessary to assure the appearance of the person as required, and shall provide the court with proof of ownership and the value of the property along with information regarding existing encumbrances as the judicial office may require;

(xii) execute a bail bond with solvent sureties; who will execute an agreement to forfeit in such amount as is reasonably necessary to assure appearance of the person as required and shall provide the court with information regarding the value of the assets and liabilities of the surety if other than an approved surety and the nature and extent of encumbrances against the surety's property; such surety shall have a net worth which shall have sufficient unencumbered value to pay the amount of the bail bond;

(xiii) return to custody for specified hours following release for employment, schooling, or other limited purposes; and

(xiv) satisfy any other condition that is reasonably necessary to assure the appearance of the person as required and to assure the safety of any other person and the community.

In any case that involves a minor victim under section 1201, 1591, 2241, 2242, 2244(a)(1), 2245, 2251, 2251A, 2252(a)(1), 2252(a)(2), 2252(a)(3), 2252A(a)(1), 2252A(a)(2), 2252A(a)(3), 2252A(a)(4), 2260, 2421, 2422, 2423, or 2425 of this title, or a failure to register offense under section 2250 of this title, any release order shall contain, at a minimum, a condition of electronic monitoring and each of the conditions specified at subparagraphs (iv), (v), (vi), (vii), and (viii).

(2)   The judicial officer may not impose a financial condition that results in the pretrial detention of the person.

(3)   The judicial officer may at any time amend the order to impose additional or different conditions of release.

(d)   Temporary detention to permit revocation of conditional release, deportation, or exclusion.—If the judicial officer determines that—

    (1)   such person—

        (A)   is, and was at the time the offense was committed, on—

            (i)   release pending trial for a felony under Federal, State, or local law;

            (ii)   release pending imposition or execution of sentence, appeal of sentence or conviction, or completion of sentence, for any offense under Federal, State, or local law; or

            (iii) probation or parole for any offense under Federal, State, or local law; or

        (B)   is not a citizen of the United States or lawfully admitted for permanent residence, as defined in section 101(a)(20) of the Immigration and Nationality Act (8 U.S.C. 1101(a)(20)); and

    (2)   such person may flee or pose a danger to any other person or the community;

such judicial officer shall order the detention of such person, for a period of not more than ten days, excluding Saturdays, Sundays, and holidays, and direct the attorney for the Government to notify the appropriate court, probation or parole official, or State or local law enforcement official, or the appropriate official of the Immigration and Naturalization Service. If the official fails or declines to take such person into custody during that period, such person shall be treated in accordance with the other provisions of this section, notwithstanding the applicability of other provisions of law governing release pending trial or deportation or exclusion proceedings. If temporary detention is sought under paragraph (1)(B) of this subsection, such person has the burden of proving to the court such person's United States citizenship or lawful admission for permanent residence.

(e)   Detention.—

    (1)   If, after a hearing pursuant to the provisions of subsection (f) of this section, the judicial officer finds that no condition or combination of conditions will reasonably assure the appearance of the person as required and the safety of any other person and the community, such judicial officer shall order the detention of the person before trial.

    (2)   In a case described in subsection (f)(1) of this section, a rebuttable presumption arises that no condition or combination of conditions will reasonably assure the safety of any other person and the community if such judicial officer finds that—

        (A)   the person has been convicted of a Federal offense that is described in subsection (f)(1) of this section, or of a State or local offense that would have been an offense described in subsection (f)(1) of this section if a circumstance giving rise to Federal jurisdiction had existed;

        (B)   the offense described in subparagraph (A) of this subsection was committed while the person was on release pending trial for a Federal, State, or local offense; and

        (C)   a period of not more than five years has elapsed since the date of conviction, or the release of the person from imprisonment, for the offense described in subparagraph (A) of this subsection, whichever is later.

(3)   Subject to rebuttal by the person, it shall be presumed that no condition or combination of conditions will reasonably assure the appearance of the person as required and the safety of the community if the judicial officer finds that there is probable cause to believe that the person committed—

(A)   an offense for which a maximum term of imprisonment of ten years or more is prescribed in the Controlled Substances Act (21 U.S.C. 801 et seq.), the Controlled Substances Import and Export Act (21 U.S.C. 951 et seq.), or chapter 705 of title 46;

(B)   an offense under section 924(c), 956(a), or 2332b of this title;

(C)   an offense listed in section 2332b(g)(5)(B) of title 18, United States Code, for which a maximum term of imprisonment of 10 years or more is prescribed;

(D)   an offense under chapter 77 of this title for which a maximum term of imprisonment of 20 years or more is prescribed; or

(E)   an offense involving a minor victim under section 1201, 1591, 2241, 2242, 2244(a)(1), 2245, 2251, 2251A, 2252(a)(1), 2252(a)(2), 2252(a)(3), 2252A(a)(1), 2252A(a)(2), 2252A(a)(3), 2252A(a)(4), 2260, 2421, 2422, 2423, or 2425 of this title.

(f)   Detention hearing.—The judicial officer shall hold a hearing to determine whether any condition or combination of conditions set forth in subsection (c) of this section will reasonably assure the appearance of such person as required and the safety of any other person and the community—

(1)   upon motion of the attorney for the Government, in a case that involves—

(A)   a crime of violence*, a violation of section 1591, or an offense listed in section 2332b(g)(5)(B) for which a maximum term of imprisonment of 10 years or more is prescribed;

(B)   an offense for which the maximum sentence is life imprisonment or death;

(C)   an offense for which a maximum term of imprisonment of ten years or more is prescribed in the Controlled Substances Act (21 U.S.C. 801 et seq.), the Controlled Substances Import and Export Act (21 U.S.C. 951 et seq.), or chapter 705 of title 46

(D)   any felony if such person has been convicted of two or more offenses described in subparagraphs (A) through (C) of this paragraph, or two or more State or local offenses that would have been offenses described in subparagraphs (A) through (C) of this paragraph if a circumstance giving rise to Federal jurisdiction had existed, or a combination of such offenses; or

(E)   any felony that is not otherwise a crime of violence that involves a minor victim or that involves the possession or use of a firearm or destructive device (as those terms are defined in section 921), or any other dangerous weapon, or involves a failure to register under section 2250 of title 18, United States Code; or

(2)   Upon motion of the attorney for the Government or upon the judicial officer's own motion, in a case that involves—

(A)   a serious risk that such person will flee; or

---

*   The phrase "crime of violence" is defined in 18 U.S.C. § 3156(a)(4) as meaning: "(A) an offense that has an element of the offense the use, attempted use, or threatened use of physical force against the person or property of another, or (B) any other offense that is a felony and that, by its nature, involves a substantial risk that physical force against the person or property of another may be used in the course of committing the offense."

(B)   a serious risk that such person will obstruct or attempt to obstruct justice, or threaten, injure, or intimidate, or attempt to threaten, injure, or intimidate, a prospective witness or juror.

The hearing shall be held immediately upon the person's first appearance before the judicial officer unless that person, or the attorney for the Government, seeks a continuance. Except for good cause, a continuance on motion of such person may not exceed five days (not including any intermediate Saturday, Sunday, or legal holiday), and a continuance on motion of the attorney for the Government may not exceed three days (not including any intermediate Saturday, Sunday, or legal holiday). During a continuance, such person shall be detained, and the judicial officer, on motion of the attorney for the Government or sua sponte, may order that, while in custody, a person who appears to be a narcotics addict receive a medical examination to determine whether such person is an addict. At the hearing, such person has the right to be represented by counsel, and, if financially unable to obtain adequate representation, to have counsel appointed. The person shall be afforded an opportunity to testify, to present witnesses, to cross-examine witnesses who appear at the hearing, and to present information by proffer or otherwise. The rules concerning admissibility of evidence in criminal trials do not apply to the presentation and consideration of information at the hearing. The facts the judicial officer uses to support a finding pursuant to subsection (e) that no condition or combination of conditions will reasonably assure the safety of any other person and the community shall be supported by clear and convincing evidence. The person may be detained pending completion of the hearing. The hearing may be reopened, before or after a determination by the judicial officer, at any time before trial if the judicial officer finds that information exists that was not known to the movant at the time of the hearing and that has a material bearing on the issue whether there are conditions of release that will reasonably assure the appearance of such person as required and the safety of any other person and the community.

(g)   Factors to be considered.—The judicial officer shall, in determining whether there are conditions of release that will reasonably assure the appearance of the person as required and the safety of any other person and the community, take into account the available information concerning—

(1)   the nature and circumstances of the offense charged, including whether the offense is a crime of violence, a violation of section 1591, a Federal crime of terrorism, or involves a minor victim or a controlled substance, firearm, explosive, or destructive device;

(2)   the weight of the evidence against the person;

(3)   the history and characteristics of the person, including—

(A)   the person's character, physical and mental condition, family ties, employment, financial resources, length of residence in the community, community ties, past conduct, history relating to drug or alcohol abuse, criminal history, and record concerning appearance at court proceedings; and

(B)   whether, at the time of the current offense or arrest, the person was on probation, on parole, or on other release pending trial, sentencing, appeal, or completion of sentence for an offense under Federal, State, or local law; and

(4)   the nature and seriousness of the danger to any person or the community that would be posed by the person's release. In considering the conditions of release described in subsection (c)(1)(B)(xi) or (c)(1)(B)(xii) of this section, the judicial officer may upon his own motion, or shall upon the motion of the Government, conduct an inquiry into the source of the property to be designated for potential forfeiture or offered as collateral to secure a bond, and shall decline to accept the designation, or the use as collateral, of property that, because of its source, will not reasonably assure the appearance of the person as required.

(h) Contents of release order.—In a release order issued under subsection (b) or (c) of this section, the judicial officer shall—

(1) include a written statement that sets forth all the conditions to which the release is subject, in a manner sufficiently clear and specific to serve as a guide for the person's conduct; and

(2) advise the person of—

(A) the penalties for violating a condition of release, including the penalties for committing an offense while on pretrial release;

(B) the consequences of violating a condition of release, including the immediate issuance of a warrant for the person's arrest; and

(C) sections 1503 of this title (relating to intimidation of witnesses, jurors, and officers of the court), 1510 (relating to obstruction of criminal investigations), 1512 (tampering with a witness, victim, or an informant), and 1513 (retaliating against a witness, victim, or an informant).

(i) Contents of detention order.—In a detention order issued under subsection (e) of this section, the judicial officer shall—

(1) include written findings of fact and a written statement of the reasons for the detention;

(2) direct that the person be committed to the custody of the Attorney General for confinement in a corrections facility separate, to the extent practicable, from persons awaiting or serving sentences or being held in custody pending appeal;

(3) direct that the person be afforded reasonable opportunity for private consultation with counsel; and

(4) direct that, on order of a court of the United States or on request of an attorney for the Government, the person in charge of the corrections facility in which the person is confined deliver the person to a United States marshal for the purpose of an appearance in connection with a court proceeding.

The judicial officer may, by subsequent order, permit the temporary release of the person, in the custody of a United States marshal or another appropriate person, to the extent that the judicial officer determines such release to be necessary for preparation of the person's defense or for another compelling reason.

(j) Presumption of innocence.—Nothing in this section shall be construed as modifying or limiting the presumption of innocence.

§ 3143. Release or detention of a defendant pending sentence or appeal

(a) Release or detention pending sentence.—

(1) Except as provided in paragraph (2), the judicial officer shall order that a person who has been found guilty of an offense and who is awaiting imposition or execution of sentence, other than a person for whom the applicable guideline promulgated pursuant to 28 U.S.C. 994 does not recommend a term of imprisonment, be detained, unless the judicial officer finds by clear and convincing evidence that the person is not likely to flee or pose a danger to the safety of any other person or the community if released under section 3142(b) or (c). If the judicial officer makes such a finding, such judicial officer shall order the release of the person in accordance with section 3142(b) or (c).

(2)   The judicial officer shall order that a person who has been found guilty of an offense in a case described in subparagraph (A), (B), or (C) of subsection (f)(1) of section 3142 and is awaiting imposition or execution of sentence be detained unless—

(A)(i)   the judicial officer finds there is a substantial likelihood that a motion for acquittal or new trial will be granted; or

(ii)   an attorney for the Government has recommended that no sentence of imprisonment be imposed on the person; and

(B)   the judicial officer finds by clear and convincing evidence that the person is not likely to flee or pose a danger to any other person or the community.

(b)   Release or detention pending appeal by the defendant.—(1) Except as provided in paragraph (2), the judicial officer shall order that a person who has been found guilty of an offense and sentenced to a term of imprisonment, and who has filed an appeal or a petition for a writ of certiorari, be detained, unless the judicial officer finds—

(A)   by clear and convincing evidence that the person is not likely to flee or pose a danger to the safety of any other person or the community if released under section 3142(b) or (c) of this title; and

(B)   that the appeal is not for the purpose of delay and raises a substantial question of law or fact likely to result in—

(i)   reversal,

(ii)   an order for a new trial,

(iii)   a sentence that does not include a term of imprisonment, or

(iv)   a reduced sentence to a term of imprisonment less than the total of the time already served plus the expected duration of the appeal process.

If the judicial officer makes such findings, such judicial officer shall order the release of the person in accordance with section 3142(b) or (c) of this title, except that in the circumstance described in subparagraph (B)(iv) of this paragraph, the judicial officer shall order the detention terminated at the expiration of the likely reduced sentence.

(2)   The judicial officer shall order that a person who has been found guilty of an offense in a case described in subparagraph (A), (B), or (C) of subsection (f)(1) of section 3142 and sentenced to a term of imprisonment, and who has filed an appeal or a petition for a writ of certiorari, be detained.

(c)   Release or detention pending appeal by the government.—The judicial officer shall treat a defendant in a case in which an appeal has been taken by the United States under section 3731 of this title, in accordance with section 3142 of this title, unless the defendant is otherwise subject to a release or detention order.

Except as provided in subsection (b) of this section, the judicial officer, in a case in which an appeal has been taken by the United States under section 3742, shall—

(1)   if the person has been sentenced to a term of imprisonment, order that person detained; and

(2)   in any other circumstance, release or detain the person under section 3142.

§ 3144.   Release or detention of a material witness

If it appears from an affidavit filed by a party that the testimony of a person is material in a criminal proceeding, and if it is shown that it may become impracticable to secure the presence of the person by subpoena, a judicial officer may order the arrest of the person and treat the person in accordance with the provisions of section 3142 of this title. No material witness may be detained because of inability to comply with any condition of release if the testimony of such witness can adequately be secured by deposition, and if further detention is not necessary to prevent a failure of justice. Release of a material witness may be delayed for a reasonable period of time until the deposition of the witness can be taken pursuant to the Federal Rules of Criminal Procedure.

§ 3145.   Review and appeal of a release or detention order

(a)   Review of a release order.—If a person is ordered released by a magistrate judge, or by a person other than a judge of a court having original jurisdiction over the offense and other than a Federal appellate court—

(1)   the attorney for the Government may file, with the court having original jurisdiction over the offense, a motion for revocation of the order or amendment of the conditions of release; and

(2)   the person may file, with the court having original jurisdiction over the offense, a motion for amendment of the conditions of release.

The motion shall be determined promptly.

(b)   Review of a detention order.—If a person is ordered detained by a magistrate judge, or by a person other than a judge of a court having original jurisdiction over the offense and other than a Federal appellate court, the person may file, with the court having original jurisdiction over the offense, a motion for revocation or amendment of the order. The motion shall be determined promptly.

(c)   Appeal from a release or detention order.—An appeal from a release or detention order, or from a decision denying revocation or amendment of such an order, is governed by the provisions of section 1291 of title 28 and section 3731 of this title. The appeal shall be determined promptly. A person subject to detention pursuant to section 3143(a)(2) or (b)(2), and who meets the conditions of release set forth in section 3143(a)(1) or (b)(1), may be ordered released, under appropriate conditions, by the judicial officer, if it is clearly shown that there are exceptional reasons why such person's detention would not be appropriate.

§ 3146.   Penalty for failure to appear

(a)   Offense.—Whoever, having been released under this chapter knowingly—

(1)   fails to appear before a court as required by the conditions of release; or

(2)   fails to surrender for service of sentence pursuant to a court order;

shall be punished as provided in subsection (b) of this section.

(b)   Punishment.—(1) The punishment for an offense under this section is—

(A)   if the person was released in connection with a charge of, or while awaiting sentence, surrender for service of sentence, or appeal or certiorari after conviction for—

(i)   an offense punishable by death, life imprisonment, or imprisonment for a term of 15 years or more, a fine under this title or imprisonment for not more than ten years, or both;

(ii)   an offense punishable by imprisonment for a term of five years or more, a fine under this title or imprisonment for not more than five years, or both;

(iii)   any other felony, a fine under this title or imprisonment for not more than two years, or both; or

(iv) a misdemeanor, a fine under this title or imprisonment for not more than one year, or both; and

(B) if the person was released for appearance as a material witness, a fine under this chapter or imprisonment for not more than one year, or both.

(2) A term of imprisonment imposed under this section shall be consecutive to the sentence of imprisonment for any other offense.

(c) Affirmative defense.—It is an affirmative defense to a prosecution under this section that uncontrollable circumstances prevented the person from appearing or surrendering, and that the person did not contribute to the creation of such circumstances in reckless disregard of the requirement to appear or surrender, and that the person appeared or surrendered as soon as such circumstances ceased to exist.

(d) Declaration of forfeiture.—If a person fails to appear before a court as required, and the person executed an appearance bond pursuant to section 3142(b) of this title or is subject to the release condition set forth in clause (xi) or (xii) of section 3142(c)(1)(B) of this title, the judicial officer may, regardless of whether the person has been charged with an offense under this section, declare any property designated pursuant to that section to be forfeited to the United States.

§ 3147. Penalty for an offense committed while on release

A person convicted of an offense committed while released under this chapter shall be sentenced, in addition to the sentence prescribed for the offense to—

(1) a term of imprisonment of not more than ten years if the offense is a felony; or

(2) a term of imprisonment of not more than one year if the offense is a misdemeanor.

A term of imprisonment imposed under this section shall be consecutive to any other sentence of imprisonment.

§ 3148. Sanctions for violation of a release condition

(a) Available sanctions.—A person who has been released under section 3142 of this title, and who has violated a condition of his release, is subject to a revocation of release, an order of detention, and a prosecution for contempt of court.

(b) Revocation of release.—The attorney for the Government may initiate a proceeding for revocation of an order of release by filing a motion with the district court. A judicial officer may issue a warrant for the arrest of a person charged with violating a condition of release, and the person shall be brought before a judicial officer in the district in which such person's arrest was ordered for a proceeding in accordance with this section. To the extent practicable, a person charged with violating the condition of release that such person not commit a Federal, State, or local crime during the period of release, shall be brought before the judicial officer who ordered the release and whose order is alleged to have been violated. The judicial officer shall enter an order of revocation and detention if, after a hearing, the judicial officer—

(1) finds that there is—

(A) probable cause to believe that the person has committed a Federal, State, or local crime while on release; or

(B) clear and convincing evidence that the person has violated any other condition of release; and

(2) finds that—

(A) based on the factors set forth in section 3142(g) of this title, there is no condition or combination of conditions of release that will assure that the person will not flee or pose a danger to the safety of any other person or the community; or

(B) the person is unlikely to abide by any condition or combination of conditions of release.

If there is probable cause to believe that, while on release, the person committed a Federal, State, or local felony, a rebuttable presumption arises that no condition or combination of conditions will assure that the person will not pose a danger to the safety of any other person or the community. If the judicial officer finds that there are conditions of release that will assure that the person will not flee or pose a danger to the safety of any other person or the community, and that the person will abide by such conditions, the judicial officer shall treat the person in accordance with the provisions of section 3142 of this title and may amend the conditions of release accordingly.

(c) Prosecution for contempt.—The judicial officer may commence a prosecution for contempt, under section 401 of this title, if the person has violated a condition of release.

§ 3149. Surrender of an offender by a surety

A person charged with an offense, who is released upon the execution of an appearance bond with a surety, may be arrested by the surety, and if so arrested, shall be delivered promptly to a United States marshal and brought before a judicial officer. The judicial officer shall determine in accordance with the provisions of section 3148(b) whether to revoke the release of the person, and may absolve the surety of responsibility to pay all or part of the bond in accordance with the provisions of Rule 46 of the Federal Rules of Criminal Procedure. The person so committed shall be held in official detention until released pursuant to this chapter or another provision of law.

§ 3150. Applicability to a case removed from a State court

The provisions of this chapter apply to a criminal case removed to a Federal court from a State court.

SPEEDY TRIAL ACT OF 1974 (AS AMENDED)

(18 U.S.C. §§ 3161–3162, 3164).

§ 3161. Time limits and exclusions

(a) In any case involving a defendant charged with an offense, the appropriate judicial officer, at the earliest practicable time, shall, after consultation with the counsel for the defendant and the attorney for the Government, set the case for trial on a day certain, or list it for trial on a weekly or other short-term trial calendar at a place within the judicial district, so as to assure a speedy trial.

(b) Any information or indictment charging an individual with the commission of an offense shall be filed within thirty days from the date on which such individual was arrested or served with a summons in connection with such charges. If an individual has been charged with a felony in a district in which no grand jury has been in session during such thirty-day period, the period of time for filing of the indictment shall be extended an additional thirty days.

(c)(1) In any case in which a plea of not guilty is entered, the trial of a defendant charged in an information or indictment with the commission of an offense shall commence within seventy days from the filing date (and making public) of the information or indictment, or from the date the defendant has appeared before a judicial officer of the court in which such charge is pending, whichever date last occurs. If a defendant consents in writing to be tried before a magistrate judge on a complaint, the trial shall commence within seventy days from the date of such consent.

(2)   Unless the defendant consents in writing to the contrary, the trial shall not commence less than thirty days from the date on which the defendant first appears through counsel or expressly waives counsel and elects to proceed pro se.

(d)(1)   If any indictment or information is dismissed upon motion of the defendant, or any charge contained in a complaint filed against an individual is dismissed or otherwise dropped, and thereafter a complaint is filed against such defendant or individual charging him with the same offense or an offense based on the same conduct or arising from the same criminal episode, or an information or indictment is filed charging such defendant with the same offense or an offense based on the same conduct or arising from the same criminal episode, the provisions of subsections (b) and (c) of this section shall be applicable with respect to such subsequent complaint, indictment, or information, as the case may be.

(2)   If the defendant is to be tried upon an indictment or information dismissed by a trial court and reinstated following an appeal, the trial shall commence within seventy days from the date the action occasioning the trial becomes final, except that the court retrying the case may extend the period for trial not to exceed one hundred and eighty days from the date the action occasioning the trial becomes final if the unavailability of witnesses or other factors resulting from the passage of time shall make trial within seventy days impractical. The periods of delay enumerated in section 3161(h) are excluded in computing the time limitations specified in this section. The sanctions of section 3162 apply to this subsection.

(e)   If the defendant is to be tried again following a declaration by the trial judge of a mistrial or following an order of such judge for a new trial, the trial shall commence within seventy days from the date the action occasioning the retrial becomes final. If the defendant is to be tried again following an appeal or a collateral attack, the trial shall commence within seventy days from the date the action occasioning the retrial becomes final, except that the court retrying the case may extend the period for retrial not to exceed one hundred and eighty days from the date the action occasioning the retrial becomes final if unavailability of witnesses or other factors resulting from passage of time shall make trial within seventy days impractical. The periods of delay enumerated in section 3161(h) are excluded in computing the time limitations specified in this section. The sanctions of section 3162 apply to this subsection.

(f)   Notwithstanding the provisions of subsection (b) of this section, for the first twelve-calendar-month period following the effective date of this section as set forth in section 3163(a) of this chapter the time limit imposed with respect to the period between arrest and indictment by subsection (b) of this section shall be sixty days, for the second such twelve-month period such time limit shall be forty-five days and for the third such period such time limit shall be thirty-five days.

(g)   Notwithstanding the provisions of subsection (c) of this section, for the first twelve-calendar-month period following the effective date of this section as set forth in section 3163(b) of this chapter, the time limit with respect to the period between arraignment and trial imposed by subsection (c) of this section shall be one hundred and eighty days, for the second such twelve-month period such time limit shall be one hundred and twenty days, and for the third such period such time limit with respect to the period between arraignment and trial shall be eighty days.

(h)   The following periods of delay shall be excluded in computing the time within which an information or an indictment must be filed, or in computing the time within which the trial of any such offense must commence:

(1)   Any period of delay resulting from other proceedings concerning the defendant, including but not limited to—

(A)   delay resulting from any proceeding, including any examinations, to determine the mental competency or physical capacity of the defendant;

(B)   delay resulting from trial with respect to other charges against the defendant;

(C)   delay resulting from any interlocutory appeal;

(D)   delay resulting from any pretrial motion, from the filing of the motion through the conclusion of the hearing on, or other prompt disposition of, such motion;

(E)   delay resulting from any proceeding relating to the transfer of a case or the removal of any defendant from another district under the Federal Rules of Criminal Procedure;

(F)   delay resulting from transportation of any defendant from another district, or to and from places of examination or hospitalization, except that any time consumed in excess of ten days from the date an order of removal or an order directing such transportation, and the defendant's arrival at the destination shall be presumed to be unreasonable;

(G)   delay resulting from consideration by the court of a proposed plea agreement to be entered into by the defendant and the attorney for the Government; and

(H)   delay reasonably attributable to any period, not to exceed thirty days, during which any proceeding concerning the defendant is actually under advisement by the court.

(2)   Any period of delay during which prosecution is deferred by the attorney for the Government pursuant to written agreement with the defendant, with the approval of the court, for the purpose of allowing the defendant to demonstrate his good conduct.

(3)(A)   Any period of delay resulting from the absence or unavailability of the defendant or an essential witness.

(B)   For purposes of subparagraph (A) of this paragraph, a defendant or an essential witness shall be considered absent when his whereabouts are unknown and, in addition, he is attempting to avoid apprehension or prosecution or his whereabouts cannot be determined by due diligence. For purposes of such subparagraph, a defendant or an essential witness shall be considered unavailable whenever his whereabouts are known but his presence for trial cannot be obtained by due diligence or he resists appearing at or being returned for trial.

(4)   Any period of delay resulting from the fact that the defendant is mentally incompetent or physically unable to stand trial.

(5)   If the information or indictment is dismissed upon motion of the attorney for the Government and thereafter a charge is filed against the defendant for the same offense, or any offense required to be joined with that offense, any period of delay from the date the charge was dismissed to the date the time limitation would commence to run as to the subsequent charge had there been no previous charge.

(6)   A reasonable period of delay when the defendant is joined for trial with a codefendant as to whom the time for trial has not run and no motion for severance has been granted.

(7)(A)   Any period of delay resulting from a continuance granted by any judge on his own motion or at the request of the defendant or his counsel or at the request of the attorney for the Government, if the judge granted such continuance on the basis of his findings that the ends of justice served by taking such action outweigh the best interest of the public and the defendant in a speedy trial. No such period of delay resulting from a continuance granted by the court in accordance with this paragraph shall be excludable under this subsection unless the court sets forth, in the record of the case, either orally or in writing, its reasons for finding that the ends of justice served by the granting of such continuance outweigh the best interests of the public and the defendant in a speedy trial.

(B) The factors, among others, which a judge shall consider in determining whether to grant a continuance under subparagraph (A) of this paragraph in any case are as follows:

(i) Whether the failure to grant such a continuance in the proceeding would be likely to make a continuation of such proceeding impossible, or result in a miscarriage of justice.

(ii) Whether the case is so unusual or so complex, due to the number of defendants, the nature of the prosecution, or the existence of novel questions of fact or law, that it is unreasonable to expect adequate preparation for pretrial proceedings or for the trial itself within the time limits established by this section.

(iii) Whether, in a case in which arrest precedes indictment, delay in the filing of the indictment is caused because the arrest occurs at a time such that it is unreasonable to expect return and filing of the indictment within the period specified in section 3161(b), or because the facts upon which the grand jury must base its determination are unusual or complex.

(iv) Whether the failure to grant such a continuance in a case which, taken as a whole, is not so unusual or so complex as to fall within clause (ii), would deny the defendant reasonable time to obtain counsel, would unreasonably deny the defendant or the Government continuity of counsel, or would deny counsel for the defendant or the attorney for the Government the reasonable time necessary for effective preparation, taking into account the exercise of due diligence.

(C) No continuance under subparagraph (A) of this paragraph shall be granted because of general congestion of the court's calendar, or lack of diligent preparation or failure to obtain available witnesses on the part of the attorney for the Government.

(8) Any period of delay, not to exceed one year, ordered by a district court upon an application of a party and a finding by a preponderance of the evidence that an official request, as defined in section 3292 of this title, has been made for evidence of any such offense and that it reasonably appears, or reasonably appeared at the time the request was made, that such evidence is, or was, in such foreign country.

(i) If trial did not commence within the time limitation specified in section 3161 because the defendant had entered a plea of guilty or nolo contendere subsequently withdrawn to any or all charges in an indictment or information, the defendant shall be deemed indicted with respect to all charges therein contained within the meaning of section 3161, on the day the order permitting withdrawal of the plea becomes final.

(j)(1) If the attorney for the Government knows that a person charged with an offense is serving a term of imprisonment in any penal institution, he shall promptly—

(A) undertake to obtain the presence of the prisoner for trial; or

(B) cause a detainer to be filed with the person having custody of the prisoner and request him to so advise the prisoner and to advise the prisoner of his right to demand trial.

(2) If the person having custody of such prisoner receives a detainer, he shall promptly advise the prisoner of the charge and of the prisoner's right to demand trial. If at any time thereafter the prisoner informs the person having custody that he does demand trial, such person shall cause notice to that effect to be sent promptly to the attorney for the Government who caused the detainer to be filed.

(3)   Upon receipt of such notice, the attorney for the Government shall promptly seek to obtain the presence of the prisoner for trial.

(4)   When the person having custody of the prisoner receives from the attorney for the Government a properly supported request for temporary custody of such prisoner for trial, the prisoner shall be made available to that attorney for the Government (subject, in cases of interjurisdictional transfer, to any right of the prisoner to contest the legality of his delivery).

(k)(1)   If the defendant is absent (as defined by subsection (h)(3)) on the day set for trial, and the defendant's subsequent appearance before the court on a bench warrant or other process or surrender to the court occurs more than 21 days after the day set for trial, the defendant shall be deemed to have first appeared before a judicial officer of the court in which the information or indictment is pending within the meaning of subsection (c) on the date of the defendant's subsequent appearance before the court.

(2)   If the defendant is absent (as defined by subsection (h)(3)) on the day set for trial, and the defendant's subsequent appearance before the court on a bench warrant or other process or surrender to the court occurs not more than 21 days after the day set for trial, the time limit required by subsection (c), as extended by subsection (h), shall be further extended by 21 days.

§ 3162.   Sanctions

(a)(1)   If, in the case of any individual against whom a complaint is filed charging such individual with an offense, no indictment or information is filed within the time limit required by section 3161(b) as extended by section 3161(h) of this chapter, such charge against that individual contained in such complaint shall be dismissed or otherwise dropped. In determining whether to dismiss the case with or without prejudice, the court shall consider, among others, each of the following factors: the seriousness of the offense; the facts and circumstances of the case which led to the dismissal; and the impact of a reprosecution on the administration of this chapter and on the administration of justice.

(2)   If a defendant is not brought to trial within the time limit required by section 3161(c) as extended by section 3161(h), the information or indictment shall be dismissed on motion of the defendant. The defendant shall have the burden of proof of supporting such motion but the Government shall have the burden of going forward with the evidence in connection with any exclusion of time under subparagraph 3161(h) (3). In determining whether to dismiss the case with or without prejudice, the court shall consider, among others, each of the following factors: the seriousness of the offense; the facts and circumstances of the case which led to the dismissal; and the impact of a reprosecution on the administration of this chapter and on the administration of justice. Failure of the defendant to move for dismissal prior to trial or entry of a plea of guilty or nolo contendere shall constitute a waiver of the right to dismissal under this section.

(b)   In any case in which counsel for the defendant or the attorney for the Government (1) knowingly allows the case to be set for trial without disclosing the fact that a necessary witness would be unavailable for trial; (2) files a motion solely for the purpose of delay which he knows is totally frivolous and without merit; (3) makes a statement for the purpose of obtaining a continuance which he knows to be false and which is material to the granting of a continuance; or (4) otherwise willfully fails to proceed to trial without justification consistent with section 3161 of this chapter, the court may punish any such counsel or attorney, as follows:

(A)   in the case of an appointed defense counsel, by reducing the amount of compensation that otherwise would have been paid to such counsel pursuant to section 3006A of this title in an amount not to exceed 25 per centum thereof;

(B)   in the case of a counsel retained in connection with the defense of a defendant, by imposing on such counsel a fine of not to exceed 25 per centum of the compensation to which he is entitled in connection with his defense of such defendant;

(C)   by imposing on any attorney for the Government a fine of not to exceed $250;

(D)   by denying any such counsel or attorney for the Government the right to practice before the court considering such case for a period of not to exceed ninety days; or

(E)   by filing a report with an appropriate disciplinary committee.

The authority to punish provided for by this subsection shall be in addition to any other authority or power available to such court.

(c)   The court shall follow procedures established in the Federal Rules of Criminal Procedure in punishing any counsel or attorney for the Government pursuant to this section.

§ 3164.   Persons detained or designated as being of high risk

(a)   The trial or other disposition of cases involving—

(1)   a detained person who is being held in detention solely because he is awaiting trial, and

(2)   a released person who is awaiting trial and has been designated by the attorney for the Government as being of high risk,

shall be accorded priority.

(b)   The trial of any person described in subsection (a) (1) or (a) (2) of this section shall commence not later than ninety days following the beginning of such continuous detention or designation of high risk by the attorney for the Government. The periods of delay enumerated in section 3161(h) are excluded in computing the time limitation specified in this section.

(c)   Failure to commence trial of a detainee as specified in subsection (b), through no fault of the accused or his counsel, or failure to commence trial of a designated releasee as specified in subsection (b), through no fault of the attorney for the Government, shall result in the automatic review by the court of the conditions of release. No detainee, as defined in subsection (a), shall be held in custody pending trial after the expiration of such ninety-day period required for the commencement of his trial. A designated releasee, as defined in subsection (a), who is found by the court to have intentionally delayed the trial of his case shall be subject to an order of the court modifying his nonfinancial conditions of release under this title to insure that he shall appear at trial as required.

JENCKS ACT

(18 U.S.C. § 3500).

§ 3500.   Demands for production of statements and reports of witnesses

(a)   In any criminal prosecution brought by the United States, no statement or report in the possession of the United States which was made by a Government witness or prospective Government witness (other than the defendant) shall be the subject of subpena, discovery, or inspection until said witness has testified on direct examination in the trial of the case.

(b)   After a witness called by the United States has testified on direct examination, the court shall, on motion of the defendant, order the United States to produce any statement (as hereinafter defined) of the witness in the possession of the United States which relates to the subject matter as to which the witness has testified. If the entire contents of any such statement relate to the subject matter of the testimony of the witness, the court shall order it to be delivered directly to the defendant for his examination and use.

(c)   If the United States claims that any statement ordered to be produced under this section contains matter which does not relate to the subject matter of the testimony of the witness, the court shall order the United States to deliver such statement for the inspection of the court in camera. Upon such delivery the court shall excise the portions of such statement which do not relate to the subject matter of the testimony of the witness. With such material excised, the court shall then direct delivery of such statement to the defendant for his use. If, pursuant to such procedure, any portion of such statement is withheld from the defendant and the defendant objects to such withholding, and the trial is continued to an adjudication of the guilt of the defendant, the entire text of such statement shall be preserved by the United States and, in the event the defendant appeals, shall be made available to the appellate court for the purpose of determining the correctness of the ruling of the trial judge. Whenever any statement is delivered to a defendant pursuant to this section, the court in its discretion, upon application of said defendant, may recess proceedings in the trial for such time as it may determine to be reasonably required for the examination of such statement by said defendant and his preparation for its use in the trial.

(d)   If the United States elects not to comply with an order of the court under subsection (b) or (c) hereof to deliver to the defendant any such statement, or such portion thereof as the court may direct, the court shall strike from the record the testimony of the witness, and the trial shall proceed unless the court in its discretion shall determine that the interests of justice require that a mistrial be declared.

(e)   The term "statement", as used in subsections (b), (c), and (d) of this section in relation to any witness called by the United States, means—

(1)   a written statement made by said witness and signed or otherwise adopted or approved by him;

(2)   a stenographic, mechanical, electrical, or other recording, or a transcription thereof, which is a substantially verbatim recital of an oral statement made by said witness and recorded contemporaneously with the making of such oral statement; or

(3)   a statement, however taken or recorded, or a transcription thereof, if any, made by said witness to a grand jury.

LITIGATION CONCERNING SOURCES OF EVIDENCE

(18 U.S.C. § 3504).

§ 3504.   Litigation concerning sources of evidence

(a)   In any trial, hearing, or other proceeding in or before any court, grand jury, department, officer, agency, regulatory body, or other authority of the United States—

(1)   upon a claim by a party aggrieved that evidence is inadmissible because it is the primary product of an unlawful act or because it was obtained by the exploitation of an unlawful act, the opponent of the claim shall affirm or deny the occurrence of the alleged unlawful act;

(2)   disclosure of information for a determination if evidence is inadmissible because it is the primary product of an unlawful act occurring prior to June 19, 1968, or because it was obtained by the exploitation of an unlawful act occurring prior to June 19, 1968, shall not be required unless such information may be relevant to a pending claim of such inadmissibility; and

(3) no claim shall be considered that evidence of an event is inadmissible on the ground that such evidence was obtained by the exploitation of an unlawful act occurring prior to June 19, 1968, if such event occurred more than five years after such allegedly unlawful act.

(b) As used in this section "unlawful act" means any act the use of any electronic, mechanical, or other device (as defined in section 2510(5) of this title) in violation of the Constitution or laws of the United States or any regulation or standard promulgated pursuant thereto.

CRIMINAL APPEALS ACT OF 1970
(AS AMENDED)
(18 U.S.C. § 3731).

§ 3731. Appeal by United States

In a criminal case an appeal by the United States shall lie to a court of appeals from a decision, judgment, or order of a district court dismissing an indictment or information or granting a new trial after verdict or judgment, as to any one or more counts, or any part thereof, except that no appeal shall lie where the double jeopardy clause of the United States Constitution prohibits further prosecution.

An appeal by the United States shall lie to a court of appeals from a decision or order of a district court suppressing or excluding evidence or requiring the return of seized property in a criminal proceeding, not made after the defendant has been put in jeopardy and before the verdict or finding on an indictment or information, if the United States attorney certifies to the district court that the appeal is not taken for purpose of delay and that the evidence is a substantial proof of a fact material in the proceeding.

An appeal by the United States shall lie to a court of appeals from a decision or order, entered by a district court of the United States, granting the release of a person charged with or convicted of an offense, or denying a motion for revocation of, or modification of the conditions of, a decision or order granting release.

The appeal in all such cases shall be taken within thirty days after the decision, judgment or order has been rendered and shall be diligently prosecuted.

The provisions of this section shall be liberally construed to effectuate its purposes.

CRIME VICTIMS' RIGHTS
(18 U.S.C. § 3771).

§ 3771. Crime victims' rights

(a) Rights of crime victims.—A crime victim has the following rights:

(1) The right to be reasonably protected from the accused.

(2) The right to reasonable, accurate, and timely notice of any public court proceeding, or any parole proceeding, involving the crime or of any release or escape of the accused.

(3) The right not to be excluded from any such public court proceeding, unless the court, after receiving clear and convincing evidence, determines that testimony by the victim would be materially altered if the victim heard other testimony at that proceeding.

(4) The right to be reasonably heard at any public proceeding in the district court involving release, plea, sentencing, or any parole proceeding.

(5)   The reasonable right to confer with the attorney for the Government in the case.

(6)   The right to full and timely restitution as provided in law.

(7)   The right to proceedings free from unreasonable delay.

(8)   The right to be treated with fairness and with respect for the victim's dignity and privacy.

(b)   Rights afforded.—

(1)   In general.—

In any court proceeding involving an offense against a crime victim, the court shall ensure that the crime victim is afforded the rights described in subsection (a). Before making a determination described in subsection (a)(3), the court shall make every effort to permit the fullest attendance possible by the victim and shall consider reasonable alternatives to the exclusion of the victim from the criminal proceeding. The reasons for any decision denying relief under this chapter shall be clearly stated on the record.

(2)   Habeas corpus proceedings.—

(A)   In general.—In a Federal habeas corpus proceeding arising out of a State conviction, the court shall ensure that a crime victim is afforded the rights described in paragraphs (3), (4), (7), and (8) of subsection (a).

(B)   Enforcement.—

(i)   In general.—These rights may be enforced by the crime victim or the crime victim's lawful representative in the manner described in paragraphs (1) and (3) of subsection (d).

(ii)   Multiple victims.—In a case involving multiple victims, subsection (d)(2) shall also apply.

(C)   Limitation.—This paragraph relates to the duties of a court in relation to the rights of a crime victim in Federal habeas corpus proceedings arising out of a State conviction, and does not give rise to any obligation or requirement applicable to personnel of any agency of the Executive Branch of the Federal Government.

(D)   Definition.—For purposes of this paragraph, the term "crime victim" means the person against whom the State offense is committed or, if that person is killed or incapacitated, that person's family member or other lawful representative.

(c)   Best efforts to accord rights.—

(1)   Government.—Officers and employees of the Department of Justice and other departments and agencies of the United States engaged in the detection, investigation, or prosecution of crime shall make their best efforts to see that crime victims are notified of, and accorded, the rights described in subsection (a).

(2)   Advice of attorney.—The prosecutor shall advise the crime victim that the crime victim can seek the advice of an attorney with respect to the rights described in subsection (a).

(3)   Notice.—Notice of release otherwise required pursuant to this chapter shall not be given if such notice may endanger the safety of any person.

(d)   Enforcement and limitations.—

(1) Rights.—The crime victim or the crime victim's lawful representative, and the attorney for the Government may assert the rights described in subsection (a). A person accused of the crime may not obtain any form of relief under this chapter.

(2) Multiple crime victims.—In a case where the court finds that the number of crime victims makes it impracticable to accord all of the crime victims the rights described in subsection (a), the court shall fashion a reasonable procedure to give effect to this chapter that does not unduly complicate or prolong the proceedings.

(3) Motion for relief and writ of mandamus.—The rights described in subsection (a) shall be asserted in the district court in which a defendant is being prosecuted for the crime or, if no prosecution is underway, in the district court in the district in which the crime occurred. The district court shall take up and decide any motion asserting a victim's right forthwith. If the district court denies the relief sought, the movant may petition the court of appeals for a writ of mandamus. The court of appeals may issue the writ on the order of a single judge pursuant to circuit rule or the Federal Rules of Appellate Procedure. The court of appeals shall take up and decide such application forthwith within 72 hours after the petition has been filed. In no event shall proceedings be stayed or subject to a continuance of more than five days for purposes of enforcing this chapter. If the court of appeals denies the relief sought, the reasons for the denial shall be clearly stated on the record in a written opinion.

(4) Error.—In any appeal in a criminal case, the Government may assert as error the district court's denial of any crime victim's right in the proceeding to which the appeal relates.

(5) Limitation on relief.—In no case shall a failure to afford a right under this chapter provide grounds for a new trial. A victim may make a motion to re-open a plea or sentence only if—

(A) the victim has asserted the right to be heard before or during the proceeding at issue and such right was denied;

(B) the victim petitions the court of appeals for a writ of mandamus within 14 days; and

(C) in the case of a plea, the accused has not pled to the highest offense charged.

This paragraph does not affect the victim's right to restitution as provided in title 18, United States Code.

(6) No cause of action.—Nothing in this chapter shall be construed to authorize a cause of action for damages or to create, to enlarge, or to imply any duty or obligation to any victim or other person for the breach of which the United States or any of its officers or employees could be held liable in damages. Nothing in this chapter shall be construed to impair the prosecutorial discretion of the Attorney General or any officer under his direction.

(e) Definitions.—For the purposes of this chapter, the term "crime victim" means a person directly and proximately harmed as a result of the commission of a Federal offense or an offense in the District of Columbia. In the case of a crime victim who is under 18 years of age, incompetent, incapacitated, or deceased, the legal guardians of the crime victim or the representatives of the crime victim's estate, family members, or any other persons appointed as suitable by the court, may assume the crime victim's rights under this chapter, but in no event shall the defendant be named as such guardian or representative.

(f) Procedures to promote compliance.—

(1) Regulations.—Not later than 1 year after the date of enactment of this chapter, the Attorney General of the United States shall promulgate regulations to enforce the rights of

crime victims and to ensure compliance by responsible officials with the obligations described in law respecting crime victims.

(2)   Contents.—The regulations promulgated under paragraph (1) shall—

(A)   designate an administrative authority within the Department of Justice to receive and investigate complaints relating to the provision or violation of the rights of a crime victim;

(B)   require a course of training for employees and offices of the Department of Justice that fail to comply with provisions of Federal law pertaining to the treatment of crime victims, and otherwise assist such employees and offices in responding more effectively to the needs of crime victims;

(C)   contain disciplinary sanctions, including suspension or termination from employment, for employees of the Department of Justice who willfully or wantonly fail to comply with provisions of Federal law pertaining to the treatment of crime victims; and

(D)   provide that the Attorney General, or the designee of the Attorney General, shall be the final arbiter of the complaint, and that there shall be no judicial review of the final decision of the Attorney General by a complainant.

JURY SELECTION AND SERVICE ACT OF 1968 (AS AMENDED)

(28 U.S.C. §§ 1861–1863, 1865–1867).

§ 1861.   Declaration of policy

It is the policy of the United States that all litigants in Federal courts entitled to trial by jury shall have the right to grand and petit juries selected at random from a fair cross section of the community in the district or division wherein the court convenes. It is further the policy of the United States that all citizens shall have the opportunity to be considered for service on grand and petit juries in the district courts of the United States, and shall have an obligation to serve as jurors when summoned for that purpose.

§ 1862.   Discrimination prohibited

No citizen shall be excluded from service as a grand or petit juror in the district courts of the United States or in the Court of International Trade on account of race, color, religion, sex, national origin, or economic status.

§ 1863.   Plan for random jury selection

(a)   Each United States district court shall devise and place into operation a written plan for random selection of grand and petit jurors that shall be designed to achieve the objectives of sections 1861 and 1862 of this title, and that shall otherwise comply with the provisions of this title. The plan shall be placed into operation after approval by a reviewing panel consisting of the members of the judicial council of the circuit and either the chief judge of the district whose plan is being reviewed or such other active district judge of that district as the chief judge of the district may designate. The panel shall examine the plan to ascertain that it complies with the provisions of this title. If the reviewing panel finds that the plan does not comply, the panel shall state the particulars in which the plan fails to comply and direct the district court to present within a reasonable time an alternative plan remedying the defect or defects. Separate plans may be adopted for each division or combination of divisions within a judicial district. The district court may modify a plan at any time and it shall modify the plan when so directed by the reviewing panel. The district court shall promptly notify the panel, the Administrative Office of the United States Courts, and the Attorney General of the United States, of the initial adoption and future modifications of the plan by filing copies therewith. Modifications of the plan made at the instance of the district court shall become effective after approval by the panel. Each district court shall submit a report on the jury selection process within its jurisdiction to the Administrative Office of the United States Courts in such form and at such times as the Judicial Conference of the United States may specify. The Judicial Conference of the United States may, from time to time, adopt rules and regulations governing the provisions and the operation of the plans formulated under this title.

(b)   Among other things, such plan shall—

(1)   either establish a jury commission, or authorize the clerk of the court, to manage the jury selection process. If the plan establishes a jury commission, the district court shall appoint one citizen to serve with the clerk of the court as the jury commission: *Provided, however,* That the plan for the District of Columbia may establish a jury commission consisting of three citizens. The citizen jury commissioner shall not belong to the same political party as the clerk serving with him. The clerk or the jury commission, as the case may be, shall act under the supervision and control of the chief judge of the district court or such other judge of the district court as the plan may provide. Each jury commissioner shall, during his tenure in office, reside in the judicial district or division for which he is appointed. Each citizen jury commissioner shall receive compensation to be fixed by the district court plan at a rate not to exceed $50 per day for each day necessarily employed in the performance of his duties, plus reimbursement for travel, subsistence, and other necessary expenses incurred by him in the performance of such duties. The Judicial Conference of the United States may establish standards for allowance of travel, subsistence, and other necessary expenses incurred by jury commissioners.

(2)   specify whether the names of prospective jurors shall be selected from the voter registration lists or the lists of actual voters of the political subdivisions within the district or division. The plan shall prescribe some other source or sources of names in addition to voter lists where necessary to foster the policy and protect the rights secured by sections 1861 and 1862 of this title. The plan for the District of Columbia may require the names of prospective jurors to be selected from the city directory rather than from voter lists. The plans for the districts of Puerto Rico and the Canal Zone may prescribe some other source or sources of names of prospective jurors in lieu of voter lists, the use of which shall be consistent with the policies declared and rights secured by sections 1861 and 1862 of this title. The plan for the district of Massachusetts may require the names of prospective jurors to be selected from the resident list provided for in chapter 234A, Massachusetts General Laws, or comparable authority, rather than from voter lists.

(3)   specify detailed procedures to be followed by the jury commission or clerk in selecting names from the sources specified in paragraph (2) of this subsection. These procedures shall be designed to ensure the random selection of a fair cross section of the persons residing in the community in the district or division wherein the court convenes. They shall ensure that names of persons residing in each of the counties, parishes, or similar political subdivisions within the judicial district or division are placed in a master jury wheel; and shall ensure that each county, parish, or similar political subdivision within the district or division is substantially proportionally represented in the master jury wheel for that judicial district, division, or combination of divisions. For the purposes of determining proportional representation in the master jury wheel, either the number of actual voters at the last general election in each county, parish, or similar political subdivision, or the number

of registered voters if registration of voters is uniformly required throughout the district or division, may be used.

(4)   provide for a master jury wheel (or a device similar in purpose and function) into which the names of those randomly selected shall be placed. The plan shall fix a minimum number of names to be placed initially in the master jury wheel, which shall be at least one-half of 1 per centum of the total number of persons on the lists used as a source of names for the district or division; but if this number of names is believed to be cumbersome and unnecessary, the plan may fix a smaller number of names to be placed in the master wheel, but in no event less than one thousand. The chief judge of the district court, or such other district court judge as the plan may provide, may order additional names to be placed in the master jury wheel from time to time as necessary. The plan shall provide for periodic emptying and refilling of the master jury wheel at specified times, the interval for which shall not exceed four years.

(5)(A)   except as provided in subparagraph (B), specify those groups of persons or occupational classes whose members shall, on individual request therefor, be excused from jury service. Such groups or classes shall be excused only if the district court finds, and the plan states, that jury service by such class or group would entail undue hardship or extreme inconvenience to the members thereof, and excuse of members thereof would not be inconsistent with sections 1861 and 1862 of this title.

(B)   specify that volunteer safety personnel, upon individual request, shall be excused from jury service. For purposes of this subparagraph, the term "volunteer safety personnel" means individuals serving a public agency (as defined in section 1203(6) of title I of the Omnibus Crime Control and Safe Streets Act of 1968) in an official capacity, without compensation, as firefighters or members of a rescue squad or ambulance crew.

(6)   specify that the following persons are barred from jury service on the ground that they are exempt: (A) members in active service in the Armed Forces of the United States; (B) members of the fire or police departments of any State, the District of Columbia, any territory or possession of the United States, or any subdivision of a State, the District of Columbia, or such territory or possession; (C) public officers in the executive, legislative, or judicial branches of the Government of the United States, or of any State, the District of Columbia, any territory or possession of the United States, or any subdivision of a State, the District of Columbia, or such territory or possession, who are actively engaged in the performance of official duties.

(7)   fix the time when the names drawn from the qualified jury wheel shall be disclosed to parties and to the public. If the plan permits these names to be made public, it may nevertheless permit the chief judge of the district court, or such other district court judge as the plan may provide, to keep these names confidential in any case where the interests of justice so require.

(8)   specify the procedures to be followed by the clerk or jury commission in assigning persons whose names have been drawn from the qualified jury wheel to grand and petit jury panels.

(c)   The initial plan shall be devised by each district court and transmitted to the reviewing panel specified in subsection (a) of this section within one hundred and twenty days of the date of enactment of the Jury Selection and Service Act of 1968. The panel shall approve or direct the modification of each plan so submitted within sixty days thereafter. Each plan or modification made at the direction of the panel shall become effective after approval at such time thereafter as the panel directs, in no event to exceed ninety days from the date of approval. Modifications made at the instance of the district court under subsection (a) of this section shall be effective at such time thereafter as the panel directs, in no event to exceed ninety days from the date of modification.

(d)   State, local, and Federal officials having custody, possession, or control of voter registration lists, lists of actual voters, or other appropriate records shall make such lists and records available to the jury commission or clerks for inspection, reproduction, and copying at all reasonable times as the commission or clerk may deem necessary and proper for the performance of duties under this title. The district courts shall have jurisdiction upon application by the Attorney General of the United States to compel compliance with this subsection by appropriate process.

§ 1865.   Qualifications for jury service

(a)   The chief judge of the district court, or such other district court judge as the plan may provide, on his initiative or upon recommendation of the clerk or jury commission, or the clerk under supervision of the court if the court's jury selection plan so authorizes, shall determine solely on the basis of information provided on the juror qualification form and other competent evidence whether a person is unqualified for, or exempt, or to be excused from jury service. The clerk shall enter such determination in the space provided on the juror qualification form and in any alphabetical list of names drawn from the master jury wheel. If a person did not appear in response to a summons, such fact shall be noted on said list.

(b)   In making such determination the chief judge of the district court, or such other district court judge as the plan may provide, or the clerk if the court's jury selection plan so provides, shall deem any person qualified to serve on grand and petit juries in the district court unless he—

(1)   is not a citizen of the United States eighteen years old who has resided for a period of one year within the judicial district;

(2)   is unable to read, write, and understand the English language with a degree of proficiency sufficient to fill out satisfactorily the juror qualification form;

(3)   is unable to speak the English language;

(4)   is incapable, by reason of mental or physical infirmity, to render satisfactory jury service; or

(5)   has a charge pending against him for the commission of, or has been convicted in a State or Federal court of record of, a crime punishable by imprisonment for more than one year and his civil rights have not been restored.

§ 1866.   Selection and summoning of jury panels

(a)   The jury commission, or in the absence thereof the clerk, shall maintain a qualified jury wheel and shall place in such wheel names of all persons drawn from the master jury wheel who are determined to be qualified as jurors and not exempt or excused pursuant to the district court plan. From time to time, the jury commission or the clerk shall draw at random from the qualified jury wheel such number of names of persons as may be required for assignment to grand and petit jury panels. The clerk or jury commission shall post a general notice for public review in the clerk's office and on the court's website explaining the process by which names are periodically and randomly drawn. The jury commission or the clerk shall prepare a separate list of names of persons assigned to each grand and petit jury panel.

(b)   When the court orders a grand or petit jury to be drawn, the clerk or jury commission or their duly designated deputies shall issue summonses for the required number of jurors.

Each person drawn for jury service may be served personally, or by registered, certified, or first-class mail addressed to such person at his usual residence or business address.

If such service is made personally, the summons shall be delivered by the clerk or the jury commission or their duly designated deputies to the marshal who shall make such service.

If such service is made by mail, the summons may be served by the marshal or by the clerk, the jury commission or their duly designated deputies, who shall make affidavit of service and shall attach thereto any receipt from the addressee for a registered or certified summons.

(c) Except as provided in section 1865 of this title or in any jury selection plan provision adopted pursuant to paragraph (5) or (6) of section 1863(b) of this title, no person or class of persons shall be disqualified, excluded, excused, or exempt from service as jurors: *Provided*, That any person summoned for jury service may be (1) excused by the court, or by the clerk under supervision of the court if the court's jury selection plan so authorizes, upon a showing of undue hardship or extreme inconvenience, for such period as the court deems necessary, at the conclusion of which such person either shall be summoned again for jury service under subsections (b) and (c) of this section or, if the court's jury selection plan so provides, the name of such person shall be reinserted into the qualified jury wheel for selection pursuant to subsection (a) of this section, or (2) excluded by the court on the ground that such person may be unable to render impartial jury service or that his service as a juror would be likely to disrupt the proceedings, or (3) excluded upon peremptory challenge as provided by law, or (4) excluded pursuant to the procedure specified by law upon a challenge by any party for good cause shown, or (5) excluded upon determination by the court that his service as a juror would be likely to threaten the secrecy of the proceedings, or otherwise adversely affect the integrity of jury deliberations. No person shall be excluded under clause (5) of this subsection unless the judge, in open court, determines that such is warranted and that exclusion of the person will not be inconsistent with sections 1861 and 1862 of this title. The number of persons excluded under clause (5) of this subsection shall not exceed one per centum of the number of persons who return executed jury qualification forms during the period, specified in the plan, between two consecutive fillings of the master jury wheel. The names of persons excluded under clause (5) of this subsection, together with detailed explanations for the exclusions, shall be forwarded immediately to the judicial council of the circuit, which shall have the power to make any appropriate order, prospective or retroactive, to redress any misapplication of clause (5) of this subsection, but otherwise exclusions effectuated under such clause shall not be subject to challenge under the provisions of this title. Any person excluded from a particular jury under clause (2), (3), or (4) of this subsection shall be eligible to sit on another jury if the basis for his initial exclusion would not be relevant to his ability to serve on such other jury.

(d) Whenever a person is disqualified, excused, exempt, or excluded from jury service, the jury commission or clerk shall note in the space provided on his juror qualification form or on the juror's card drawn from the qualified jury wheel the specific reason therefor.

(e) In any two-year period, no person shall be required to (1) serve or attend court for prospective service as a petit juror for a total of more than thirty days, except when necessary to complete service in a particular case, or (2) serve on more than one grand jury, or (3) serve as both a grand and petit juror.

(f) When there is an unanticipated shortage of available petit jurors drawn from the qualified jury wheel, the court may require the marshal to summon a sufficient number of petit jurors selected at random from the voter registration lists, lists of actual voters, or other lists specified in the plan, in a manner ordered by the court consistent with sections 1861 and 1862 of this title.

(g) Any person summoned for jury service who fails to appear as directed may be ordered by the district court to appear forthwith and show cause for failure to comply with the summons. Any person who fails to show good cause for noncompliance with a summons may be fined not more than $1,000, imprisoned not more than three days, ordered to perform community service, or any combination thereof.

§ 1867.   Challenging compliance with selection procedures

(a)   In criminal cases, before the voir dire examination begins, or within seven days after the defendant discovered or could have discovered, by the exercise of diligence, the grounds therefor, whichever is earlier, the defendant may move to dismiss the indictment or stay the proceedings against him on the ground of substantial failure to comply with the provisions of this title in selecting the grand or petit jury.

(b)   In criminal cases, before the voir dire examination begins, or within seven days after the Attorney General of the United States discovered or could have discovered, by the exercise of diligence, the grounds therefor, whichever is earlier, the Attorney General may move to dismiss the indictment or stay the proceedings on the ground of substantial failure to comply with the provisions of this title in selecting the grand or petit jury.

(c)   In civil cases, before the voir dire examination begins, or within seven days after the party discovered or could have discovered, by the exercise of diligence, the grounds therefor, whichever is earlier, any party may move to stay the proceedings on the ground of substantial failure to comply with the provisions of this title in selecting the petit jury.

(d)   Upon motion filed under subsection (a), (b), or (c) of this section, containing a sworn statement of facts which, if true, would constitute a substantial failure to comply with the provisions of this title, the moving party shall be entitled to present in support of such motion the testimony of the jury commission or clerk, if available, any relevant records and papers not public or otherwise available used by the jury commissioner or clerk, and any other relevant evidence. If the court determines that there has been a substantial failure to comply with the provisions of this title in selecting the grand jury, the court shall stay the proceedings pending the selection of a grand jury in conformity with this title or dismiss the indictment, whichever is appropriate. If the court determines that there has been a substantial failure to comply with the provisions of this title in selecting the petit jury, the court shall stay the proceedings pending the selection of a petit jury in conformity with this title.

(e)   The procedures prescribed by this section shall be the exclusive means by which a person accused of a Federal crime, the Attorney General of the United States or a party in a civil case may challenge any jury on the ground that such jury was not selected in conformity with the provisions of this title. Nothing in this section shall preclude any person or the United States from pursuing any other remedy, civil or criminal, which may be available for the vindication or enforcement of any law prohibiting discrimination on account of race, color, religion, sex, national origin or economic status in the selection of persons for service on grand or petit juries.

(f)   The contents of records or papers used by the jury commission or clerk in connection with the jury selection process shall not be disclosed, except pursuant to the district court plan or as may be necessary in the preparation or presentation of a motion under subsection (a), (b), or (c) of this section, until after the master jury wheel has been emptied and refilled pursuant to section 1863(b)(4) of this title and all persons selected to serve as jurors before the master wheel was emptied have completed such service. The parties in a case shall be allowed to inspect, reproduce, and copy such records or papers at all reasonable times during the preparation and pendency of such a motion. Any person who discloses the contents of any record or paper in violation of this subsection may be fined not more than $1,000 or imprisoned not more than one year, or both.

HABEAS CORPUS

(28 U.S.C. §§ 2241–2244, 2253–2255, 2261–2266).

§ 2241.   Power to grant writ

(a)   Writs of habeas corpus may be granted by the Supreme Court, any justice thereof, the district courts and any circuit judge within their respective jurisdictions. The order of a circuit judge shall be entered in the records of the district court of the district wherein the restraint complained of is had.

(b)   The Supreme Court, any justice thereof, and any circuit judge may decline to entertain an application for a writ of habeas corpus and may transfer the application for hearing and determination to the district court having jurisdiction to entertain it.

(c)   The writ of habeas corpus shall not extend to a prisoner unless—

(1)   He is in custody under or by color of the authority of the United States or is committed for trial before some court thereof; or

(2)   He is in custody for an act done or omitted in pursuance of an Act of Congress, or an order, process, judgment or decree of a court or judge of the United States; or

(3)   He is in custody in violation of the Constitution or laws or treaties of the United States; or

(4)   He, being a citizen of a foreign state and domiciled therein is in custody for an act done or omitted under any alleged right, title, authority, privilege, protection, or exemption claimed under the commission, order or sanction of any foreign state, or under color thereof, the validity and effect of which depend upon the law of nations; or

(5)   It is necessary to bring him into court to testify or for trial.

(d)   Where an application for a writ of habeas corpus is made by a person in custody under the judgment and sentence of a State court of a State which contains two or more Federal judicial districts, the application may be filed in the district court for the district wherein such person is in custody or in the district court for the district within which the State court was held which convicted and sentenced him and each of such district courts shall have concurrent jurisdiction to entertain the application. The district court for the district wherein such an application is filed in the exercise of its discretion and in furtherance of justice may transfer the application to the other district court for hearing and determination.

(e)(1)   No court, justice, or judge shall have jurisdiction to hear or consider an application for a writ of habeas corpus filed by or on behalf of an alien detained by the United States who has been determined by the United States to have been properly detained as an enemy combatant or is awaiting such determination.

(2)   Except as provided in paragraphs (2) and (3) of section 1005(e) of the Detainee Treatment Act of 2005 (10 U.S.C. 801 note), no court, justice, or judge shall have jurisdiction to hear or consider any other action against the United States or its agents relating to any aspect of the detention, transfer, treatment, trial, or conditions of confinement of an alien who is or was detained by the United States and has been determined by the United States to have been properly detained as an enemy combatant or is awaiting such determination.

§ 2242.   Application

Application for a writ of habeas corpus shall be in writing signed and verified by the person for whose relief it is intended or by someone acting in his behalf.

It shall allege the facts concerning the applicant's commitment or detention, the name of the person who has custody over him and by virtue of what claim or authority, if known.

It may be amended or supplemented as provided in the rules of procedure applicable to civil actions.

If addressed to the Supreme Court, a justice thereof or a circuit judge it shall state the reasons for not making application to the district court of the district in which the applicant is held.

§ 2243. Issuance of writ; return; hearing; decision

A court, justice or judge entertaining an application for a writ of habeas corpus shall forthwith award the writ or issue an order directing the respondent to show cause why the writ should not be granted, unless it appears from the application that the applicant or person detained is not entitled thereto.

The writ, or order to show cause shall be directed to the person having custody of the person detained. It shall be returned within three days unless for good cause additional time, not exceeding twenty days, is allowed.

The person to whom the writ or order is directed shall make a return certifying the true cause of the detention.

When the writ or order is returned a day shall be set for hearing, not more than five days after the return unless for good cause additional time is allowed.

Unless the application for the writ and the return present only issues of law the person to whom the writ is directed shall be required to produce at the hearing the body of the person detained.

The applicant or the person detained may, under oath, deny any of the facts set forth in the return or allege any other material facts.

The return and all suggestions made against it may be amended, by leave of court, before or after being filed.

The court shall summarily hear and determine the facts, and dispose of the matter as law and justice require.

§ 2244. Finality of determination

(a)   No circuit or district judge shall be required to entertain an application for a writ of habeas corpus to inquire into the detention of a person pursuant to a judgment of a court of the United States if it appears that the legality of such detention has been determined by a judge or court of the United States on a prior application for a writ of habeas corpus, except as provided in section 2255.

(b)(1)   A claim presented in a second or successive habeas corpus application under section 2254 that was presented in a prior application shall be dismissed.

(2)   A claim presented in a second or successive habeas corpus application under section 2254 that was not presented in a prior application shall be dismissed unless—

(A)   the applicant shows that the claim relies on a new rule of constitutional law, made retroactive to cases on collateral review by the Supreme Court, that was previously unavailable; or

(B)(i)   the factual predicate for the claim could not have been discovered previously through the exercise of due diligence; and

(ii)   the facts underlying the claim, if proven and viewed in light of the evidence as a whole, would be sufficient to establish by clear and convincing evidence that, but for constitutional error, no reasonable factfinder would have found the applicant guilty of the underlying offense.

(3)(A)   Before a second or successive application permitted by this section is filed in the district court, the applicant shall move in the appropriate court of appeals for an order authorizing the district court to consider the application.

(B)   A motion in the court of appeals for an order authorizing the district court to consider a second or successive application shall be determined by a three-judge panel of the court of appeals.

(C)   The court of appeals may authorize the filing of a second or successive application only if it determines that the application makes a prima facie showing that the application satisfies the requirements of this subsection.

(D)   The court of appeals shall grant or deny the authorization to file a second or successive application not later than 30 days after the filing of the motion.

(E)   The grant or denial of an authorization by a court of appeals to file a second or successive application shall not be appealable and shall not be the subject of a petition for rehearing or for a writ of certiorari.

(4)   A district court shall dismiss any claim presented in a second or successive application that the court of appeals has authorized to be filed unless the applicant shows that the claim satisfies the requirements of this section.

(c)   In a habeas corpus proceeding brought in behalf of a person in custody pursuant to the judgment of a State court, a prior judgment of the Supreme Court of the United States on an appeal or review by a writ of certiorari at the instance of the prisoner of the decision of such State court, shall be conclusive as to all issues of fact or law with respect to an asserted denial of a Federal right which constitutes ground for discharge in a habeas corpus proceeding, actually adjudicated by the Supreme Court therein, unless the applicant for the writ of habeas corpus shall plead and the court shall find the existence of a material and controlling fact which did not appear in the record of the proceeding in the Supreme Court and the court shall further find that the applicant for the writ of habeas corpus could not have caused such fact to appear in such record by the exercise of reasonable diligence.

(d)(1)   A 1-year period of limitation shall apply to an application for a writ of habeas corpus by a person in custody pursuant to the judgment of a State court. The limitation period shall run from the latest of—

(A)   the date on which the judgment became final by the conclusion of direct review or the expiration of the time for seeking such review;

(B)   the date on which the impediment to filing an application created by State action in violation of the Constitution or laws of the United States is removed, if the applicant was prevented from filing by such State action;

(C)   the date on which the constitutional right asserted was initially recognized by the Supreme Court, if the right has been newly recognized by the Supreme Court and made retroactively applicable to cases on collateral review; or

(D)   the date on which the factual predicate of the claim or claims presented could have been discovered through the exercise of due diligence.

(2)   The time during which a properly filed application for State post-conviction or other collateral review with respect to the pertinent judgment or claim is pending shall not be counted toward any period of limitation under this subsection.

§ 2253.   Appeal

(a)   In a habeas corpus proceeding or a proceeding under section 2255 before a district judge, the final order shall be subject to review, on appeal, by the court of appeals for the circuit in which the proceeding is held.

(b)   There shall be no right of appeal from a final order in a proceeding to test the validity of a warrant to remove to another district or place for commitment or trial a person charged with a criminal offense against the United States, or to test the validity of such person's detention pending removal proceedings.

(c)(1)   Unless a circuit justice or judge issues a certificate of appealability, an appeal may not be taken to the court of appeals from—

(A)   the final order in a habeas corpus proceeding in which the detention complained of arises out of process issued by a State court; or

(B)   the final order in a proceeding under section 2255.

(2)   A certificate of appealability may issue under paragraph (1) only if the applicant has made a substantial showing of the denial of a constitutional right.

(3)   The certificate of appealability under paragraph (1) shall indicate which specific issue or issues satisfy the showing required by paragraph (2).

§ 2254.   State custody; remedies in Federal courts

(a)   The Supreme Court, a Justice thereof, a circuit judge, or a district court shall entertain an application for a writ of habeas corpus in behalf of a person in custody pursuant to the judgment of a State court only on the ground that he is in custody in violation of the Constitution or laws or treaties of the United States.

(b)(1)   An application for a writ of habeas corpus on behalf of a person in custody pursuant to the judgment of a State court shall not be granted unless it appears that—

(A)   the applicant has exhausted the remedies available in the courts of the State; or

(B)(i)   there is an absence of available State corrective process; or

(ii)   circumstances exist that render such process ineffective to protect the rights of the applicant.

(2)   An application for a writ of habeas corpus may be denied on the merits, notwithstanding the failure of the applicant to exhaust the remedies available in the courts of the State.

(3)   A State shall not be deemed to have waived the exhaustion requirement or be estopped from reliance upon the requirement unless the State, through counsel, expressly waives the requirement.

(c)   An applicant shall not be deemed to have exhausted the remedies available in the courts of the State, within the meaning of this section, if he has the right under the law of the State to raise, by any available procedure, the question presented.

(d)   An application for a writ of habeas corpus on behalf of a person in custody pursuant to the judgment of a State court shall not be granted with respect to any claim that was adjudicated on the merits in State court proceedings unless the adjudication of the claim—

(1)   resulted in a decision that was contrary to, or involved an unreasonable application of, clearly established Federal law, as determined by the Supreme Court of the United States; or

(2)   resulted in a decision that was based on an unreasonable determination of the facts in light of the evidence presented in the State court proceeding.

(e)(1)   In a proceeding instituted by an application for a writ of habeas corpus by a person in custody pursuant to the judgment of a State court, a determination of a factual issue made by a State court shall be presumed to be correct. The applicant shall have the burden of rebutting the presumption of correctness by clear and convincing evidence.

(2)   If the applicant has failed to develop the factual basis of a claim in State court proceedings, the court shall not hold an evidentiary hearing on the claim unless the applicant shows that—

(A)   the claim relies on—

(i)   a new rule of constitutional law, made retroactive to cases on collateral review by the Supreme Court, that was previously unavailable; or

(ii)   a factual predicate that could not have been previously discovered through the exercise of due diligence; and

(B)   the facts underlying the claim would be sufficient to establish by clear and convincing evidence that but for constitutional error, no reasonable factfinder would have found the applicant guilty of the underlying offense.

(f)   If the applicant challenges the sufficiency of the evidence adduced in such State court proceeding to support the State court's determination of a factual issue made therein, the applicant, if able, shall produce that part of the record pertinent to a determination of the sufficiency of the evidence to support such determination. If the applicant, because of indigency or other reason is unable to produce such part of the record, then the State shall produce such part of the record and the Federal court shall direct the State to do so by order directed to an appropriate State official. If the State cannot provide such pertinent part of the record, then the court shall determine under the existing facts and circumstances what weight shall be given to the State court's factual determination.

(g)   A copy of the official records of the State court, duly certified by the clerk of such court to be a true and correct copy of a finding, judicial opinion, or other reliable written indicia showing such a factual determination by the State court shall be admissible in the Federal court proceeding.

(h)   Except as provided in section 408 of the Controlled Substances Act, in all proceedings brought under this section, and any subsequent proceedings on review, the court may appoint counsel for an applicant who is or becomes financially unable to afford counsel, except as provided by a rule promulgated by the Supreme Court pursuant to statutory authority. Appointment of counsel under this section shall be governed by section 3006A of title 18.

(i)   The ineffectiveness or incompetence of counsel during Federal or State collateral post-conviction proceedings shall not be a ground for relief in a proceeding arising under section 2254.

§ 2255.   Federal custody; remedies on motion attacking sentence

(a)   A prisoner in custody under sentence of a court established by Act of Congress claiming the right to be released upon the ground that the sentence was imposed in violation of the Constitution or laws of the United States, or that the court was without jurisdiction to impose such sentence, or that the sentence was in excess of the maximum authorized by law, or is otherwise subject to collateral attack, may move the court which imposed the sentence to vacate, set aside or correct the sentence.

(b)   Unless the motion and the files and records of the case conclusively show that the prisoner is entitled to no relief, the court shall cause notice thereof to be served upon the United States attorney, grant a prompt hearing thereon, determine the issues and make findings of fact and conclusions of law with respect thereto. If the court finds that the judgment was rendered without jurisdiction, or that the sentence imposed was not authorized by law or otherwise open to collateral attack, or that there has been such a denial or infringement of the constitutional rights of the prisoner as to render the judgment vulnerable to collateral attack, the court shall vacate and set the judgment aside and shall discharge the prisoner or resentence him or grant a new trial or correct the sentence as may appear appropriate.

(c)   A court may entertain and determine such motion without requiring the production of the prisoner at the hearing.

(d)   An appeal may be taken to the court of appeals from the order entered on the motion as from a final judgment on application for a writ of habeas corpus.

(e)   An application for a writ of habeas corpus in behalf of a prisoner who is authorized to apply for relief by motion pursuant to this section, shall not be entertained if it appears that the applicant has failed to apply for relief, by motion, to the court which sentenced him, or that such court has denied him relief, unless it also appears that the remedy by motion is inadequate or ineffective to test the legality of his detention.

(f)   A 1-year period of limitation shall apply to a motion under this section. The limitation period shall run from the latest of—

(1)   the date on which the judgment of conviction becomes final;

(2)   the date on which the impediment to making a motion created by governmental action in violation of the Constitution or laws of the United States is removed, if the movant was prevented from making a motion by such governmental action;

(3)   the date on which the right asserted was initially recognized by the Supreme Court, if that right has been newly recognized by the Supreme Court and made retroactively applicable to cases on collateral review; or

(4)   the date on which the facts supporting the claim or claims presented could have been discovered through the exercise of due diligence.

(g)   Except as provided in section 408 of the Controlled Substances Act, in all proceedings brought under this section, and any subsequent proceedings on review, the court may appoint counsel, except as provided by a rule promulgated by the Supreme Court pursuant to statutory authority. Appointment of counsel under this section shall be governed by section 3006A of title 18.

(h)   A second or successive motion must be certified as provided in section 2244 by a panel of the appropriate court of appeals to contain—

(1)   newly discovered evidence that, if proven and viewed in light of the evidence as a whole, would be sufficient to establish by clear and convincing evidence that no reasonable factfinder would have found the movant guilty of the offense; or

(2)   a new rule of constitutional law, made retroactive to cases on collateral review by the Supreme Court, that was previously unavailable.

§ 2261.   Prisoners in State custody subject to capital sentence; appointment of counsel; requirement of rule of court or statute; procedures for appointment

(a)   This chapter shall apply to cases arising under section 2254 brought by prisoners in State custody who are subject to a capital sentence. It shall apply only if the provisions of subsections (b) and (c) are satisfied.

(b)   Counsel.—This chapter is applicable if—

(1)   the Attorney General of the United States certifies that a State has established a mechanism for providing counsel in postconviction proceedings as provided in section 2265; and

(2)   counsel was appointed pursuant to that mechanism, petitioner validly waived counsel, petitioner retained counsel, or petitioner was found not to be indigent.

(c)   Any mechanism for the appointment, compensation, and reimbursement of counsel as provided in subsection (b) must offer counsel to all State prisoners under capital sentence and must provide for the entry of an order by a court of record—

(1)   appointing one or more counsels to represent the prisoner upon a finding that the prisoner is indigent and accepted the offer or is unable competently to decide whether to accept or reject the offer;

(2)   finding, after a hearing if necessary, that the prisoner rejected the offer of counsel and made the decision with an understanding of its legal consequences; or

(3)   denying the appointment of counsel upon a finding that the prisoner is not indigent.

(d)   No counsel appointed pursuant to subsections (b) and (c) to represent a State prisoner under capital sentence shall have previously represented the prisoner at trial in the case for which the appointment is made unless the prisoner and counsel expressly request continued representation.

(e)   The ineffectiveness or incompetence of counsel during State or Federal post-conviction proceedings in a capital case shall not be a ground for relief in a proceeding arising under section 2254. This limitation shall not preclude the appointment of different counsel, on the court's own motion or at the request of the prisoner, at any phase of State or Federal post-conviction proceedings on the basis of the ineffectiveness or incompetence of counsel in such proceedings.

§ 2262.   Mandatory stay of execution; duration; limits on stays of execution; successive petitions

(a)   Upon the entry in the appropriate State court of record of an order under section 2261(c), a warrant or order setting an execution date for a State prisoner shall be stayed upon application to any court that would have jurisdiction over any proceedings filed under section 2254. The application shall recite that the State has invoked the post-conviction review procedures of this chapter and that the scheduled execution is subject to stay.

(b)   A stay of execution granted pursuant to subsection (a) shall expire if—

(1)   a State prisoner fails to file a habeas corpus application under section 2254 within the time required in section 2263;

(2)   before a court of competent jurisdiction, in the presence of counsel, unless the prisoner has competently and knowingly waived such counsel, and after having been advised of the consequences, a State prisoner under capital sentence waives the right to pursue habeas corpus review under section 2254; or

(3)   a State prisoner files a habeas corpus petition under section 2254 within the time required by section 2263 and fails to make a substantial showing of the denial of a Federal right or is denied relief in the district court or at any subsequent stage of review.

(c)   If one of the conditions in subsection (b) has occurred, no Federal court thereafter shall have the authority to enter a stay of execution in the case, unless the court of appeals approves the filing of a second or successive application under section 2244(b).

§ 2263.   Filing of habeas corpus application; time requirements; tolling rules

(a)   Any application under this chapter for habeas corpus relief under section 2254 must be filed in the appropriate district court not later than 180 days after final State court affirmance of the conviction and sentence on direct review or the expiration of the time for seeking such review.

(b)   The time requirements established by subsection (a) shall be tolled—

(1)   from the date that a petition for certiorari is filed in the Supreme Court until the date of final disposition of the petition if a State prisoner files the petition to secure review by the Supreme Court of the affirmance of a capital sentence on direct review by the court of last resort of the State or other final State court decision on direct review;

(2)   from the date on which the first petition for post-conviction review or other collateral relief is filed until the final State court disposition of such petition; and

(3)   during an additional period not to exceed 30 days, if—

(A)   a motion for an extension of time is filed in the Federal district court that would have jurisdiction over the case upon the filing of a habeas corpus application under section 2254; and

(B)   a showing of good cause is made for the failure to file the habeas corpus application within the time period established by this section.

§ 2264.   Scope of Federal review; district court adjudications

(a)   Whenever a State prisoner under capital sentence files a petition for habeas corpus relief to which this chapter applies, the district court shall only consider a claim or claims that have been raised and decided on the merits in the State courts, unless the failure to raise the claim properly is—

(1)   the result of State action in violation of the Constitution or laws of the United States;

(2)   the result of the Supreme Court's recognition of a new Federal right that is made retroactively applicable; or

(3)   based on a factual predicate that could not have been discovered through the exercise of due diligence in time to present the claim for State or Federal post-conviction review.

(b)   Following review subject to subsections (a), (d), and (e) of section 2254, the court shall rule on the claims properly before it.

§ 2265.   Certification and judicial review

(a)   Certification.—

(1)   In general.—If requested by an appropriate State official, the Attorney General of the United States shall determine—

(A)   whether the State has established a mechanism for the appointment, compensation, and payment of reasonable litigation expenses of competent counsel in

State postconviction proceedings brought by indigent prisoners who have been sentenced to death;

(B) the date on which the mechanism described in subparagraph (A) was established; and

(C) whether the State provides standards of competency for the appointment of counsel in proceedings described in subparagraph (A).

(2) Effective date.—The date the mechanism described in paragraph (1)(A) was established shall be the effective date of the certification under this subsection.

(3) Only express requirements.—There are no requirements for certification or for application of this chapter other than those expressly stated in this chapter.

(b) Regulations.—The Attorney General shall promulgate regulations to implement the certification procedure under subsection (a).

(c) Review of certification.—

(1) In general.—The determination by the Attorney General regarding whether to certify a State under this section is subject to review exclusively as provided under chapter 158 of this title.

(2) Venue.—The Court of Appeals for the District of Columbia Circuit shall have exclusive jurisdiction over matters under paragraph (1), subject to review by the Supreme Court under section 2350 of this title.

(3) Standard of review.—The determination by the Attorney General regarding whether to certify a State under this section shall be subject to de novo review.

§ 2266.   Limitation periods for determining applications and motions

(a) The adjudication of any application under section 2254 that is subject to this chapter, and the adjudication of any motion under section 2255 by a person under sentence of death, shall be given priority by the district court and by the court of appeals over all noncapital matters.

(b)(1)(A) A district court shall render a final determination and enter a final judgment on any application for a writ of habeas corpus brought under this chapter in a capital case not later than 450 days after the date on which the application is filed, or 60 days after the date on which the case is submitted for decision, whichever is earlier.

(B) A district court shall afford the parties at least 120 days in which to complete all actions, including the preparation of all pleadings and briefs, and if necessary, a hearing, prior to the submission of the case for decision.

(C)(i) A district court may delay for not more than one additional 30-day period beyond the period specified in subparagraph (A), the rendering of a determination of an application for a writ of habeas corpus if the court issues a written order making a finding, and stating the reasons for the finding, that the ends of justice that would be served by allowing the delay outweigh the best interests of the public and the applicant in a speedy disposition of the application.

(ii) The factors, among others, that a court shall consider in determining whether a delay in the disposition of an application is warranted are as follows:

(I) Whether the failure to allow the delay would be likely to result in a miscarriage of justice.

(II) Whether the case is so unusual or so complex, due to the number of defendants, the nature of the prosecution, or the existence of novel questions of fact or law, that it is unreasonable to expect adequate briefing within the time limitations established by subparagraph (A).

(III) Whether the failure to allow a delay in a case that, taken as a whole, is not so unusual or so complex as described in subclause (II), but would otherwise deny the applicant reasonable time to obtain counsel, would unreasonably deny the applicant or the government continuity of counsel, or would deny counsel for the applicant or the government the reasonable time necessary for effective preparation, taking into account the exercise of due diligence.

(iii) No delay in disposition shall be permissible because of general congestion of the court's calendar.

(iv) The court shall transmit a copy of any order issued under clause (i) to the Director of the Administrative Office of the United States Courts for inclusion in the report under paragraph (5).

(2) The time limitations under paragraph (1) shall apply to—

(A) an initial application for a writ of habeas corpus;

(B) any second or successive application for a writ of habeas corpus; and

(C) any redetermination of an application for a writ of habeas corpus following a remand by the court of appeals or the Supreme Court for further proceedings, in which case the limitation period shall run from the date the remand is ordered.

(3)(A) The time limitations under this section shall not be construed to entitle an applicant to a stay of execution, to which the applicant would otherwise not be entitled, for the purpose of litigating any application or appeal.

(B) No amendment to an application for a writ of habeas corpus under this chapter shall be permitted after the filing of the answer to the application, except on the grounds specified in section 2244(b).

(4)(A) The failure of a court to meet or comply with a time limitation under this section shall not be a ground for granting relief from a judgment of conviction or sentence.

(B) The State may enforce a time limitation under this section by petitioning for a writ of mandamus to the court of appeals. The court of appeals shall act on the petition for a writ of mandamus not later than 30 days after the filing of the petition.

(5)(A) The Administrative Office of the United States Courts shall submit to Congress an annual report on the compliance by the district courts with the time limitations under this section.*

(B) The report described in subparagraph (A) shall include copies of the orders submitted by the district courts under paragraph (1)(B)(iv).

(c)(1)(A) A court of appeals shall hear and render a final determination of any appeal of an order granting or denying, in whole or in part, an application brought under this chapter in a capital case not later than 120 days after the date on which the reply brief is filed, or if no reply brief is filed, not later than 120 days after the date on which the answering brief is filed.

(B)(i) A court of appeals shall decide whether to grant a petition for rehearing or other request for rehearing en banc not later than 30 days after the date on which the petition for rehearing is filed unless a responsive pleading is required, in which case the court shall decide whether to grant the petition not later than 30 days after the date on which the responsive pleading is filed.

---

* The enacting legislation states that new sections 2261–2266 "shall apply to cases pending on or after the date of enactment of this Act."

(ii) If a petition for rehearing or rehearing en banc is granted, the court of appeals shall hear and render a final determination of the appeal not later than 120 days after the date on which the order granting rehearing or rehearing en banc is entered.

(2) The time limitations under paragraph (1) shall apply to—

(A) an initial application for a writ of habeas corpus;

(B) any second or successive application for a writ of habeas corpus; and

(C) any redetermination of an application for a writ of habeas corpus or related appeal following a remand by the court of appeals en banc or the Supreme Court for further proceedings, in which case the limitation period shall run from the date the remand is ordered.

(3) The time limitations under this section shall not be construed to entitle an applicant to a stay of execution, to which the applicant would otherwise not be entitled, for the purpose of litigating any application or appeal.

(4)(A) The failure of a court to meet or comply with a time limitation under this section shall not be a ground for granting relief from a judgment of conviction or sentence.

(B) The State may enforce a time limitation under this section by applying for a writ of mandamus to the Supreme Court.

(5) The Administrative Office of the United States Courts shall submit to Congress an annual report on the compliance by the courts of appeals with the time limitations under this section.*

PRIVACY PROTECTION ACT OF 1980

(42 U.S.C. §§ 2000aa–2000aa–12); Guidelines (28 C.F.R. § 59.4).

§ 2000aa.   Searches and seizures by government officers and employees in connection with investigation or prosecution of criminal offenses

(a) Work product materials

Notwithstanding any other law, it shall be unlawful for a government officer or employee, in connection with the investigation or prosecution of a criminal offense, to search for or seize any work product materials possessed by a person reasonably believed to have a purpose to disseminate to the public a newspaper, book, broadcast, or other similar form of public communication, in or affecting interstate or foreign commerce; but this provision shall not impair or affect the ability of any government officer or employee, pursuant to otherwise applicable law, to search for or seize such materials, if—

(1) there is probable cause to believe that the person possessing such materials has committed or is committing the criminal offense to which the materials relate: *Provided, however,* That a government officer or employee may not search for or seize such materials under the provisions of this paragraph if the offense to which the materials relate consists of the receipt, possession, communication, or withholding of such materials or the information contained therein (but such a search or seizure may be conducted under the provisions of this paragraph if the offense consists of the receipt, possession, or communication of information relating to the national defense, classified information, or restricted data under the provisions of section 793, 794, 797, or 798 of Title 18, or section 2274, 2275 or 2277 of this

---

* The enacting legislation states that the new §§ 2216–2266 "shall apply to cases pending on or after the date of enactment of this Act."

title, or section 783 of Title 50, or if the offense involves the production, possession, receipt, mailing, sale, distribution, shipment, or transportation of child pornography, the sexual exploitation of children, or the sale or purchase of children under section 2251, 2251A, 2252, or 2252A of Title 18); or

(2)   there is reason to believe that the immediate seizure of such materials is necessary to prevent the death of, or serious bodily injury to, a human being.

(b)   Other documents

Notwithstanding any other law, it shall be unlawful for a government officer or employee, in connection with the investigation or prosecution of a criminal offense, to search for or seize documentary materials, other than work product materials, possessed by a person in connection with a purpose to disseminate to the public a newspaper, book, broadcast, or other similar form of public communication, in or affecting interstate or foreign commerce; but this provision shall not impair or affect the ability of any government officer or employee, pursuant to otherwise applicable law, to search for or seize such materials, if—

(1)   there is probable cause to believe that the person possessing such materials has committed or is committing the criminal offense to which the materials relate: *Provided, however,* That a government officer or employee may not search for or seize such materials under the provisions of this paragraph if the offense to which the materials relate consists of the receipt, possession, communication, or withholding of such materials or the information contained therein (but such a search or seizure may be conducted under the provisions of this paragraph if the offense consists of the receipt, possession, or communication of information relating to the national defense, classified information, or restricted data under the provisions of section 793, 794, 797, or 798 of Title 18, or section 2274, 2275, or 2277 of this title, or section 783 of Title 50, or if the offense involves the production, possession, receipt, mailing, sale, distribution, shipment, or transportation of child pornography, the sexual exploitation of children, or the sale or purchase of children under section 2251, 2251A, 2252, or 2252A of Title 18);

(2)   there is reason to believe that the immediate seizure of such materials is necessary to prevent the death of, or serious bodily injury to, a human being;

(3)   there is reason to believe that the giving of notice pursuant to a subpena duces tecum would result in the destruction, alteration, or concealment of such materials; or

(4)   such materials have not been produced in response to a court order directing compliance with a subpena duces tecum, and—

(A)   all appellate remedies have been exhausted; or

(B)   there is reason to believe that the delay in an investigation or trial occasioned by further proceedings relating to the subpena would threaten the interests of justice.

(c)   Objections to court ordered subpoenas; affidavits

In the event a search warrant is sought pursuant to paragraph (4)(B) of subsection (b) of this section, the person possessing the materials shall be afforded adequate opportunity to submit an affidavit setting forth the basis for any contention that the materials sought are not subject to seizure.

§ 2000aa–5.   Border and customs searches

This chapter shall not impair or affect the ability of a government officer or employee, pursuant to otherwise applicable law, to conduct searches and seizures at the borders of, or at international points of, entry into the United States in order to enforce the customs laws of the United States.

§ 2000aa–6.   Civil actions by aggrieved persons

(a)   Right of action

A person aggrieved by a search for or seizure of materials in violation of this chapter shall have a civil cause of action for damages for such search or seizure—

(1)   against the United States, against a State which has waived its sovereign immunity under the Constitution to a claim for damages resulting from a violation of this chapter, or against any other governmental unit, all of which shall be liable for violations of this chapter by their officers or employees while acting within the scope or under color of their office or employment; and

(2)   against an officer or employee of a State who has violated this chapter while acting within the scope or under color of his office or employment, if such State has not waived its sovereign immunity as provided in paragraph (1).

(b)   Good faith defense

It shall be a complete defense to a civil action brought under paragraph (2) of subsection (a) of this section that the officer or employee had a reasonable good faith belief in the lawfulness of his conduct.

(c)   Official immunity

The United States, a State, or any other governmental unit liable for violations of this chapter under subsection (a)(1) of this section, may not assert as a defense to a claim arising under this chapter the immunity of the officer or employee whose violation is complained of or his reasonable good faith belief in the lawfulness of his conduct, except that such a defense may be asserted if the violation complained of is that of a judicial officer.

(d)   Exclusive nature of remedy

The remedy provided by subsection (a)(1) of this section against the United States, a State, or any other governmental unit is exclusive of any other civil action or proceeding for conduct constituting a violation of this chapter, against the officer or employee whose violation gave rise to the claim, or against the estate of such officer or employee.

(e)   Admissibility of evidence

Evidence otherwise admissible in a proceeding shall not be excluded on the basis of a violation of this chapter.

(f)   Damages; costs and attorneys' fees

A person having a cause of action under this section shall be entitled to recover actual damages but not less than liquidated damages of $1,000, and such reasonable attorneys' fees and other litigation costs reasonably incurred as the court, in its discretion, may award: *Provided, however,* That the United States, a State, or any other governmental unit shall not be liable for interest prior to judgment.

(g)   Attorney General; claims settlement; regulations

The Attorney General may settle a claim for damages brought against the United States under this section, and shall promulgate regulations to provide for the commencement of an administrative inquiry following a determination of a violation of this chapter by an officer or employee of the United States and for the imposition of administrative sanctions against such officer or employee, if warranted.

(h)   Jurisdiction

The district courts shall have original jurisdiction of all civil actions arising under this section.

§ 2000aa–7.   Definitions

(a)   "Documentary materials", as used in this chapter, means materials upon which information is recorded, and includes, but is not limited to, written or printed materials, photographs, motion picture films, negatives, video tapes, audio tapes, and other mechanically, magentically[1] or electronically recorded cards, tapes, or discs, but does not include contraband or the fruits of a crime or things otherwise criminally possessed, or property designed or intended for use, or which is or has been used as, the means of committing a criminal offense.

(b)   "Work product materials", as used in this chapter, means materials, other than contraband or the fruits of a crime or things otherwise criminally possessed, or property designed or intended for use, or which is or has been used, as the means of committing a criminal offense, and—

(1)   in anticipation of communicating such materials to the public, are prepared, produced, authored, or created, whether by the person in possession of the materials or by any other person;

(2)   are possessed for the purposes of communicating such materials to the public; and

(3)   include mental impressions, conclusions, opinions, or theories of the person who prepared, produced, authored, or created such material.

(c)   "Any other governmental unit", as used in this chapter, includes the District of Columbia, the Commonwealth of Puerto Rico, any territory or possession of the United States, and any local government, unit of local government, or any unit of State government.

§ 2000aa–11.   Guidelines for Federal officers and employees

(a)   Procedures to obtain documentary evidence; protection of certain privacy interests

The Attorney General shall, within six months of October 13, 1980, issue guidelines for the procedures to be employed by any Federal officer or employee, in connection with the investigation or prosecution of an offense, to obtain documentary materials in the private possession of a person when the person is not reasonably believed to be a suspect in such offense or related by blood or marriage to such a suspect, and when the materials sought are not contraband or the fruits or instrumentalities of an offense. The Attorney General shall incorporate in such guidelines—

(1)   a recognition of the personal privacy interests of the person in possession of such documentary materials;

(2)   a requirement that the least intrusive method or means of obtaining such materials be used which do not substantially jeopardize the availability or usefulness of the materials sought to be obtained;

(3)   a recognition of special concern for privacy interests in cases in which a search or seizure for such documents would intrude upon a known confidential relationship such as that which may exist between clergyman and parishioner; lawyer and client; or doctor and patient; and

(4)   a requirement that an application for a warrant to conduct a search governed by this subchapter be approved by an attorney for the government, except that in an emergency

---

[1]   So in original. Probably should be "magnetically".

situation the application may be approved by another appropriate supervisory official if within 24 hours of such emergency the appropriate United States Attorney is notified.

(b)   Use of search warrants; reports to Congress

The Attorney General shall collect and compile information on, and report annually to the Committees on the Judiciary of the Senate and the House of Representatives on the use of search warrants by Federal officers and employees for documentary materials described in subsection (a)(3) of this section.

§ 2000aa–12. Binding nature of guidelines; disciplinary actions for violations; legal proceedings for non-compliance prohibited

Guidelines issued by the Attorney General under this subchapter shall have the full force and effect of Department of Justice regulations and any violation of these guidelines shall make the employee or officer involved subject to appropriate administrative disciplinary action. However, an issue relating to the compliance, or the failure to comply, with guidelines issued pursuant to this subchapter may not be litigated, and a court may not entertain such an issue as the basis for the suppression or exclusion of evidence.

[Editor's Note: These guidelines appear in 28 C.F.R. Pt. 59. The procedural provisions are set out below.]

GUIDELINES

(28 C.F.R. § 59.4).

§ 59.4   Procedures.[1]

(a)   Provisions governing the use of search warrants generally.

(1)   A search warrant should not be used to obtain documentary materials believed to be in the private possession of a disinterested third party unless it appears that the use of a subpoena, summons, request, or other less intrusive alternative means of obtaining the materials would substantially jeopardize the availability or usefulness of the materials sought, and the application for the warrant has been authorized as provided in paragraph (a)(2) of this section.

(2)   No federal officer or employee shall apply for a warrant to search for and seize documentary materials believed to be in the private possession of a disinterested third party unless the application for the warrant has been authorized by an attorney for the government. Provided, however, that in an emergency situation in which the immediacy of the need to seize the materials does not permit an opportunity to secure the authorization of an attorney for the government, the application may be authorized by a supervisory law enforcement officer in the applicant's department or agency, if the appropriate U.S. Attorney (or where the case is not being handled by a U.S. Attorney's Office, the appropriate supervisory official of the Department of Justice) is notified of the authorization and the basis for justifying such authorization under this part within 24 hours of the authorization.

(b)   Provisions governing the use of search warrants which may intrude upon professional, confidential relationships.

---

[1]   Notwithstanding the provisions of this section, any application for a warrant to search for evidence of a criminal tax offense under the jurisdiction of the Tax Division must be specifically approved in advance by the Tax Division pursuant to section 6–2.330 of the U.S. Attorneys' Manual.

(1)   A search warrant should not be used to obtain documentary materials believed to be in the private possession of a disinterested third party physician,[2] lawyer, or clergyman, under circumstances in which the materials sought, or other materials likely to be reviewed during the execution of the warrant, contain confidential information on patients, clients, or parishioners which was furnished or developed for the purposes of professional counseling or treatment, unless—

(i)   It appears that the use of a subpoena, summons, request or other less intrusive alternative means of obtaining the materials would substantially jeopardize the availability or usefulness of the materials sought;

(ii)   Access to the documentary materials appears to be of substantial importance to the investigation or prosecution for which they are sought; and

(iii)   The application for the warrant has been approved as provided in paragraph (b)(2) of this section.

(2)   No federal officer or employee shall apply for a warrant to search for and seize documentary materials believed to be in the private possession of a disinterested third party physician, lawyer, or clergyman under the circumstances described in paragraph (b)(1) of this section, unless, upon the recommendation of the U.S. Attorney (or where a case is not being handled by a U.S. Attorney's Office, upon the recommendation of the appropriate supervisory official of the Department of Justice), an appropriate Deputy Assistant Attorney General has authorized the application for the warrant. Provided, however, that in an emergency situation in which the immediacy of the need to seize the materials does not permit an opportunity to secure the authorization of a Deputy Assistant Attorney General, the application may be authorized by the U.S. Attorney (or where the case is not being handled by a U.S. Attorney's Office, by the appropriate supervisory official of the Department of Justice) if an appropriate Deputy Assistant Attorney General is notified of the authorization and the basis for justifying such authorization under this part within 72 hours of the authorization.

(3)   Whenever possible, a request for authorization by an appropriate Deputy Assistant Attorney General of a search warrant application pursuant to paragraph (b)(2) of this section shall be made in writing and shall include:

(i)   The application for the warrant; and

(ii)   A brief description of the facts and circumstances advanced as the basis for recommending authorization of the application under this part.

If a request for authorization of the application is made orally or if, in an emergency situation, the application is authorized by the U.S. Attorney or a supervisory official of the Department of Justice as provided in paragraph (b)(2) of this section, a written record of the request including the materials specified in paragraphs (b)(3)(i) and (ii) of this section shall be transmitted to an appropriate Deputy Assistant Attorney General within 7 days. The Deputy Assistant Attorneys General shall keep a record of the disposition of all requests for authorizations of search warrant applications made under paragraph (b) of this section.

(4)   A search warrant authorized under paragraph (b)(2) of this section shall be executed in such a manner as to minimize, to the greatest extent practicable, scrutiny of confidential materials.

---

[2]   Documentary materials created or compiled by a physician, but retained by the physician as a matter of practice at a hospital or clinic shall be deemed to be in the private possession of the physician, unless the clinic or hospital is a suspect in the offense.

(5)   Although it is impossible to define the full range of additional doctor-like therapeutic relationships which involve the furnishing or development of private information, the U.S. Attorney (or where a case is not being handled by a U.S. Attorney's Office, the appropriate supervisory official of the Department of Justice) should determine whether a search for documentary materials held by other disinterested third party professionals involved in such relationships (e.g. psychologists or psychiatric social workers or nurses) would implicate the special privacy concerns which are addressed in paragraph (b) of this section. If the U.S. Attorney (or other supervisory official of the Department of Justice) determines that such a search would require review of extremely confidential information furnished or developed for the purposes of professional counseling or treatment, the provisions of this subsection should be applied. Otherwise, at a minimum, the requirements of paragraph (a) of this section must be met.

(c)   Considerations bearing on choice of methods. In determining whether, as an alternative to the use of a search warrant, the use of a subpoena or other less intrusive means of obtaining documentary materials would substantially jeopardize the availability or usefulness of the materials sought, the following factors, among others, should be considered:

(1)   Whether it appears that the use of a subpoena or other alternative which gives advance notice of the government's interest in obtaining the materials would be likely to result in the destruction, alteration, concealment, or transfer of the materials sought; considerations, among others, bearing on this issue may include:

(i)   Whether a suspect has access to the materials sought;

(ii)   Whether there is a close relationship of friendship, loyalty, or sympathy between the possessor of the materials and a suspect;

(iii)   Whether the possessor of the materials is under the domination or control of a suspect;

(iv)   Whether the possessor of the materials has an interest in preventing the disclosure of the materials to the government;

(v)   Whether the possessor's willingness to comply with a subpoena or request by the government would be likely to subject him to intimidation or threats of reprisal;

(vi)   Whether the possessor of the materials has previously acted to obstruct a criminal investigation or judicial proceeding or refused to comply with or acted in defiance of court orders; or

(vii)   Whether the possessor has expressed an intent to destroy, conceal, alter, or transfer the materials;

(2)   The immediacy of the government's need to obtain the materials; considerations, among others, bearing on this issue may include:

(i)   Whether the immediate seizure of the materials is necessary to prevent injury to persons or property;

(ii)   Whether the prompt seizure of the materials is necessary to preserve their evidentiary value;

(iii)   Whether delay in obtaining the materials would significantly jeopardize an ongoing investigation or prosecution; or

(iv)   Whether a legally enforceable form of process, other than a search warrant, is reasonably available as a means of obtaining the materials.

The fact that the disinterested third party possessing the materials may have grounds to challenge a subpoena or other legal process is not in itself a legitimate basis for the use of a search warrant.

FOREIGN INTELLIGENCE SURVEILLANCE ACT

(50 U.S.C. § 1861).

§ 1861.   Access to certain business records for foreign intelligence and international terrorism investigations

(a)   Application for order; conduct of investigation generally

(1)   Subject to paragraph (3), the Director of the Federal Bureau of Investigation or a designee of the Director (whose rank shall be no lower than Assistant Special Agent in Charge) may make an application for an order requiring the production of any tangible things (including books, records, papers, documents, and other items) for an investigation to obtain foreign intelligence information not concerning a United States person or to protect against international terrorism or clandestine intelligence activities, provided that such investigation of a United States person is not conducted solely upon the basis of activities protected by the first amendment to the Constitution.

(2)   An investigation conducted under this section shall

(A)   be conducted under guidelines approved by the Attorney General under Executive Order 12333 (or a successor order); and

(B)   not be conducted of a United States person solely upon the basis of activities protected by the first amendment to the Constitution of the United States.

(3)   In the case of an application for an order requiring the production of library circulation records, library patron lists, book sales records, book customer lists, firearms sales records, tax return records, educational records, or medical records containing information that would identify a person, the Director of the Federal Bureau of Investigation may delegate the authority to make such application to either the Deputy Director of the Federal Bureau of Investigation or the Executive Assistant Director for National Security (or any successor position). The Deputy Director or the Executive Assistant Director may not further delegate such authority.

(b)   Recipient and contents of application

Each application under this section

(1)   shall be made to—

(A)   a judge of the court established by section 1803(a) of this title; or

(B)   a United States Magistrate Judge under chapter 43 of Title 28, who is publicly designated by the Chief Justice of the United States to have the power to hear applications and grant orders for the production of tangible things under this section on behalf of a judge of that court; and

(2)   shall include—

(A)   a specific selection term to be used as the basis for the production of the tangible things sought;

(B)   in the case of an application other than an application described in subparagraph (C) (including an application for the production of call detail records other than in the manner described in subparagraph (C)), a statement of facts showing that there are reasonable grounds to believe that the tangible things sought are relevant to an authorized investigation (other than a threat assessment) conducted in accordance with subsection (a)(2) to obtain foreign intelligence information not concerning a United States person or to protect against international terrorism or clandestine intelligence activities, such things being presumptively relevant to an authorized investigation if the applicant shows in the statement of the facts that they pertain to—

      (i)   a foreign power or an agent of a foreign power;

      (ii)   the activities of a suspected agent of a foreign power who is the subject of such authorized investigation; or

      (iii)   an individual in contact with, or known to, a suspected agent of a foreign power who is the subject of such authorized investigation;

      (C)   in the case of an application for the production on an ongoing basis of call detail records created before, on, or after the date of the application relating to an authorized investigation (other than a threat assessment) conducted in accordance with subsection (a)(2) to protect against international terrorism, a statement of facts showing that—

      (i)   there are reasonable grounds to believe that the call detail records sought to be produced based on the specific selection term required under subparagraph (A) are relevant to such investigation; and

      (ii)   there is a reasonable, articulable suspicion that such specific selection term is associated with a foreign power engaged in international terrorism or activities in preparation therefor, or an agent of a foreign power engaged in international terrorism or activities in preparation therefor; and

      (D)   an enumeration of the minimization procedures adopted by the Attorney General under subsection (g) that are applicable to the retention and dissemination by the Federal Bureau of Investigation of any tangible things to be made available to the Federal Bureau of Investigation based on the order requested in such application.

(c)   Ex parte judicial order of approval

(1)   Upon an application made pursuant to this section, if the judge finds that the application meets the requirements of subsections (a) and (b) and that the minimization procedures submitted in accordance with subsection (b)(2)(D) meet the definition of minimization procedures under subsection (g), the judge shall enter an ex parte order as requested, or as modified, approving the release of tangible things. Such order shall direct that minimization procedures adopted pursuant to subsection (g) be followed.

(2)   An order under this subsection—

      (A)   shall describe the tangible things that are ordered to be produced with sufficient particularity to permit them to be fairly identified, including each specific selection term to be used as the basis for the production;

      (B)   shall include the date on which the tangible things must be provided, which shall allow a reasonable period of time within which the tangible things can be assembled and made available;

      (C)   shall provide clear and conspicuous notice of the principles and procedures described in subsection (d);

      (D)   may only require the production of a tangible thing if such thing can be obtained with a subpoena duces tecum issued by a court of the United States in aid of a grand jury investigation or with any other order issued by a court of the United States directing the production of records or tangible things;

      (E)   shall not disclose that such order is issued for purposes of an investigation described in subsection (a); and

(F)   in the case of an application described in subsection (b)(2)(C), shall—

(i)   authorize the production on a daily basis of call detail records for a period not to exceed 180 days;

(ii)   provide that an order for such production may be extended upon application under subsection (b) and the judicial finding under paragraph (1) of this subsection;

(iii)   provide that the Government may require the prompt production of a first set of call detail records using the specific selection term that satisfies the standard required under subsection (b)(2)(C)(ii);

(iv)   provide that the Government may require the prompt production of a second set of call detail records using session-identifying information or a telephone calling card number identified by the specific selection term used to produce call detail records under clause (iii);

(v)   provide that, when produced, such records be in a form that will be useful to the Government;

(vi)   direct each person the Government directs to produce call detail records under the order to furnish the Government forthwith all information, facilities, or technical assistance necessary to accomplish the production in such a manner as will protect the secrecy of the production and produce a minimum of interference with the services that such person is providing to each subject of the production; and

(vii)   direct the Government to—

(I)   adopt minimization procedures that require the prompt destruction of all call detail records produced under the order that the Government determines are not foreign intelligence information; and

(II)   destroy all call detail records produced under the order as prescribed by such procedures.

(3)   No order issued under this subsection may authorize the collection of tangible things without the use of a specific selection term that meets the requirements of subsection (b)(2).

(4)   A denial of the application made under this subsection may be reviewed as provided in section 103.

(d)   Nondisclosure

(1)   No person shall disclose to any other person that the Federal Bureau of Investigation has sought or obtained tangible things pursuant to an order issued or an emergency production required under this section, other than to

(A)   those persons to whom disclosure is necessary to comply with such order or such emergency production;

(B)   an attorney to obtain legal advice or assistance with respect to the production of things in response to the order or the emergency production; or

(C)   other persons as permitted by the Director of the Federal Bureau of Investigation or the designee of the Director.

(2)(A) A person to whom disclosure is made pursuant to paragraph (1) shall be subject to the nondisclosure requirements applicable to a person to whom an order or emergency production is directed under this section in the same manner as such person.

(B) Any person who discloses to a person described in subparagraph (A), (B), or (C) of paragraph (1) that the Federal Bureau of Investigation has sought or obtained tangible things pursuant to an order or emergency production under this section shall notify such person of the nondisclosure requirements of this subsection.

(C) At the request of the Director of the Federal Bureau of Investigation or the designee of the Director, any person making or intending to make a disclosure under subparagraph (A) or (C) of paragraph (1) shall identify to the Director or such designee the person to whom such disclosure will be made or to whom such disclosure was made prior to the request.

(e) Liability for good faith disclosure; waiver

(1) No cause of action shall lie in any court against a person who—

(A) produces tangible things or provides information, facilities, or technical assistance in accordance with an order issued or an emergency production required under this section; or

(B) otherwise provides technical assistance to the Government under this section or to implement the amendments made to this section by the USA FREEDOM Act of 2015.

(2) A production or provision of information, facilities, or technical assistance described in paragraph (1) shall not be deemed to constitute a waiver of any privilege in any other proceeding or context.

(f) Judicial review of FISA orders

(1) In this subsection—

(A) the term "production order" means an order to produce any tangible thing under this section; and

(B) the term "nondisclosure order" means an order imposed under subsection (d).

(2)(A)(i) A person receiving a production order may challenge the legality of the production order or any nondisclosure order imposed in connection with the production order by filing a petition with the pool established by section 1803(e)(1) of this title.

(ii) The presiding judge shall immediately assign a petition under clause (i) to 1 of the judges serving in the pool established by section 1803(e)(1) of this title. Not later than 72 hours after the assignment of such petition, the assigned judge shall conduct an initial review of the petition. If the assigned judge determines that the petition is frivolous, the assigned judge shall immediately deny the petition and affirm the production order or nondisclosure order. If the assigned judge determines the petition is not frivolous, the assigned judge shall promptly consider the petition in accordance with the procedures established under section 1803(e)(2) of this title.

(iii) The assigned judge shall promptly provide a written statement for the record of the reasons for any determination under this subsection. Upon the request of the Government, any order setting aside a nondisclosure order shall be stayed pending review pursuant to paragraph (3).

(B) A judge considering a petition to modify or set aside a production order may grant such petition only if the judge finds that such order does not meet the requirements of this section or is otherwise unlawful. If the judge does not modify or set aside the production order, the judge shall immediately affirm such order, and order the recipient to comply therewith.

(C)(i) A judge considering a petition to modify or set aside a nondisclosure order may grant such petition only if the judge finds that there is no reason to believe that disclosure may endanger the national security of the United States, interfere with a criminal, counterterrorism, or counterintelligence investigation, interfere with diplomatic relations, or endanger the life or physical safety of any person.

(ii) If the judge denies a petition to modify or set aside a nondisclosure order, the recipient of such order shall be precluded for a period of 1 year from filing another such petition with respect to such nondisclosure order.

(iii) Redesignated (ii)

(D) Any production or nondisclosure order not explicitly modified or set aside consistent with this subsection shall remain in full effect.

(3) A petition for review of a decision under paragraph (2) to affirm, modify, or set aside an order by the Government or any person receiving such order shall be made to the court of review established under section 1803(b) of this title, which shall have jurisdiction to consider such petitions. The court of review shall provide for the record a written statement of the reasons for its decision and, on petition by the Government or any person receiving such order for writ of certiorari, the record shall be transmitted under seal to the Supreme Court of the United States, which shall have jurisdiction to review such decision.

(4) Judicial proceedings under this subsection shall be concluded as expeditiously as possible. The record of proceedings, including petitions filed, orders granted, and statements of reasons for decision, shall be maintained under security measures established by the Chief Justice of the United States, in consultation with the Attorney General and the Director of National Intelligence.

(5) All petitions under this subsection shall be filed under seal. In any proceedings under this subsection, the court shall, upon request of the Government, review ex parte and in camera any Government submission, or portions thereof, which may include classified information.

(g) Minimization procedures

(1) In general

The Attorney General shall adopt, and update as appropriate, specific minimization procedures governing the retention and dissemination by the Federal Bureau of Investigation of any tangible things, or information therein, received by the Federal Bureau of Investigation in response to an order under this subchapter.

(2) Defined

In this section, the term "minimization procedures" means—

(A) specific procedures that are reasonably designed in light of the purpose and technique of an order for the production of tangible things, to minimize the retention, and prohibit the dissemination, of nonpublicly available information concerning unconsenting United States persons consistent with the need of the United States to obtain, produce, and disseminate foreign intelligence information;

(B) procedures that require that nonpublicly available information, which is not foreign intelligence information, as defined in section 1801(e)(1) of this title, shall not be disseminated in a manner that identifies any United States person, without such person's consent, unless such person's identity is necessary to understand foreign intelligence information or assess its importance; and

(C) notwithstanding subparagraphs (A) and (B), procedures that allow for the retention and dissemination of information that is evidence of a crime which has been, is being, or is about to be committed and that is to be retained or disseminated for law enforcement purposes.

(3) Rule of construction

Nothing in this subsection shall limit the authority of the court established under section 1803(a) of this title to impose additional, particularized minimization procedures with regard to the production, retention, or dissemination of nonpublicly available information concerning unconsenting United States persons, including additional, particularized procedures related to the destruction of information within a reasonable time period.

(h) Use of information

Information acquired from tangible things received by the Federal Bureau of Investigation in response to an order under this subchapter concerning any United States person may be used and disclosed by Federal officers and employees without the consent of the United States person only in accordance with the minimization procedures adopted pursuant to subsection (g). No otherwise privileged information acquired from tangible things received by the Federal Bureau of Investigation in accordance with the provisions of this subchapter shall lose its privileged character. No information acquired from tangible things received by the Federal Bureau of Investigation in response to an order under this subchapter may be used or disclosed by Federal officers or employees except for lawful purposes.

(i) Emergency authority for production of tangible things

(1) Notwithstanding any other provision of this section, the Attorney General may require the emergency production of tangible things if the Attorney General—

(A) reasonably determines that an emergency situation requires the production of tangible things before an order authorizing such production can with due diligence be obtained;

(B) reasonably determines that the factual basis for the issuance of an order under this section to approve such production of tangible things exists;

(C) informs, either personally or through a designee, a judge having jurisdiction under this section at the time the Attorney General requires the emergency production of tangible things that the decision has been made to employ the authority under this subsection; and

(D) makes an application in accordance with this section to a judge having jurisdiction under this section as soon as practicable, but not later than 7 days after the Attorney General requires the emergency production of tangible things under this subsection.

(2) If the Attorney General requires the emergency production of tangible things under paragraph (1), the Attorney General shall require that the minimization procedures required by this section for the issuance of a judicial order be followed.

(3)   In the absence of a judicial order approving the production of tangible things under this subsection, the production shall terminate when the information sought is obtained, when the application for the order is denied, or after the expiration of 7 days from the time the Attorney General begins requiring the emergency production of such tangible things, whichever is earliest.

(4)   A denial of the application made under this subsection may be reviewed as provided in section 1803 of this title.

(5)   If such application for approval is denied, or in any other case where the production of tangible things is terminated and no order is issued approving the production, no information obtained or evidence derived from such production shall be received in evidence or otherwise disclosed in any trial, hearing, or other proceeding in or before any court, grand jury, department, office, agency, regulatory body, legislative committee, or other authority of the United States, a State, or a political subdivision thereof, and no information concerning any United States person acquired from such production shall subsequently be used or disclosed in any other manner by Federal officers or employees without the consent of such person, except with the approval of the Attorney General if the information indicates a threat of death or serious bodily harm to any person.

(6)   The Attorney General shall assess compliance with the requirements of paragraph (5).

(j)   Compensation

The Government shall compensate a person for reasonable expenses incurred for—

(1)   producing tangible things or providing information, facilities, or assistance in accordance with an order issued with respect to an application described in subsection (b)(2)(C) or an emergency production under subsection (i) that, to comply with subsection (i)(1)(D), requires an application described in subsection (b)(2)(C); or

(2)   otherwise providing technical assistance to the Government under this section or to implement the amendments made to this section by the USA FREEDOM Act of 2015.

(k)   Definitions

In this section:

(1)   In general

The terms "foreign power", "agent of a foreign power", "international terrorism", "foreign intelligence information", "Attorney General", "United States person", "United States", "person", and "State" have the meanings provided those terms in section 1801 of this title.

(2)   Address

The term "address" means a physical address or electronic address, such as an electronic mail address or temporarily assigned network address (including an Internet protocol address).

(3)   Call detail record

The term "call detail record"—

(A)   means session-identifying information (including an originating or terminating telephone number, an International Mobile Subscriber Identity number, or an International Mobile Station Equipment Identity number), a telephone calling card number, or the time or duration of a call; and

(B)   does not include—

(i)   the contents (as defined in section 2510(8) of Title 18) of any communication;

(ii)   the name, address, or financial information of a subscriber or customer; or

(iii)   cell site location or global positioning system information.

(4)   Specific selection term

(A)   Tangible things

(i)   In general

Except as provided in subparagraph (B), a "specific selection term"—

(I)   is a term that specifically identifies a person, account, address, or personal device, or any other specific identifier; and

(II)   is used to limit, to the greatest extent reasonably practicable, the scope of tangible things sought consistent with the purpose for seeking the tangible things.

(ii)   Limitation

A specific selection term under clause (i) does not include an identifier that does not limit, to the greatest extent reasonably practicable, the scope of tangible things sought consistent with the purpose for seeking the tangible things, such as an identifier that—

(I)   identifies an electronic communication service provider (as that term is defined in section 1881 of this title) or a provider of remote computing service (as that term is defined in section 2711 of Title 18), when not used as part of a specific identifier as described in clause (i), unless the provider is itself a subject of an authorized investigation for which the specific selection term is used as the basis for the production; or

(II)   identifies a broad geographic region, including the United States, a city, a county, a State, a zip code, or an area code, when not used as part of a specific identifier as described in clause (i).

(iii)   Rule of construction

Nothing in this paragraph shall be construed to preclude the use of multiple terms or identifiers to meet the requirements of clause (i).

(B)   Call detail record applications

For purposes of an application submitted under subsection (b)(2)(C), the term "specific selection term" means a term that specifically identifies an individual, account, or personal device.

Appendix C

Federal Rules of Criminal Procedure for the United States District Courts

■ ■ ■

TITLE I. APPLICABILITY
Rule 1. Scope; Definitions
Rule 2. Interpretation
TITLE II. PRELIMINARY PROCEEDINGS
Rule 3. The Complaint
Rule 4. Arrest Warrant or Summons on a Complaint
Rule 4.1. Complaint, Warrant, or Summons by Telephone or Other Reliable Electronic Means
Rule 5. Initial Appearance
Rule 5.1. Preliminary Hearing
TITLE III. THE GRAND JURY, THE INDICTMENT, AND THE INFORMATION
Rule 6. The Grand Jury
Rule 7. The Indictment and the Information
Rule 8. Joinder of Offenses or Defendants
Rule 9. Arrest Warrant or Summons on an Indictment or Information
TITLE IV. ARRAIGNMENT AND PREPARATION FOR TRIAL
Rule 10. Arraignment
Rule 11. Pleas
Rule 12. Pleadings and Pretrial Motions
Rule 12.1. Notice of an Alibi Defense
Rule 12.2. Notice of an Insanity Defense; Mental Examination
Rule 12.3. Notice of a Public-Authority Defense
Rule 12.4. Disclosure Statement
Rule 13. Joint Trial of Separate Cases
Rule 14. Relief from Prejudicial Joinder
Rule 15. Depositions
Rule 16. Discovery and Inspection
Rule 16.1. Pretrial Discovery Conference; Request for Court Action
Rule 17. Subpoena
Rule 17.1. Pretrial Conference
TITLE V. VENUE
Rule 18. Place of Prosecution and Trial
Rule 19. [Reserved]
Rule 20. Transfer for Plea and Sentence
Rule 21. Transfer for Trial
Rule 22. [Transferred]
TITLE VI. TRIAL
Rule 23. Jury or Nonjury Trial
Rule 24. Trial Jurors
Rule 25. Judge's Disability
Rule 26. Taking Testimony

Rule 26.1. Foreign Law Determination
Rule 26.2. Producing a Witness's Statement
Rule 26.3. Mistrial
Rule 27. Proving an Official Record
Rule 28. Interpreters
Rule 29. Motion for a Judgment of Acquittal
Rule 29.1. Closing Argument
Rule 30. Jury Instructions
Rule 31. Jury Verdict
TITLE VII. POST-CONVICTION PROCEDURES
Rule 32. Sentencing and Judgment
Rule 32.1. Revoking or Modifying Probation or Supervised Release
Rule 32.2. Criminal Forfeiture
Rule 33. New Trial
Rule 34. Arresting Judgment
Rule 35. Correcting or Reducing a Sentence
Rule 36. Clerical Error
Rule 37. Ruling on a Motion for Relief That Is Barred by a Pending Appeal
Rule 38. Staying a Sentence or a Disability
Rule 39. [Reserved]
TITLE VIII. SUPPLEMENTARY AND SPECIAL PROCEEDINGS
Rule 40. Arrest for Failing to Appear in Another District
Rule 41. Search and Seizure
Rule 42. Criminal Contempt
TITLE IX. GENERAL PROVISIONS
Rule 43. Defendant's Presence
Rule 44. Right to and Appointment of Counsel
Rule 45. Computing and Extending Time
Rule 46. Release from Custody; Supervising Detention
Rule 47. Motions and Supporting Affidavits
Rule 48. Dismissal
Rule 49.1. Privacy Protection for Filings Made with the Court
Rule 50. Prompt Disposition
Rule 51. Preserving Claimed Error
Rule 52. Harmless and Plain Error
Rule 53. Courtroom Photographing and Broadcasting Prohibited
Rule 54. [Transferred]
Rule 55. Records
Rule 56. When Court Is Open
Rule 57. District Court Rules
Rule 58. Petty Offenses and Other Misdemeanors
Rule 59. Matters Before a Magistrate Judge
Rule 60. Victim's Rights
Rule 61. Title

I.   SCOPE, PURPOSE AND CONSTRUCTION

Rule 1.   Scope; Definitions

(a) Scope.

(1) In General. These rules govern the procedure in all criminal proceedings in the United States district courts, the United States courts of appeals, and the Supreme Court of the United States.

(2) State or Local Judicial Officer. When a rule so states, it applies to a proceeding before a state or local judicial officer.

(3) Territorial Courts. These rules also govern the procedure in all criminal proceedings in the following courts:

(A) the district court of Guam;

(B) the district court for the Northern Mariana Islands, except as otherwise provided by law; and

(C) the district court of the Virgin Islands, except that the prosecution of offenses in that court must be by indictment or information as otherwise provided by law.

(4) Removed Proceedings. Although these rules govern all proceedings after removal from a state court, state law governs a dismissal by the prosecution.

(5) Excluded Proceedings. Proceedings not governed by these rules include:

(A) the extradition and rendition of a fugitive;

(B) a civil property forfeiture for violating a federal statute;

(C) the collection of a fine or penalty;

(D) a proceeding under a statute governing juvenile delinquency to the extent the procedure is inconsistent with the statute, unless Rule 20(d) provides otherwise;

(E) a dispute between seamen under 22 U.S.C. §§ 256–258; and

(F) a proceeding against a witness in a foreign country under 28 U.S.C. § 1784.

(b) Definitions. The following definitions apply to these rules:

(1) "Attorney for the government" means:

(A) the Attorney General or an authorized assistant;

(B) a United States attorney or an authorized assistant;

(C) when applicable to cases arising under Guam law, the Guam Attorney General or other person whom Guam law authorizes to act in the matter; and

(D) any other attorney authorized by law to conduct proceedings under these rules as a prosecutor.

(2) "Court" means a federal judge performing functions authorized by law.

(3) "Federal judge" means:

(A) a justice or judge of the United States as these terms are defined in 28 U.S.C. § 451;

(B) a magistrate judge; and

(C) a judge confirmed by the United States Senate and empowered by statute in any commonwealth, territory, or possession to perform a function to which a particular rule relates.

(4) "Judge" means a federal judge or a state or local judicial officer.

(5) "Magistrate judge" means a United States magistrate judge as defined in 28 U.S.C. §§ 631–639.

(6) "Oath" includes an affirmation.

(7) "Organization" is defined in 18 U.S.C. § 18.

(8) "Petty offense" is defined in 18 U.S.C. § 19.

(9) "State" includes the District of Columbia, and any commonwealth, territory, or possession of the United States.

(10) "State or local judicial officer" means:

(A) a state or local officer authorized to act under 18 U.S.C. § 3041; and

(B) a judicial officer empowered by statute in the District of Columbia or in any commonwealth, territory, or possession to perform a function to which a particular rule relates.

(11) "Telephone" means any technology for transmitting live electronic voice communication.

(12) "Victim" means a "crime victim" as defined in 18 U.S.C. § 3771(e).

(c) Authority of a Justice or Judge of the United States. When these rules authorize a magistrate judge to act, any other federal judge may also act.

Rule 2. Interpretation

These rules are to be interpreted to provide for the just determination of every criminal proceeding, to secure simplicity in procedure and fairness in administration, and to eliminate unjustifiable expense and delay.

Rule 3. The Complaint

The complaint is a written statement of the essential facts constituting the offense charged. Except as provided in Rule 4.1, it must be made under oath before a magistrate judge or, if none is reasonably available, before a state or local judicial officer.

Rule 4. Arrest Warrant or Summons on a Complaint

(a) Issuance. If the complaint or one or more affidavits filed with the complaint establish probable cause to believe that an offense has been committed and that the defendant committed it, the judge must issue an arrest warrant to an officer authorized to execute it. At the request of an attorney for the government, the judge must issue a summons, instead of a warrant, to a person authorized to serve it. A judge may issue more than one warrant or summons on the same complaint. If an individual defendant fails to appear in response to a summons, a judge may, and upon request of an attorney for the government must, issue a warrant. If an organizational defendant fails to appear in response to a summons, a judge may take any action authorized by United States law.

(b) Form.

(1) Warrant. A warrant must:

(A) contain the defendant's name or, if it is unknown, a name or description by which the defendant can be identified with reasonable certainty;

(B) describe the offense charged in the complaint;

(C) command that the defendant be arrested and brought without unnecessary delay before a magistrate judge or, if none is reasonably available, before a state or local judicial officer; and

(D) be signed by a judge.

(2) Summons. A summons must be in the same form as a warrant except that it must require the defendant to appear before a magistrate judge at a stated time and place.

(c) Execution or Service, and Return.

(1) By Whom. Only a marshal or other authorized officer may execute a warrant. Any person authorized to serve a summons in a federal civil action may serve a summons.

(2) Location. A warrant may be executed, or a summons served, within the jurisdiction of the United States or anywhere else a federal statute authorizes an arrest. A summons to an organization under Rule 4(c)(3)(D) may also be served at a place not within a judicial district of the United States.

(3) Manner.

(A) A warrant is executed by arresting the defendant. Upon arrest, an officer possessing the original or a duplicate original warrant must show it to the defendant. If the officer does not possess the warrant, the officer must inform the defendant of the warrant's existence and of the offense charged and, at the defendant's request, must show the original or a duplicate original warrant to the defendant as soon as possible.

(B) A summons is served on an individual defendant:

(i) by delivering a copy to the defendant personally; or

(ii) by leaving a copy at the defendant's residence or usual place of abode with a person of suitable age and discretion residing at that location and by mailing a copy to the defendant's last known address.

(C) A summons is served on an organization in a judicial district of the United States by delivering a copy to an officer, to a managing or general agent, or to another agent appointed or legally authorized to receive service of process. If the agent is one authorized by statute and the statute so requires, a copy must also be mailed to the organization.

(D) A summons is served on an organization not within a judicial district of the United States:

(i) by delivering a copy, in a manner authorized by the foreign jurisdiction's law, to an officer, to a managing or general agent, or to an agent appointed or legally authorized to receive service of process; or

(ii) by any other means that gives notice, including one that is:

(a) stipulated by the parties;

(b) undertaken by a foreign authority in response to a letter rogatory, a letter of request, or a request submitted under an applicable international agreement; or

(c) permitted by an applicable international agreement.

(4) Return.

(A) After executing a warrant, the officer must return it to the judge before whom the defendant is brought in accordance with Rule 5. The officer may do so by reliable electronic means. At the request of an attorney for the government, an unexecuted warrant must be brought back to and canceled by a magistrate judge or, if none is reasonably available, by a state or local judicial officer.

(B) The person to whom a summons was delivered for service must return it on or before the return day.

(C) At the request of an attorney for the government, a judge may deliver an unexecuted warrant, an unserved summons, or a copy of the warrant or summons to the marshal or other authorized person for execution or service.

(d) Warrant by Telephone or Other Reliable Electronic Means. In accordance with Rule 4.1, a magistrate judge may issue a warrant or summons based on information communicated by telephone or other reliable electronic means.

Rule 4.1. Complaint, Warrant, or Summons by Telephone or Other Reliable Electronic Means

(a) In General. A magistrate judge may consider information communicated by telephone or other reliable electronic means when deciding whether to approve a complaint or to issue a warrant or summons.

(b) Procedures. If a magistrate judge decides to proceed under this rule, the following procedures apply:

(1) Taking Testimony Under Oath. The judge must place under oath—and may examine—the applicant and any person on whose testimony the application is based.

(2) Creating a Record of the Testimony and Exhibits.

(A) Testimony Limited to Attestation. If the applicant does no more than attest to the contents of a written affidavit submitted by reliable electronic means, the judge must acknowledge the attestation in writing on the affidavit.

(B) Additional Testimony or Exhibits. If the judge considers additional testimony or exhibits, the judge must:

(i) have the testimony recorded verbatim by an electronic recording device, by a court reporter, or in writing;

(ii) have any recording or reporter's notes transcribed, have the transcription certified as accurate, and file it;

(iii) sign any other written record, certify its accuracy, and file it; and

(iv) make sure that the exhibits are filed.

(3) Preparing a Proposed Duplicate Original of a Complaint, Warrant, or Summons. The applicant must prepare a proposed duplicate original of a complaint, warrant, or summons, and must read or otherwise transmit its contents verbatim to the judge.

(4) Preparing an Original Complaint, Warrant, or Summons. If the applicant reads the contents of the proposed duplicate original, the judge must enter those contents into an original complaint, warrant, or summons. If the applicant transmits the contents by reliable electronic means, the transmission received by the judge may serve as the original.

(5) Modification. The judge may modify the complaint, warrant, or summons. The judge must then:

  (A) transmit the modified version to the applicant by reliable electronic means; or

  (B) file the modified original and direct the applicant to modify the proposed duplicate original accordingly.

(6) Issuance. To issue the warrant or summons, the judge must:

  (A) sign the original documents;

  (B) enter the date and time of issuance on the warrant or summons; and

  (C) transmit the warrant or summons by reliable electronic means to the applicant or direct the applicant to sign the judge's name and enter the date and time on the duplicate original.

(c) Suppression Limited. Absent a finding of bad faith, evidence obtained from a warrant issued under this rule is not subject to suppression on the ground that issuing the warrant in this manner was unreasonable under the circumstances.

Rule 5. Initial Appearance

(a) In General.

  (1) Appearance Upon an Arrest.

    (A) A person making an arrest within the United States must take the defendant without unnecessary delay before a magistrate judge, or before a state or local judicial officer as Rule 5(c) provides, unless a statute provides otherwise.

    (B) A person making an arrest outside the United States must take the defendant without unnecessary delay before a magistrate judge, unless a statute provides otherwise.

  (2) Exceptions.

    (A) An officer making an arrest under a warrant issued upon a complaint charging solely a violation of 18 U.S.C. § 1073 need not comply with this rule if:

      (i) the person arrested is transferred without unnecessary delay to the custody of appropriate state or local authorities in the district of arrest; and

      (ii) an attorney for the government moves promptly, in the district where the warrant was issued, to dismiss the complaint.

    (B) If a defendant is arrested for violating probation or supervised release, Rule 32.1 applies.

    (C) If a defendant is arrested for failing to appear in another district, Rule 40 applies.

  (3) Appearance Upon a Summons. When a defendant appears in response to a summons under Rule 4, a magistrate judge must proceed under Rule 5(d) or (e), as applicable.

(b) Arrest Without a Warrant. If a defendant is arrested without a warrant, a complaint meeting Rule 4(a)'s requirement of probable cause must be promptly filed in the district where the offense was allegedly committed.

(c) Place of Initial Appearance; Transfer to Another District.

(1) Arrest in the District Where the Offense Was Allegedly Committed. If the defendant is arrested in the district where the offense was allegedly committed:

    (A) the initial appearance must be in that district; and

    (B) if a magistrate judge is not reasonably available, the initial appearance may be before a state or local judicial officer.

(2) Arrest in a District Other Than Where the Offense Was Allegedly Committed. If the defendant was arrested in a district other than where the offense was allegedly committed, the initial appearance must be:

    (A) in the district of arrest; or

    (B) in an adjacent district if:

        (i) the appearance can occur more promptly there; or

        (ii) the offense was allegedly committed there and the initial appearance will occur on the day of arrest.

(3) Procedures in a District Other Than Where the Offense Was Allegedly Committed. If the initial appearance occurs in a district other than where the offense was allegedly committed, the following procedures apply:

    (A) the magistrate judge must inform the defendant about the provisions of Rule 20;

    (B) if the defendant was arrested without a warrant, the district court where the offense was allegedly committed must first issue a warrant before the magistrate judge transfers the defendant to that district;

    (C) the magistrate judge must conduct a preliminary hearing if required by Rule 5.1;

    (D) the magistrate judge must transfer the defendant to the district where the offense was allegedly committed if:

        (i) the government produces the warrant, a certified copy of the warrant, reliable electronic form of either; and

        (ii) the judge finds that the defendant is the same person named in the indictment, information, or warrant; and

    (E) when a defendant is transferred and discharged, the clerk must promptly transmit the papers and any bail to the clerk in the district where the offense was allegedly committed.

(4) Procedure for Persons Extradited to the United States. If the defendant is surrendered to the United States in accordance with a request for the defendant's extradition, the initial appearance must be in the district (or one of the districts) where the offense is charged.

(d) Procedure in a Felony Case.

(1) Advice. If the defendant is charged with a felony, the judge must inform the defendant of the following:

    (A) the complaint against the defendant, and any affidavit filed with it;

    (B) the defendant's right to retain counsel or to request that counsel be appointed if the defendant cannot obtain counsel;

(C) the circumstances, if any, under which the defendant may secure pretrial release;

(D) any right to a preliminary hearing; and

(E) the defendant's right not to make a statement, and that any statement made may be used against the defendant; and

(F) that a defendant who is not a United States citizen may request that an attorney for the government or a federal law enforcement official notify a consular office from the defendant's country of nationality that the defendant has been arrested—but that even without the defendant's request, a treaty or other international agreement may require consular notification.

(2) Consulting with Counsel. The judge must allow the defendant reasonable opportunity to consult with counsel.

(3) Detention or Release. The judge must detain or release the defendant as provided by statute or these rules.

(4) Plea. A defendant may be asked to plead only under Rule 10.

(e) Procedure in a Misdemeanor Case. If the defendant is charged with a misdemeanor only, the judge must inform the defendant in accordance with Rule 58(b)(2).

(f) Reminder of Prosecutorial Obligation.

(1) In General. In all criminal proceedings, on the first scheduled court date when both prosecutor and defense counsel are present, the judge shall issue an oral and written order to prosecution and defense counsel that confirms the disclosure obligation of the prosecutor under Brady v. Maryland, 373 U.S. 83 (1963) and its progeny, and the possible consequences of violating such order under applicable law.

(2) Formation of Order. Each judicial council in which a district court is located shall promulgate a model order for the purpose of paragraph (1) that the court may use as it determines is appropriate.

(g) Video Teleconferencing. Video teleconferencing may be used to conduct an appearance under this rule if the defendant consents.

Rule 5.1. Preliminary Hearing

(a) In General. If a defendant is charged with an offense other than a petty offense, a magistrate judge must conduct a preliminary hearing unless:

(1) the defendant waives the hearing;

(2) the defendant is indicted;

(3) the government files an information under Rule 7(b) charging the defendant with a felony;

(4) the government files an information charging the defendant with a misdemeanor; or

(5) the defendant is charged with a misdemeanor and consents to trial before a magistrate judge.

(b) Selecting a District. A defendant arrested in a district other than where the offense was allegedly committed may elect to have the preliminary hearing conducted in the district where the prosecution is pending.

(c) Scheduling. The magistrate judge must hold the preliminary hearing within a reasonable time, but no later than 14 days after the initial appearance if the defendant is in custody and no later than 21 days if not in custody.

(d) Extending the Time. With the defendant's consent and upon a showing of good cause—taking into account the public interest in the prompt disposition of criminal cases—a magistrate judge may extend the time limits in Rule 5.1(c) one or more times. If the defendant does not consent, the magistrate judge may extend the time limits only on a showing that extraordinary circumstances exist and justice requires the delay.

(e) Hearing and Finding. At the preliminary hearing, the defendant may cross-examine adverse witnesses and may introduce evidence but may not object to evidence on the ground that it was unlawfully acquired. If the magistrate judge finds probable cause to believe an offense has been committed and the defendant committed it, the magistrate judge must promptly require the defendant to appear for further proceedings.

(f) Discharging the Defendant. If the magistrate judge finds no probable cause to believe an offense has been committed or the defendant committed it, the magistrate judge must dismiss the complaint and discharge the defendant. A discharge does not preclude the government from later prosecuting the defendant for the same offense.

(g) Recording the Proceedings. The preliminary hearing must be recorded by a court reporter or by a suitable recording device. A recording of the proceeding may be made available to any party upon request. A copy of the recording and a transcript may be provided to any party upon request and upon any payment required by applicable Judicial Conference regulations.

(h) Producing a Statement.

(1) In General. Rule 26.2(a)–(d) and (f) applies at any hearing under this rule, unless the magistrate judge for good cause rules otherwise in a particular case.

(2) Sanctions for Not Producing a Statement. If a party disobeys a Rule 26.2 order to deliver a statement to the moving party, the magistrate judge must not consider the testimony of a witness whose statement is withheld.

Rule 6.   The Grand Jury

(a) Summoning a Grand Jury.

(1) In General. When the public interest so requires, the court must order that one or more grand juries be summoned. A grand jury must have 16 to 23 members, and the court must order that enough legally qualified persons be summoned to meet this requirement.

(2) Alternate Jurors. When a grand jury is selected, the court may also select alternate jurors. Alternate jurors must have the same qualifications and be selected in the same manner as any other juror. Alternate jurors replace jurors in the same sequence in which the alternates were selected. An alternate juror who replaces a juror is subject to the same challenges, takes the same oath, and has the same authority as the other jurors.

(b) Objection to the Grand Jury or to a Grand Juror.

(1) Challenges. Either the government or a defendant may challenge the grand jury on the ground that it was not lawfully drawn, summoned, or selected, and may challenge an individual juror on the ground that the juror is not legally qualified.

(2) Motion to Dismiss an Indictment. A party may move to dismiss the indictment based on an objection to the grand jury or on an individual juror's lack of legal qualification, unless the court has previously ruled on the same objection under Rule 6(b)(1). The motion to dismiss is governed by 28 U.S.C. § 1867(e). The court must not dismiss the indictment on the ground that a grand juror was not legally qualified if the record shows that at least 12 qualified jurors concurred in the indictment.

(c) Foreperson and Deputy Foreperson. The court will appoint one juror as the foreperson and another as the deputy foreperson. In the foreperson's absence, the deputy foreperson will act as the foreperson. The foreperson may administer oaths and affirmations and will sign all indictments. The foreperson—or another juror designated by the foreperson—will record the number of jurors concurring in every indictment and will file the record with the clerk, but the record may not be made public unless the court so orders.

(d) Who May Be Present.

(1) While the Grand Jury Is in Session. The following persons may be present while the grand jury is in session: attorneys for the government, the witness being questioned, interpreters when needed, and a court reporter or an operator of a recording device.

(2) During Deliberations and Voting. No person other than the jurors, and any interpreter needed to assist a hearing-impaired or speech-impaired juror, may be present while the grand jury is deliberating or voting.

(e) Recording and Disclosing the Proceedings.

(1) Recording the Proceedings. Except while the grand jury is deliberating or voting, all proceedings must be recorded by a court reporter or by a suitable recording device. But the validity of a prosecution is not affected by the unintentional failure to make a recording. Unless the court orders otherwise, an attorney for the government will retain control of the recording, the reporter's notes, and any transcript prepared from those notes.

(2) Secrecy.

(A) No obligation of secrecy may be imposed on any person except in accordance with Rule 6(e)(2)(B).

(B) Unless these rules provide otherwise, the following persons must not disclose a matter occurring before the grand jury:

    (i) a grand juror;

    (ii) an interpreter;

    (iii) a court reporter;

    (iv) an operator of a recording device;

    (v) a person who transcribes recorded testimony;

    (vi) an attorney for the government; or

    (vii) a person to whom disclosure is made under Rule 6(e)(3)(A)(ii) or (iii).

(3) Exceptions.

(A) Disclosure of a grand-jury matter—other than the grand jury's deliberations or any grand juror's vote—may be made to:

    (i) an attorney for the government for use in performing that attorney's duty;

    (ii) any government personnel—including those of a state, state subdivision, Indian tribe, or foreign government—that an attorney for the government considers necessary to assist in performing that attorney's duty to enforce federal criminal law; or

(iii) a person authorized by 18 U.S.C. § 3322.

(B) A person to whom information is disclosed under Rule 6(e)(3)(A)(ii) may use that information only to assist an attorney for the government in performing that attorney's duty to enforce federal criminal law. An attorney for the government must promptly provide the court that impaneled the grand jury with the names of all persons to whom a disclosure has been made, and must certify that the attorney has advised those persons of their obligation of secrecy under this rule.

(C) An attorney for the government may disclose any grand-jury matter to another federal grand jury.

(D) An attorney for the government may disclose any grand-jury matter involving foreign intelligence, counterintelligence (as defined in 50 U.S.C. § 3003), or foreign intelligence information (as defined in Rule 16(e)(3)(D)(iii)) to any federal law enforcement, intelligence, protective, immigration, national defense, or national security official to assist the official receiving the information in the performance of that official's duties. An attorney for the government may also disclose any grand jury matter involving, within the United States or elsewhere, a threat of attack or other grave hostile acts of a foreign power or its agent, a threat of domestic or international sabotage or terrorism, or clandestine intelligence gathering activities by an intelligence service or network of a foreign power or by its agent, to any appropriate federal, state, state subdivision, Indian tribal, or foreign government official, for the purpose of preventing or responding to such threat or activities.

(i) Any official who receives information under Rule 6(e)(3)(D) may use the information only as necessary in the conduct of that person's official duties subject to any limitations on the unauthorized disclosure of such information. Any state, state subdivision, Indian tribal, or foreign government official who receives information under Rule 6(e)(3)(D) may use the information only in a manner consistent with any guidelines issued by the Attorney General and the Director of National Intelligence.

(ii) Within a reasonable time after disclosure is made under Rule 6(e)(3)(D), an attorney for the government must file, under seal, a notice with the court in the district where the grand jury convened stating that such information was disclosed and the departments, agencies, or entities to which the disclosure was made.

(iii) As used in Rule 6(e)(3)(D), the term "foreign intelligence information" means:

(a) information, whether or not it concerns a United States person, that relates to the ability of the United States to protect against—

• actual or potential attack or other grave hostile acts of a foreign power or its agent;

• sabotage or international terrorism by a foreign power or its agent; or

• clandestine intelligence activities by an intelligence service or network of a foreign power or by its agent; or

(b) information, whether or not it concerns a United States person, with respect to a foreign power or foreign territory that relates to—

• the national defense or the security of the United States; or

- the conduct of the foreign affairs of the United States.

(E) The court may authorize disclosure—at a time, in a manner, and subject to any other conditions that it directs—of a grand-jury matter:

(i) preliminarily to or in connection with a judicial proceeding;

(ii) at the request of a defendant who shows that a ground may exist to dismiss the indictment because of a matter that occurred before the grand jury;

(iii) at the request of the government, when sought by a foreign court or prosecutor for use in an official criminal investigation;

(iv) at the request of the government if it shows that the matter may disclose a violation of State, Indian tribal, or foreign criminal law, as long as the disclosure is to an appropriate state, state-subdivision, Indian tribal, or foreign government official for the purpose of enforcing that law; or

(v) at the request of the government if it shows that the matter may disclose a violation of military criminal law under the Uniform Code of Military Justice, as long as the disclosure is to an appropriate military official for the purpose of enforcing that law.

(F) A petition to disclose a grand-jury matter under Rule 6(e)(3)(E)(i) must be filed in the district where the grand jury convened. Unless the hearing is ex parte—as it may be when the government is the petitioner—the petitioner must serve the petition on, and the court must afford a reasonable opportunity to appear and be heard to:

(i) an attorney for the government;

(ii) the parties to the judicial proceeding; and

(iii) any other person whom the court may designate.

(G) If the petition to disclose arises out of a judicial proceeding in another district, the petitioned court must transfer the petition to the other court unless the petitioned court can reasonably determine whether disclosure is proper. If the petitioned court decides to transfer, it must send to the transferee court the material sought to be disclosed, if feasible, and a written evaluation of the need for continued grand-jury secrecy. The transferee court must afford those persons identified in Rule 6(e)(3)(F) a reasonable opportunity to appear and be heard.

(4) Sealed Indictment. The magistrate judge to whom an indictment is returned may direct that the indictment be kept secret until the defendant is in custody or has been released pending trial. The clerk must then seal the indictment, and no person may disclose the indictment's existence except as necessary to issue or execute a warrant or summons.

(5) Closed Hearing. Subject to any right to an open hearing in a contempt proceeding, the court must close any hearing to the extent necessary to prevent disclosure of a matter occurring before a grand jury.

(6) Sealed Records. Records, orders, and subpoenas relating to grand-jury proceedings must be kept under seal to the extent and as long as necessary to prevent the unauthorized disclosure of a matter occurring before a grand jury.

(7) Contempt. A knowing violation of Rule 6, or of guidelines jointly issued by the Attorney General and the Director of National Intelligence pursuant to Rule 6, may be punished as a contempt of court.

(f)   Indictment and Return. A grand jury may indict only if at least 12 jurors concur. The grand jury—or its foreperson or deputy foreperson—must return the indictment to a magistrate judge in open court. To avoid unnecessary cost or delay, the magistrate judge may take the return by video teleconference from the court where the grand jury sits. If a complaint or information is pending against the defendant and 12 jurors do not concur in the indictment, the foreperson must promptly and in writing report the lack of concurrence to the magistrate judge.

(g)   Discharging the Grand Jury. A grand jury must serve until the court discharges it, but it may serve more than 18 months only if the court, having determined that an extension is in the public interest, extends the grand jury's service. An extension may be granted for no more than 6 months, except as otherwise provided by statute.

(h)   Excusing a Juror. At any time, for good cause, the court may excuse a juror either temporarily or permanently, and if permanently, the court may impanel an alternate juror in place of the excused juror.

(i)   "Indian Tribe" Defined. "Indian tribe" means an Indian tribe recognized by the Secretary of the Interior on a list published in the Federal Register under 25 U.S.C. § 479a–1.

Rule 7.   The Indictment and the Information

(a)   When Used.

(1)   Felony. An offense (other than criminal contempt) must be prosecuted by an indictment if it is punishable:

(A)   by death; or

(B)   by imprisonment for more than one year.

(2)   Misdemeanor. An offense punishable by imprisonment for one year or less may be prosecuted in accordance with Rule 58(b)(1).

(b)   Waiving Indictment. An offense punishable by imprisonment for more than one year may be prosecuted by information if the defendant—in open court and after being advised of the nature of the charge and of the defendant's rights—waives prosecution by indictment.

(c)   Nature and Contents.

(1)   In General. The indictment or information must be a plain, concise, and definite written statement of the essential facts constituting the offense charged and must be signed by an attorney for the government. It need not contain a formal introduction or conclusion. A count may incorporate by reference an allegation made in another count. A count may allege that the means by which the defendant committed the offense are unknown or that the defendant committed it by one or more specified means. For each count, the indictment or information must give the official or customary citation of the statute, rule, regulation, or other provision of law that the defendant is alleged to have violated. For purposes of an indictment referred to in section 3282 of title 18, United States Code, for which the identity of the defendant is unknown, it shall be sufficient for the indictment to describe the defendant as an individual whose name is unknown, but who has a particular DNA profile, as that term is defined in that section 3282.

(2)   Citation Error. Unless the defendant was misled and thereby prejudiced, neither an error in a citation nor a citation's omission is a ground to dismiss the indictment or information or to reverse a conviction.

(d)   Surplusage. Upon the defendant's motion, the court may strike surplusage from the indictment or information.

(e) Amending an Information. Unless an additional or different offense is charged or a substantial right of the defendant is prejudiced, the court may permit an information to be amended at any time before the verdict or finding.

(f) Bill of Particulars. The court may direct the government to file a bill of particulars. The defendant may move for a bill of particulars before or within 14 days after arraignment or at a later time if the court permits. The government may amend a bill of particulars subject to such conditions as justice requires.

Rule 8.   Joinder of Offenses or Defendants

(a) Joinder of Offenses. The indictment or information may charge a defendant in separate counts with 2 or more offenses if the offenses charged—whether felonies or misdemeanors or both—are of the same or similar character, or are based on the same act or transaction, or are connected with or constitute parts of a common scheme or plan.

(b) Joinder of Defendants. The indictment or information may charge 2 or more defendants if they are alleged to have participated in the same act or transaction, or in the same series of acts or transactions, constituting an offense or offenses. The defendants may be charged in one or more counts together or separately. All defendants need not be charged in each count.

Rule 9.   Arrest Warrant or Summons on an Indictment or Information

(a) Issuance. The court must issue a warrant—or at the government's request, a summons—for each defendant named in an indictment or named in an information if one or more affidavits accompanying the information establish probable cause to believe that an offense has been committed and that the defendant committed it. The court may issue more than one warrant or summons for the same defendant. If a defendant fails to appear in response to a summons, the court may, and upon request of an attorney for the government must, issue a warrant. The court must issue the arrest warrant to an officer authorized to execute it or the summons to a person authorized to serve it.

(b) Form.

(1) Warrant. The warrant must conform to Rule 4(b)(1) except that it must be signed by the clerk and must describe the offense charged in the indictment or information.

(2) Summons. The summons must be in the same form as a warrant except that it must require the defendant to appear before the court at a stated time and place.

(c) Execution or Service; Return; Initial Appearance.

(1) Execution or Service.

(A) The warrant must be executed or the summons served as provided in Rule 4(c)(1), (2), and (3).

(B) The officer executing the warrant must proceed in accordance with Rule 5(a)(1).

(2) Return. A warrant or summons must be returned in accordance with Rule 4(c)(4).

(3) Initial Appearance. When an arrested or summoned defendant first appears before the court, the judge must proceed under Rule 5.

(d) Warrant by Telephone or Other Means. In accordance with Rule 4.1, a magistrate judge may issue an arrest warrant or summons based on information communicated by telephone or other reliable electronic means.

Rule 10. Arraignment

(a) In General. An arraignment must be conducted in open court and must consist of:

(1) ensuring that the defendant has a copy of the indictment or information;

(2) reading the indictment or information to the defendant or stating to the defendant the substance of the charge; and then

(3) asking the defendant to plead to the indictment or information.

(b) Waiving Appearance. A defendant need not be present for the arraignment if:

(1) the defendant has been charged by indictment or misdemeanor information;

(2) the defendant, in a written waiver signed by both the defendant and defense counsel, has waived appearance and has affirmed that the defendant received a copy of the indictment or information and that the plea is not guilty; and

(3) the court accepts the waiver.

(c) Video Teleconferencing. Video teleconferencing may be used to arraign a defendant if the defendant consents.

Rule 11. Pleas

(a) Entering a Plea.

(1) In General. A defendant may plead not guilty, guilty, or (with the court's consent) nolo contendere.

(2) Conditional Plea. With the consent of the court and the government, a defendant may enter a conditional plea of guilty or nolo contendere, reserving in writing the right to have an appellate court review an adverse determination of a specified pretrial motion. A defendant who prevails on appeal may then withdraw the plea.

(3) Nolo Contendere Plea. Before accepting a plea of nolo contendere, the court must consider the parties' views and the public interest in the effective administration of justice.

(4) Failure to Enter a Plea. If a defendant refuses to enter a plea or if a defendant organization fails to appear, the court must enter a plea of not guilty.

(b) Considering and Accepting a Guilty or Nolo Contendere Plea.

(1) Advising and Questioning the Defendant. Before the court accepts a plea of guilty or nolo contendere, the defendant may be placed under oath, and the court must address the defendant personally in open court. During this address, the court must inform the defendant of, and determine that the defendant understands, the following:

(A) the government's right, in a prosecution for perjury or false statement, to use against the defendant any statement that the defendant gives under oath;

(B) the right to plead not guilty, or having already so pleaded, to persist in that plea;

(C) the right to a jury trial;

(D) the right to be represented by counsel—and if necessary have the court appoint counsel—at trial and at every other stage of the proceeding;

(E) the right at trial to confront and cross-examine adverse witnesses, to be protected from compelled self-incrimination, to testify and present evidence, and to compel the attendance of witnesses;

(F) the defendant's waiver of these trial rights if the court accepts a plea of guilty or nolo contendere;

(G) the nature of each charge to which the defendant is pleading;

(H) any maximum possible penalty, including imprisonment, fine, and term of supervised release;

(I) any mandatory minimum penalty;

(J) any applicable forfeiture;

(K) the court's authority to order restitution;

(L) the court's obligation to impose a special assessment;

(M) in determining a sentence, the court's obligation to calculate the applicable sentencing-guideline range and to consider that range, possible departures under the Sentencing Guidelines, and other sentencing factors under 18 U.S.C. § 3553(a);

(N) the terms of any plea-agreement provision waiving the right to appeal or to collaterally attack the sentence; and

(O) that, if convicted, a defendant who is not a United States citizen may be removed from the United States, denied citizenship, and denied admission to the United States in the future.

(2) Ensuring That a Plea Is Voluntary. Before accepting a plea of guilty or nolo contendere, the court must address the defendant personally in open court and determine that the plea is voluntary and did not result from force, threats, or promises (other than promises in a plea agreement).

(3) Determining the Factual Basis for a Plea. Before entering judgment on a guilty plea, the court must determine that there is a factual basis for the plea.

(c) Plea Agreement Procedure.

(1) In General. An attorney for the government and the defendant's attorney, or the defendant when proceeding pro se, may discuss and reach a plea agreement. The court must not participate in these discussions. If the defendant pleads guilty or nolo contendere to either a charged offense or a lesser or related offense, the plea agreement may specify that an attorney for the government will:

(A) not bring, or will move to dismiss, other charges;

(B) recommend, or agree not to oppose the defendant's request, that a particular sentence or sentencing range is appropriate or that a particular provision of the Sentencing Guidelines, or policy statement, or sentencing factor does or does not apply (such a recommendation or request does not bind the court); or

(C) agree that a specific sentence or sentencing range is the appropriate disposition of the case, or that a particular provision of the Sentencing Guidelines, or policy statement, or sentencing factor does or does not apply (such a recommendation or request binds the court once the court accepts the plea agreement).

(2) Disclosing a Plea Agreement. The parties must disclose the plea agreement in open court when the plea is offered, unless the court for good cause allows the parties to disclose the plea agreement in camera.

(3) Judicial Consideration of a Plea Agreement.

(A) To the extent the plea agreement is of the type specified in Rule 11(c)(1)(A) or (C), the court may accept the agreement, reject it, or defer a decision until the court has reviewed the presentence report.

(B) To the extent the plea agreement is of the type specified in Rule 11(c)(1)(B), the court must advise the defendant that the defendant has no right to withdraw the plea if the court does not follow the recommendation or request.

(4) Accepting a Plea Agreement. If the court accepts the plea agreement, it must inform the defendant that to the extent the plea agreement is of the type specified in Rule 11(c)(1)(A) or (C), the agreed disposition will be included in the judgment.

(5) Rejecting a Plea Agreement. If the court rejects a plea agreement containing provisions of the type specified in Rule 11(c)(1)(A) or (C), the court must do the following on the record and in open court (or, for good cause, in camera):

(A) inform the parties that the court rejects the plea agreement;

(B) advise the defendant personally that the court is not required to follow the plea agreement and give the defendant an opportunity to withdraw the plea; and

(C) advise the defendant personally that if the plea is not withdrawn, the court may dispose of the case less favorably toward the defendant than the plea agreement contemplated.

(d) Withdrawing a Guilty or Nolo Contendere Plea. A defendant may withdraw a plea of guilty or nolo contendere:

(1) before the court accepts the plea, for any reason or no reason; or

(2) after the court accepts the plea, but before it imposes sentence if:

(A) the court rejects a plea agreement under Rule 11(c)(5); or

(B) the defendant can show a fair and just reason for requesting the withdrawal.

(e) Finality of a Guilty or Nolo Contendere Plea. After the court imposes sentence, the defendant may not withdraw a plea of guilty or nolo contendere, and the plea may be set aside only on direct appeal or collateral attack.

(f) Admissibility or Inadmissibility of a Plea, Plea Discussions, and Related Statements. The admissibility or inadmissibility of a plea, a plea discussion, and any related statement is governed by Federal Rule of Evidence 410.

(g) Recording the Proceedings. The proceedings during which the defendant enters a plea must be recorded by a court reporter or by a suitable recording device. If there is a guilty plea or a nolo contendere plea, the record must include the inquiries and advice to the defendant required under Rule 11(b) and (c).

(h) Harmless Error. A variance from the requirements of this rule is harmless error if it does not affect substantial rights.

Rule 12. Pleadings and Pretrial Motions

(a) Pleadings. The pleadings in a criminal proceeding are the indictment, the information, and the pleas of not guilty, guilty, and nolo contendere.

(b) Pretrial Motions.

(1) In General. A party may raise by pretrial motion any defense, objection, or request that the court can determine without a trial on the merits. Rule 47 applies to a pretrial motion.

(2) Motions That May Be Made at Any Time. A motion that the court lacks jurisdiction may be made at any time while the case is pending.

(3) Motions That Must Be Made Before Trial. The following defenses, objections, and requests must be raised by pretrial motion if the basis for the motion is then reasonably available and the motion can be determined without a trial on the merits:

    (A) a defect in instituting the prosecution, including:

        (i) improper venue;

        (ii) preindictment delay;

        (iii) a violation of the constitutional right to a speedy trial;

        (iv) selective or vindictive prosecution; and

        (v) an error in the grand-jury proceeding or preliminary hearing;

    (B) a defect in the indictment or information, including:

        (i) joining two or more offenses in the same count (duplicity);

        (ii) charging the same offense in more than one count (multiplicity);

        (iii) lack of specificity;

        (iv) improper joinder; and

        (v) failure to state an offense;

    (C) suppression of evidence;

    (D) severance of charges or defendants under Rule 14; and

    (E) discovery under Rule 16.

(4) Notice of the Government's Intent to Use Evidence.

    (A) At the Government's Discretion. At the arraignment or as soon afterward as practicable, the government may notify the defendant of its intent to use specified evidence at trial in order to afford the defendant an opportunity to object before trial under Rule 12(b)(3)(C).

    (B) At the Defendant's Request. At the arraignment or as soon afterward as practicable, the defendant may, in order to have an opportunity to move to suppress evidence under Rule 12(b)(3)(C), request notice of the government's intent to use (in its evidence-in-chief at trial) any evidence that the defendant may be entitled to discover under Rule 16.

(c) Deadline for a Pretrial Motion; Consequences of Not Making a Timely Motion.

(1) Setting the Deadline. The court may, at the arraignment or as soon afterward as practicable, set a deadline for the parties to make pretrial motions and may also schedule a motion hearing. If the court does not set one, the deadline is the start of trial.

(2) Extending or Resetting the Deadline. At any time before trial, the court may extend or reset the deadline for pretrial motions.

(3) Consequences of Not Making a Timely Motion Under Rule 12(b)(3). If a party does not meet the deadline for making a Rule 12(b)(3) motion, the motion is untimely. But a court may consider the defense, objection, or request if the party shows good cause.

(d) Ruling on a Motion. The court must decide every pretrial motion before trial unless it finds good cause to defer a ruling. The court must not defer ruling on a pretrial motion if the deferral will adversely affect a party's right to appeal. When factual issues are involved in deciding a motion, the court must state its essential findings on the record.

(e) [Reserved]

(f) Recording the Proceedings. All proceedings at a motion hearing, including any findings of fact and conclusions of law made orally by the court, must be recorded by a court reporter or a suitable recording device.

(g) Defendant's Continued Custody or Release Status. If the court grants a motion to dismiss based on a defect in instituting the prosecution, in the indictment, or in the information, it may order the defendant to be released or detained under 18 U.S.C. § 3142 for a specified time until a new indictment or information is filed. This rule does not affect any federal statutory period of limitations.

(h) Producing Statements at a Suppression Hearing. Rule 26.2 applies at a suppression hearing under Rule 12(b)(3)(C). At a suppression hearing, a law enforcement officer is considered a government witness.

Rule 12.1. Notice of an Alibi Defense

(a) Government's Request for Notice and Defendant's Response.

(1) Government's Request. An attorney for the government may request in writing that the defendant notify an attorney for the government of any intended alibi defense. The request must state the time, date, and place of the alleged offense.

(2) Defendant's Response. Within 14 days after the request, or at some other time the court sets, the defendant must serve written notice on an attorney for the government of any intended alibi defense. The defendant's notice must state:

(A) each specific place where the defendant claims to have been at the time of the alleged offense; and

(B) the name, address, and telephone number of each alibi witness on whom the defendant intends to rely.

(b) Disclosing Government Witnesses.

(1) Disclosure.

(A) In General. If the defendant serves a Rule 12.1(a)(2) notice, an attorney for the government must disclose in writing to the defendant or the defendant's attorney:

(i) the name of each witness—and the address and telephone number of each witness other than a victim—that the government intends to rely on to establish that the defendant was present at the scene of the alleged offense; and

(ii) each government rebuttal witness to the defendant's alibi defense.

(B) Victim's Address and Telephone Number. If the government intends to rely on a victim's testimony to establish that the defendant was present at the scene of the alleged offense and the defendant establishes a need for the victim's address and telephone number, the court may:

(i) order the government to provide the information in writing to the defendant or the defendant's attorney; or

(ii) fashion a reasonable procedure that allows preparation of the defense and also protects the victim's interests.

(2) Time to Disclose. Unless the court directs otherwise, an attorney for the government must give its Rule 12.1(b)(1) disclosure within 14 days after the defendant serves notice of an intended alibi defense under Rule 12.1(a)(2), but no later than 14 days before trial.

(c) Continuing Duty to Disclose.

(1) In General. Both an attorney for the government and the defendant must promptly disclose in writing to the other party the name of each additional witness—and the address and telephone number of each additional witness other than a victim—if:

(A) the disclosing party learns of the witness before or during trial; and

(B) the witness should have been disclosed under Rule 12.1(a) or (b) if the disclosing party had known of the witness earlier.

(2) Address and Telephone Number of an Additional Victim Witness. The address and telephone number of an additional victim witness must not be disclosed except as provided in Rule 12.1 (b)(1)(B).

(d) Exceptions. For good cause, the court may grant an exception to any requirement of Rule 12.1(a)–(c).

(e) Failure to Comply. If a party fails to comply with this rule, the court may exclude the testimony of any undisclosed witness regarding the defendant's alibi. This rule does not limit the defendant's right to testify.

(f) Inadmissibility of Withdrawn Intention. Evidence of an intention to rely on an alibi defense, later withdrawn, or of a statement made in connection with that intention, is not, in any civil or criminal proceeding, admissible against the person who gave notice of the intention.

Rule 12.2. Notice of an Insanity Defense; Mental Examination

(a) Notice of an Insanity Defense. A defendant who intends to assert a defense of insanity at the time of the alleged offense must so notify an attorney for the government in writing within the time provided for filing a pretrial motion, or at any later time the court sets, and file a copy of the notice with the clerk. A defendant who fails to do so cannot rely on an insanity defense. The court may, for good cause, allow the defendant to file the notice late, grant additional trial-preparation time, or make other appropriate orders.

(b) Notice of Expert Evidence of a Mental Condition. If a defendant intends to introduce expert evidence relating to a mental disease or defect or any other mental condition of the defendant bearing on either (1) the issue of guilt or (2) the issue of punishment in a capital case, the defendant must—within the time provided for filing a pretrial motion or at any later time the court sets—notify an attorney for the government in writing of this intention and file a copy of the notice with the clerk. The court may, for good cause, allow the defendant to file the notice late, grant the parties additional trial-preparation time, or make other appropriate orders.

(c) Mental Examination.

(1) Authority to Order an Examination; Procedures.

(A) The court may order the defendant to submit to a competency examination under 18 U.S.C. § 4241.

(B) If the defendant provides notice under Rule 12.2(a), the court must, upon the government's motion, order the defendant to be examined under 18 U.S.C. § 4242. If the defendant provides notice under Rule 12.2(b) the court may, upon the government's motion, order the defendant to be examined under procedures ordered by the court.

(2) Disclosing Results and Reports of Capital Sentencing Examination. The results and reports of any examination conducted solely under Rule 12.2(c)(1) after notice under Rule 12.2(b)(2) must be sealed and must not be disclosed to any attorney for the government or the defendant unless the defendant is found guilty of one or more capital crimes and the defendant confirms an intent to offer during sentencing proceedings expert evidence on mental condition.

(3) Disclosing Results and Reports of the Defendant's Expert Examination. After disclosure under Rule 12.2(c)(2) of the results and reports of the government's examination, the defendant must disclose to the government the results and reports of any examination on mental condition conducted by the defendant's expert about which the defendant intends to introduce expert evidence.

(4) Inadmissibility of a Defendant's Statements. No statement made by a defendant in the course of any examination conducted under this rule (whether conducted with or without the defendant's consent), no testimony by the expert based on the statement, and no other fruits of the statement may be admitted into evidence against the defendant in any criminal proceeding except on an issue regarding mental condition on which the defendant:

(A) has introduced evidence of incompetency or evidence requiring notice under Rule 12.2(a) or (b)(1), or

(B) has introduced expert evidence in a capital sentencing proceeding requiring notice under Rule 12.2(b)(2).

(d) Failure to Comply.

(1) Failure to Give Notice or to Submit to Examination. The court may exclude any expert evidence from the defendant on the issue of the defendant's mental disease, mental defect, or any other mental condition bearing on the defendant's guilt or the issue of punishment in a capital case if the defendant fails to:

(A) give notice under Rule 12.2(b); or

(B) submit to an examination when ordered under Rule 12.2(c).

(2) Failure to Disclose. The court may exclude any expert evidence for which the defendant has failed to comply with the disclosure requirement of Rule 12.2(c)(3).

(e) Inadmissibility of Withdrawn Intention. Evidence of an intention as to which notice was given under Rule 12.2(a) or (b), later withdrawn, is not, in any civil or criminal proceeding, admissible against the person who gave notice of the intention.

Rule 12.3. Notice of a Public-Authority Defense

(a) Notice of the Defense and Disclosure of Witnesses.

(1) Notice in General. If a defendant intends to assert a defense of actual or believed exercise of public authority on behalf of a law enforcement agency or federal intelligence agency at the time of the alleged offense, the defendant must so notify an attorney for the government in writing and must file a copy of the notice with the clerk within the time provided for filing a pretrial motion, or at any later time the court sets. The notice filed with the clerk must be under seal if the notice identifies a federal intelligence agency as the source of public authority.

(2) Contents of Notice. The notice must contain the following information:

(A) the law enforcement agency or federal intelligence agency involved;

(B) the agency member on whose behalf the defendant claims to have acted; and

(C) the time during which the defendant claims to have acted with public authority.

(3) Response to the Notice. An attorney for the government must serve a written response on the defendant or the defendant's attorney within 14 days after receiving the defendant's notice, but no later than 21 days before trial. The response must admit or deny that the defendant exercised the public authority identified in the defendant's notice.

(4) Disclosing Witnesses.

(A) Government's Request. An attorney for the government may request in writing that the defendant disclose the name, address, and telephone number of each witness the defendant intends to rely on to establish a public-authority defense. An attorney for the government may serve the request when the government serves its response to the defendant's notice under Rule 12.3(a)(3), or later, but must serve the request no later than 21 days before trial.

(B) Defendant's Response. Within 14 days after receiving the government's request, the defendant must serve on an attorney for the government a written statement of the name, address, and telephone number of each witness.

(C) Government's Reply. Within 14 days after receiving the defendant's statement, an attorney for the government must serve on the defendant or the defendant's attorney a written statement of the name of each witness—and the address and telephone number of each witness other than a victim—that the government intends to rely on to oppose the defendant's public-authority defense.

(D) Victim's Address and Telephone Number. If the government intends to rely on a victim's testimony to oppose the defendant's public-authority defense and the defendant establishes a need for the victim's address and telephone number, the court may:

(i) order the government to provide the information in writing to the defendant or the defendant's attorney; or

(ii) fashion a reasonable procedure that allows for preparing the defense and also protects the victim's interests.

(5) Additional Time. The court may, for good cause, allow a party additional time to comply with this rule.

(b) Continuing Duty to Disclose.

(1) In General. Both an attorney for the government and the defendant must promptly disclose in writing to the other party the name of any additional witness—and the address, and telephone number of any additional witness other than a victim—if:

(A) the disclosing party learns of the witness before or during trial; and

(B) the witness should have been disclosed under Rule 12.3(a)(4) if the disclosing party had known of the witness earlier.

(2) Address and Telephone Number of an Additional Victim-Witness. The address and telephone number of an additional victim-witness must not be disclosed except as provided in Rule 12.3(a)(4)(D).

(c) Failure to Comply. If a party fails to comply with this rule, the court may exclude the testimony of any undisclosed witness regarding the public-authority defense. This rule does not limit the defendant's right to testify.

(d) Protective Procedures Unaffected. This rule does not limit the court's authority to issue appropriate protective orders or to order that any filings be under seal.

(e) Inadmissibility of Withdrawn Intention. Evidence of an intention as to which notice was given under Rule 12.3(a), later withdrawn, is not, in any civil or criminal proceeding, admissible against the person who gave notice of the intention.

Rule 12.4. Disclosure Statement

(a) Who Must File.

(1) Nongovernmental Corporate Party. Any nongovernmental corporate party to a proceeding in a district court must file a statement that identifies any parent corporation and any publicly held corporation that owns 10% or more of its stock or states that there is no such corporation.

(2) Organizational Victim. Unless the government shows good cause, it must file a statement identifying any organizational victim of the alleged criminal activity. If the organizational victim is a corporation, the statement must also disclose the information required by Rule 12.4(a)(1) to the extent it can be obtained through due diligence.

(b) Time for Filing; Supplemental Filing. A party must:

(1) file the Rule 12.4(a) statement within 28 days after the defendant's initial appearance; and

(2) promptly file a supplemental statement upon any change in the information that the statement requires.

Rule 13. Joint Trial of Separate Cases

The court may order that separate cases be tried together as though brought in a single indictment or information if all offenses and all defendants could have been joined in a single indictment or information.

Rule 14. Relief from Prejudicial Joinder

(a) Relief. If the joinder of offenses or defendants in an indictment, an information, or a consolidation for trial appears to prejudice a defendant or the government, the court may order separate trials of counts, sever the defendants' trials, or provide any other relief that justice requires.

(b) Defendant's Statements. Before ruling on a defendant's motion to sever, the court may order an attorney for the government to deliver to the court for in camera inspection any defendant's statement that the government intends to use as evidence.

Rule 15. Depositions

(a) When Taken.

(1) In General. A party may move that a prospective witness be deposed in order to preserve testimony for trial. The court may grant the motion because of exceptional circumstances and in the interest of justice. If the court orders the deposition to be taken, it may also require the deponent to produce at the deposition any designated material that is not privileged, including any book, paper, document, record, recording, or data.

(2) Detained Material Witness. A witness who is detained under 18 U.S.C. § 3144 may request to be deposed by filing a written motion and giving notice to the parties. The court may then order that the deposition be taken and may discharge the witness after the witness has signed under oath the deposition transcript.

(b) Notice.

(1) In General. A party seeking to take a deposition must give every other party reasonable written notice of the deposition's date and location. The notice must state the name and address of each deponent. If requested by a party receiving the notice, the court may, for good cause, change the deposition's date or location.

(2) To the Custodial Officer. A party seeking to take the deposition must also notify the officer who has custody of the defendant of the scheduled date and location.

(c) Defendant's Presence.

(1) Defendant in Custody. Except as authorized by Rule 15(c)(3), the officer who has custody of the defendant must produce the defendant at the deposition and keep the defendant in the witness's presence during the examination, unless the defendant:

    (A) waives in writing the right to be present; or

    (B) persists in disruptive conduct justifying exclusion after being warned by the court that disruptive conduct will result in the defendant's exclusion.

(2) Defendant Not in Custody. Except as authorized by Rule 15(c)(3), a defendant who is not in custody has the right upon request to be present at the deposition, subject to any conditions imposed by the court. If the government tenders the defendant's expenses as provided in Rule 15(d) but the defendant still fails to appear, the defendant—absent good cause—waives both the right to appear and any objection to the taking and use of the deposition based on that right.

(3) Taking Depositions Outside the United States Without the Defendant's Presence. The deposition of a witness who is outside the United States may be taken without the defendant's presence if the court makes case-specific findings of all the following:

    (A) the witness's testimony could provide substantial proof of a material fact in a felony prosecution;

    (B) there is a substantial likelihood that the witness's attendance at trial cannot be obtained;

    (C) the witness's presence for a deposition in the United States cannot be obtained;

    (D) the defendant cannot be present because:

        (i) the country where the witness is located will not permit the defendant to attend the deposition;

        (ii) for an in-custody defendant, secure transportation and continuing custody cannot be assured at the witness's location; or

        (iii) for an out-of-custody defendant, no reasonable conditions will assure an appearance at the deposition or at trial or sentencing; and

(E) the defendant can meaningfully participate in the deposition through reasonable means.

(d) Expenses. If the deposition was requested by the government, the court may—or if the defendant is unable to bear the deposition expenses, the court must—order the government to pay:

(1) any reasonable travel and subsistence expenses of the defendant and the defendant's attorney to attend the deposition; and

(2) the costs of the deposition transcript.

(e) Manner of Taking. Unless these rules or a court order provides otherwise, a deposition must be taken and filed in the same manner as a deposition in a civil action, except that:

(1) A defendant may not be deposed without that defendant's consent.

(2) The scope and manner of the deposition examination and cross-examination must be the same as would be allowed during trial.

(3) The government must provide to the defendant or the defendant's attorney, for use at the deposition, any statement of the deponent in the government's possession to which the defendant would be entitled at trial.

(f) Admissibility and Use as Evidence. An order authorizing a deposition to be taken under this rule does not determine its admissibility. A party may use all or part of a deposition as provided by the Federal Rules of Evidence.

(g) Objections. A party objecting to deposition testimony or evidence must state the grounds for the objection during the deposition.

(h) Depositions by Agreement Permitted. The parties may by agreement take and use a deposition with the court's consent.

Rule 16. Discovery and Inspection

(a) Government's Disclosure.

(1) Information Subject to Disclosure.

(A) Defendant's Oral Statement. Upon a defendant's request, the government must disclose to the defendant the substance of any relevant oral statement made by the defendant, before or after arrest, in response to interrogation by a person the defendant knew was a government agent if the government intends to use the statement at trial.

(B) Defendant's Written or Recorded Statement. Upon a defendant's request, the government must disclose to the defendant, and make available for inspection, copying, or photographing, all of the following:

(i) any relevant written or recorded statement by the defendant if:

• the statement is within the government's possession, custody, or control; and

• the attorney for the government knows—or through due diligence could know—that the statement exists;

(ii) the portion of any written record containing the substance of any relevant oral statement made before or after arrest if the defendant made the statement in response to interrogation by a person the defendant knew was a government agent; and

(iii) the defendant's recorded testimony before a grand jury relating to the charged offense.

(C) Organizational Defendant. Upon a defendant's request, if the defendant is an organization, the government must disclose to the defendant any statement described in Rule 16(a)(1)(A) and (B) if the government contends that the person making the statement:

    (i) was legally able to bind the defendant regarding the subject of the statement because of that person's position as the defendant's director, officer, employee, or agent; or

    (ii) was personally involved in the alleged conduct constituting the offense and was legally able to bind the defendant regarding that conduct because of that person's position as the defendant's director, officer, employee, or agent.

(D) Defendant's Prior Record. Upon a defendant's request, the government must furnish the defendant with a copy of the defendant's prior criminal record that is within the government's possession, custody, or control if the attorney for the government knows—or through due diligence could know—that the record exists.

(E) Documents and Objects. Upon a defendant's request, the government must permit the defendant to inspect and to copy or photograph books, papers, documents, data, photographs, tangible objects, buildings or places, or copies or portions of any of these items, if the item is within the government's possession, custody, or control and:

    (i) the item is material to preparing the defense;

    (ii) the government intends to use the item in its case-in-chief at trial; or

    (iii) the item was obtained from or belongs to the defendant.

(F) Reports of Examinations and Tests. Upon a defendant's request, the government must permit a defendant to inspect and to copy or photograph the results or reports of any physical or mental examination and of any scientific test or experiment if:

    (i) the item is within the government's possession, custody, or control;

    (ii) the attorney for the government knows—or through due diligence could know—that the item exists; and

    (iii) the item is material to preparing the defense or the government intends to use the item in its case-in-chief at trial.

(G) Expert witnesses. At the defendant's request, the government must give to the defendant a written summary of any testimony that the government intends to use under Rules 702, 703, or 705 of the Federal Rules of Evidence during its case-in-chief at trial. If the government requests discovery under subdivision (b)(1)(C)(ii) and the defendant complies, the government must, at the defendant's request, give to the defendant a written summary of testimony that the government intends to use under Rules 702, 703, or 705 of the Federal Rules of Evidence as evidence at trial on the issue of the defendant's mental condition. The summary provided under this subparagraph must describe the witness's opinions, the bases and reasons for those opinions, and the witness's qualifications.

(2) Information Not Subject to Disclosure. Except as permitted by Rule 16(a)(1)(A)–(D), (F), and (G), this rule does not authorize the discovery or inspection of reports, memoranda, or other internal government documents made by an attorney for the government or other government agent in connection with investigating or prosecuting the case. Nor does this rule authorize the discovery or inspection of statements made by prospective government witnesses except as provided in 18 U.S.C. 3 § 3500.*

(3) Grand Jury Transcripts. This rule does not apply to the discovery or inspection of a grand jury's recorded proceedings, except as provided in Rules 6, 12(h), 16(a)(1), and 26.2.

(b) Defendant's Disclosure.

(1) Information Subject to Disclosure.

(A) Documents and Objects. If a defendant requests disclosure under Rule 16(a)(1)(E) and the government complies, then the defendant must permit the government, upon request, to inspect and to copy or photograph books, papers, documents, data, photographs, tangible objects, buildings or places, or copies or portions of any of these items if:

(i) the item is within the defendant's possession, custody, or control; and

(ii) the defendant intends to use the item in the defendant's case-in-chief at trial.

(B) Reports of Examinations and Tests. If a defendant requests disclosure under Rule 16(a)(1)(F) and the government complies, the defendant must permit the government, upon request, to inspect and to copy or photograph the results or reports of any physical or mental examination and of any scientific test or experiment if:

(i) the item is within the defendant's possession, custody, or control; and

(ii) the defendant intends to use the item in the defendant's case-in-chief at trial, or intends to call the witness who prepared the report and the report relates to the witness's testimony.

(C) Expert witnesses. The defendant must, at the government's request, give to the government a written summary of any testimony that the defendant intends to use under Rules 702, 703, or 705 of the Federal Rules of Evidence as evidence at trial, if—

(i) the defendant requests disclosure under subdivision (a)(1)(G) and the government complies; or

(ii) the defendant has given notice under Rule 12.2(b) of an intent to present expert testimony on the defendant's mental condition.

This summary must describe the witness's opinions, the bases and reasons for those opinions, and the witness's qualifications.

(2) Information Not Subject to Disclosure. Except for scientific or medical reports, Rule 16(b)(1) does not authorize discovery or inspection of:

(A) reports, memoranda, or other documents made by the defendant, or the defendant's attorney or agent, during the case's investigation or defense; or

(B) a statement made to the defendant, or the defendant's attorney or agent, by:

(i) the defendant;

(ii) a government or defense witness; or

(iii) a prospective government or defense witness.

---

* This provision is set out in Appendix B.

(c) Continuing Duty to Disclose. A party who discovers additional evidence or material before or during trial must promptly disclose its existence to the other party or the court if:

> **(1)** the evidence or material is subject to discovery or inspection under this rule; and

> **(2)** the other party previously requested, or the court ordered, its production.

(d) Regulating Discovery.

> **(1) Protective and Modifying Orders.** At any time the court may, for good cause, deny, restrict, or defer discovery or inspection, or grant other appropriate relief. The court may permit a party to show good cause by a written statement that the court will inspect ex parte. If relief is granted, the court must preserve the entire text of the party's statement under seal.

> **(2) Failure to Comply.** If a party fails to comply with this rule, the court may:

>> **(A)** order that party to permit the discovery or inspection; specify its time, place, and manner; and prescribe other just terms and conditions;

>> **(B)** grant a continuance;

>> **(C)** prohibit that party from introducing the undisclosed evidence; or

>> **(D)** enter any other order that is just under the circumstances.

Rule 16.1. Pretrial Discovery Conference; Request for Court Action

(a) Discovery Conference. No later than 14 days after the arraignment, the attorney for the government and the defendants attorney must confer and try to agree on a timetable and procedures for pretrial disclosure under Rule 16.

(b) Request for Court Action. After the discovery conference, one or both parties may ask the court to determine or modify the time, place, manner, or other aspects of disclosure to facilitate preparation for trial.

Rule 17. Subpoena

(a) Content. A subpoena must state the court's name and the title of the proceeding, include the seal of the court, and command the witness to attend and testify at the time and place the subpoena specifies. The clerk must issue a blank subpoena—signed and sealed—to the party requesting it, and that party must fill in the blanks before the subpoena is served.

(b) Defendant Unable to Pay. Upon a defendant's ex parte application, the court must order that a subpoena be issued for a named witness if the defendant shows an inability to pay the witness's fees and the necessity of the witness's presence for an adequate defense. If the court orders a subpoena to be issued, the process costs and witness fees will be paid in the same manner as those paid for witnesses the government subpoenas.

(c) Producing Documents and Objects.

> **(1) In General.** A subpoena may order the witness to produce any books, papers, documents, data, or other objects the subpoena designates. The court may direct the witness to produce the designated items in court before trial or before they are to be offered in evidence. When the items arrive, the court may permit the parties and their attorneys to inspect all or part of them.

> **(2) Quashing or Modifying the Subpoena.** On motion made promptly, the court may quash or modify the subpoena if compliance would be unreasonable or oppressive.

> **(3) Subpoena for Personal or Confidential Information About a Victim.** After a complaint, indictment, or information is filed, a subpoena requiring the production of

personal or confidential information about a victim may be served on a third party only by court order. Before entering the order and unless there are exceptional circumstances, the court must require giving notice to the victim so that the victim can move to quash or modify the subpoena or otherwise object.

(d) Service. A marshal, a deputy marshal, or any nonparty who is at least 18 years old may serve a subpoena. The server must deliver a copy of the subpoena to the witness and must tender to the witness one day's witness-attendance fee and the legal mileage allowance. The server need not tender the attendance fee or mileage allowance when the United States, a federal officer, or a federal agency has requested the subpoena.

(e) Place of Service.

(1) In the United States. A subpoena requiring a witness to attend a hearing or trial may be served at any place within the United States.

(2) In a Foreign Country. If the witness is in a foreign country, 28 U.S.C. § 1783 governs the subpoena's service.

(f) Issuing a Deposition Subpoena.

(1) Issuance. A court order to take a deposition authorizes the clerk in the district where the deposition is to be taken to issue a subpoena for any witness named or described in the order.

(2) Place. After considering the convenience of the witness and the parties, the court may order—and the subpoena may require—the witness to appear anywhere the court designates.

(g) Contempt. The court (other than a magistrate judge) may hold in contempt a witness who, without adequate excuse, disobeys a subpoena issued by a federal court in that district. A magistrate judge may hold in contempt a witness who, without adequate excuse, disobeys a subpoena issued by that magistrate judge as provided in 28 U.S.C. § 636(e).

(h) Information Not Subject to a Subpoena. No party may subpoena a statement of a witness or of a prospective witness under this rule. Rule 26.2 governs the production of the statement.

Rule 17.1. Pretrial Conference

On its own, or on a party's motion, the court may hold one or more pretrial conferences to promote a fair and expeditious trial. When a conference ends, the court must prepare and file a memorandum of any matters agreed to during the conference. The government may not use any statement made during the conference by the defendant or the defendant's attorney unless it is in writing and is signed by the defendant and the defendant's attorney.

Rule 18. Place of Prosecution and Trial

Unless a statute or these rules permit otherwise, the government must prosecute an offense in a district where the offense was committed. The court must set the place of trial within the district with due regard for the convenience of the defendant, any victim, and the witnesses, and the prompt administration of justice.

Rule 19. [Reserved]

Rule 20. Transfer for Plea and Sentence

(a) Consent to Transfer. A prosecution may be transferred from the district where the indictment or information is pending, or from which a warrant on a complaint has been issued, to the district where the defendant is arrested, held, or present if:

(1) the defendant states in writing a wish to plead guilty or nolo contendere and to waive trial in the district where the indictment, information, or complaint is pending, consents in writing to the court's disposing of the case in the transferee district, and files the statement in the transferee district; and

(2) the United States attorneys in both districts approve the transfer in writing.

(b) Clerk's Duties. After receiving the defendant's statement and the required approvals, the clerk where the indictment, information, or complaint is pending must send the file, or a certified copy, to the clerk in the transferee district.

(c) Effect of a Not Guilty Plea. If the defendant pleads not guilty after the case has been transferred under Rule 20(a), the clerk must return the papers to the court where the prosecution began, and that court must restore the proceeding to its docket. The defendant's statement that the defendant wished to plead guilty or nolo contendere is not, in any civil or criminal proceeding, admissible against the defendant.

(d) Juveniles.

(1) Consent to Transfer. A juvenile, as defined in 18 U.S.C. § 5031, may be proceeded against as a juvenile delinquent in the district where the juvenile is arrested, held, or present if:

(A) the alleged offense that occurred in the other district is not punishable by death or life imprisonment;

(B) an attorney has advised the juvenile;

(C) the court has informed the juvenile of the juvenile's rights—including the right to be returned to the district where the offense allegedly occurred—and the consequences of waiving those rights;

(D) the juvenile, after receiving the court's information about rights, consents in writing to be proceeded against in the transferee district, and files the consent in the transferee district;

(E) the United States attorneys for both districts approve the transfer in writing; and

(F) the transferee court approves the transfer.

(2) Clerk's Duties. After receiving the juvenile's written consent and the required approvals, the clerk where the indictment, information, or complaint is pending or where the alleged offense occurred must send the file, or a certified copy, to the clerk in the transferee district.

Rule 21. Transfer for Trial

(a) For Prejudice. Upon the defendant's motion, the court must transfer the proceeding against that defendant to another district if the court is satisfied that so great a prejudice against the defendant exists in the transferring district that the defendant cannot obtain a fair and impartial trial there.

(b) For Convenience. Upon the defendant's motion, the court may transfer the proceeding, or one or more counts, against that defendant to another district for the convenience of the parties, any victim, and the witnesses, and in the interest of justice.

(c) Proceedings on Transfer. When the court orders a transfer, the clerk must send to the transferee district the file, or a certified copy, and any bail taken. The prosecution will then continue in the transferee district.

(d) Time to File a Motion to Transfer. A motion to transfer may be made at or before arraignment or at any other time the court or these rules prescribe.

Rule 22. [Transferred]

Rule 23. Jury or Nonjury Trial

(a) Jury Trial. If the defendant is entitled to a jury trial, the trial must be by jury unless:

> **(1)** the defendant waives a jury trial in writing;
>
> **(2)** the government consents; and
>
> **(3)** the court approves.

(b) Jury Size.

> **(1) In General.** A jury consists of 12 persons unless this rule provides otherwise.
>
> **(2) Stipulation for a Smaller Jury.** At any time before the verdict, the parties may, with the court's approval, stipulate in writing that:
>
>> **(A)** the jury may consist of fewer than 12 persons; or
>>
>> **(B)** a jury of fewer than 12 persons may return a verdict if the court finds it necessary to excuse a juror for good cause after the trial begins.
>
> **(3) Court Order for a Jury of 11.** After the jury has retired to deliberate, the court may permit a jury of 11 persons to return a verdict, even without a stipulation by the parties, if the court finds good cause to excuse a juror.

(c) Nonjury Trial. In a case tried without a jury, the court must find the defendant guilty or not guilty. If a party requests before the finding of guilty or not guilty, the court must state its specific findings of fact in open court or in a written decision or opinion.

Rule 24. Trial Jurors

(a) Examination.

> **(1) In General.** The court may examine prospective jurors or may permit the attorneys for the parties to do so.
>
> **(2) Court Examination.** If the court examines the jurors, it must permit the attorneys for the parties to:
>
>> **(A)** ask further questions that the court considers proper; or
>>
>> **(B)** submit further questions that the court may ask if it considers them proper.

(b) Peremptory Challenges. Each side is entitled to the number of peremptory challenges to prospective jurors specified below. The court may allow additional peremptory challenges to multiple defendants, and may allow the defendants to exercise those challenges separately or jointly.

> **(1) Capital Case.** Each side has 20 peremptory challenges when the government seeks the death penalty.
>
> **(2) Other Felony Case.** The government has 6 peremptory challenges and the defendant or defendants jointly have 10 peremptory challenges when the defendant is charged with a crime punishable by imprisonment of more than one year.
>
> **(3) Misdemeanor Case.** Each side has 3 peremptory challenges when the defendant is charged with a crime punishable by fine, imprisonment of one year or less, or both.

(c) Alternate Jurors.

(1) In General. The court may impanel up to 6 alternate jurors to replace any jurors who are unable to perform or who are disqualified from performing their duties.

(2) Procedure.

(A) Alternate jurors must have the same qualifications and be selected and sworn in the same manner as any other juror.

(B) Alternate jurors replace jurors in the same sequence in which the alternates were selected. An alternate juror who replaces a juror has the same authority as the other jurors.

(3) Retaining Alternate Jurors. The court may retain alternate jurors after the jury retires to deliberate. The court must ensure that a retained alternate does not discuss the case with anyone until that alternate replaces a juror or is discharged. If an alternate replaces a juror after deliberations have begun, the court must instruct the jury to begin its deliberations anew.

(4) Peremptory Challenges. Each side is entitled to the number of additional peremptory challenges to prospective alternate jurors specified below. These additional challenges may be used only to remove alternate jurors.

(A) One or Two Alternates. One additional peremptory challenge is permitted when one or two alternates are impaneled.

(B) Three or Four Alternates. Two additional peremptory challenges are permitted when three or four alternates are impaneled.

(C) Five or Six Alternates. Three additional peremptory challenges are permitted when five or six alternates are impaneled.

Rule 25. Judge's Disability

(a) During Trial. Any judge regularly sitting in or assigned to the court may complete a jury trial if:

(1) the judge before whom the trial began cannot proceed because of death, sickness, or other disability; and

(2) the judge completing the trial certifies familiarity with the trial record.

(b) After a Verdict or Finding of Guilty.

(1) In General. After a verdict or finding of guilty, any judge regularly sitting in or assigned to a court may complete the court's duties if the judge who presided at trial cannot perform those duties because of absence, death, sickness, or other disability.

(2) Granting a New Trial. The successor judge may grant a new trial if satisfied that:

(A) a judge other than the one who presided at the trial cannot perform the post-trial duties; or

(B) a new trial is necessary for some other reason.

Rule 26. Taking Testimony

In every trial the testimony of witnesses must be taken in open court, unless otherwise provided by a statute or by rules adopted under 28 U.S.C. §§ 2072–2077.

Rule 26.1. Foreign Law Determination

A party intending to raise an issue of foreign law must provide the court and all parties with reasonable written notice. Issues of foreign law are questions of law, but in deciding such issues a court may consider any relevant material or source—including testimony—without regard to the Federal Rules of Evidence.

Rule 26.2. Producing a Witness's Statement

(a) Motion to Produce. After a witness other than the defendant has testified on direct examination, the court, on motion of a party who did not call the witness, must order an attorney for the government or the defendant and the defendant's attorney to produce, for the examination and use of the moving party, any statement of the witness that is in their possession and that relates to the subject matter of the witness's testimony.

(b) Producing the Entire Statement. If the entire statement relates to the subject matter of the witness's testimony, the court must order that the statement be delivered to the moving party.

(c) Producing a Redacted Statement. If the party who called the witness claims that the statement contains information that is privileged or does not relate to the subject matter of the witness's testimony, the court must inspect the statement in camera. After excising any privileged or unrelated portions, the court must order delivery of the redacted statement to the moving party. If the defendant objects to an excision, the court must preserve the entire statement with the excised portion indicated, under seal, as part of the record.

(d) Recess to Examine a Statement. The court may recess the proceedings to allow time for a party to examine the statement and prepare for its use.

(e) Sanction for Failure to Produce or Deliver a Statement. If the party who called the witness disobeys an order to produce or deliver a statement, the court must strike the witness's testimony from the record. If an attorney for the government disobeys the order, the court must declare a mistrial if justice so requires.

(f) "Statement" Defined. As used in this rule, a witness's "statement" means:

(1) a written statement that the witness makes and signs, or otherwise adopts or approves;

(2) a substantially verbatim, contemporaneously recorded recital of the witness's oral statement that is contained in any recording or any transcription of a recording; or

(3) the witness's statement to a grand jury, however taken or recorded, or a transcription of such a statement.

(g) Scope. This rule applies at trial, at a suppression hearing under Rule 12, and to the extent specified in the following rules:

(1) Rule 5.1(h) (preliminary hearing);

(2) Rule 32(i)(2) (sentencing);

(3) Rule 32.1(e) (hearing to revoke or modify probation or supervised release);

(4) Rule 46(j) (detention hearing); and

(5) Rule 8 of the Rules Governing Proceedings under 28 U.S.C. § 2255.

Rule 26.3. Mistrial

Before ordering a mistrial, the court must give each defendant and the government an opportunity to comment on the propriety of the order, to state whether that party consents or objects, and to suggest alternatives.

Rule 27. Proving an Official Record

A party may prove an official record, an entry in such a record, or the lack of a record or entry in the same manner as in a civil action.

Rule 28. Interpreters

The court may select, appoint, and set the reasonable compensation for an interpreter. The compensation must be paid from funds provided by law or by the government, as the court may direct.

Rule 29. Motion for a Judgment of Acquittal

(a) Before Submission to the Jury. After the government closes its evidence or after the close of all the evidence, the court on the defendant's motion must enter a judgment of acquittal of any offense for which the evidence is insufficient to sustain a conviction. The court may on its own consider whether the evidence is insufficient to sustain a conviction. If the court denies a motion for a judgment of acquittal at the close of the government's evidence, the defendant may offer evidence without having reserved the right to do so.

(b) Reserving Decision. The court may reserve decision on the motion, proceed with the trial (where the motion is made before the close of all the evidence), submit the case to the jury, and decide the motion either before the jury returns a verdict or after it returns a verdict of guilty or is discharged without having returned a verdict. If the court reserves decision, it must decide the motion on the basis of the evidence at the time the ruling was reserved.

(c) After Jury Verdict or Discharge.

    (1) Time for a Motion. A defendant may move for a judgment of acquittal, or renew such a motion, within 14 days after a guilty verdict or after the court discharges the jury, whichever is later.

    (2) Ruling on the Motion. If the jury has returned a guilty verdict, the court may set aside the verdict and enter an acquittal. If the jury has failed to return a verdict, the court may enter a judgment of acquittal.

    (3) No Prior Motion Required. A defendant is not required to move for a judgment of acquittal before the court submits the case to the jury as a prerequisite for making such a motion after jury discharge.

(d) Conditional Ruling on a Motion for a New Trial.

    (1) Motion for a New Trial. If the court enters a judgment of acquittal after a guilty verdict, the court must also conditionally determine whether any motion for a new trial should be granted if the judgment of acquittal is later vacated or reversed. The court must specify the reasons for that determination.

    (2) Finality. The court's order conditionally granting a motion for a new trial does not affect the finality of the judgment of acquittal.

    (3) Appeal.

        (A) Grant of a Motion for a New Trial. If the court conditionally grants a motion for a new trial and an appellate court later reverses the judgment of acquittal, the trial court must proceed with the new trial unless the appellate court orders otherwise.

        (B) Denial of a Motion for a New Trial. If the court conditionally denies a motion for a new trial, an appellee may assert that the denial was erroneous. If the appellate court later reverses the judgment of acquittal, the trial court must proceed as the appellate court directs.

Rule 29.1. Closing Argument

Closing arguments proceed in the following order:

(a) the government argues;

(b) the defense argues; and

(c) the government rebuts.

Rule 30. Jury Instructions

(a) In General. Any party may request in writing that the court instruct the jury on the law as specified in the request. The request must be made at the close of the evidence or at any earlier time that the court reasonably sets. When the request is made, the requesting party must furnish a copy to every other party.

(b) Ruling on a Request. The court must inform the parties before closing arguments how it intends to rule on the requested instructions.

(c) Time for Giving Instructions. The court may instruct the jury before or after the arguments are completed, or at both times.

(d) Objections to Instructions. A party who objects to any portion of the instructions or to a failure to give a requested instruction must inform the court of the specific objection and the grounds for the objection before the jury retires to deliberate. An opportunity must be given to object out of the jury's hearing and, on request, out of the jury's presence. Failure to object in accordance with this rule precludes appellate review, except as permitted under Rule 52(b).

Rule 31. Jury Verdict

(a) Return. The jury must return its verdict to a judge in open court. The verdict must be unanimous.

(b) Partial Verdicts, Mistrial, and Retrial.

(1) Multiple Defendants. If there are multiple defendants, the jury may return a verdict at any time during its deliberations as to any defendant about whom it has agreed.

(2) Multiple Counts. If the jury cannot agree on all counts as to any defendant, the jury may return a verdict on those counts on which it has agreed.

(3) Mistrial and Retrial. If the jury cannot agree on a verdict on one or more counts, the court may declare a mistrial on those counts. The government may retry any defendant on any count on which the jury could not agree.

(c) Lesser Offense or Attempt. A defendant may be found guilty of any of the following:

(1) an offense necessarily included in the offense charged;

(2) an attempt to commit the offense charged; or

(3) an attempt to commit an offense necessarily included in the offense charged, if the attempt is an offense in its own right.

(d) Jury Poll. After a verdict is returned but before the jury is discharged, the court must on a party's request, or may on its own, poll the jurors individually. If the poll reveals a lack of unanimity, the court may direct the jury to deliberate further or may declare a mistrial and discharge the jury.

Rule 32. Sentencing and Judgment

(a) **[Reserved.]**

(b) **Time of Sentencing.**

(1) **In General.** The court must impose sentence without unnecessary delay.

(2) **Changing Time Limits.** The court may, for good cause, change any time limits prescribed in this rule.

(c) **Presentence Investigation.**

(1) **Required Investigation.**

(A) **In General.** The probation officer must conduct a presentence investigation and submit a report to the court before it imposes sentence unless:

(i) 18 U.S.C. § 3593(c) or another statute requires otherwise; or

(ii) the court finds that the information in the record enables it to meaningfully exercise its sentencing authority under 18 U.S.C. § 3553, and the court explains its finding on the record.

(B) **Restitution.** If the law permits restitution, the probation officer must conduct an investigation and submit a report that contains sufficient information for the court to order restitution.

(2) **Interviewing the Defendant.** The probation officer who interviews a defendant as part of a presentence investigation must, on request, give the defendant's attorney notice and a reasonable opportunity to attend the interview.

(d) **Presentence Report.**

(1) **Applying the Sentencing Guidelines.** The presentence report must:

(A) identify all applicable guidelines and policy statements of the Sentencing Commission;

(B) calculate the defendant's offense level and criminal history category;

(C) state the resulting sentencing range and kinds of sentences available;

(D) identify any factor relevant to:

(i) the appropriate kind of sentence, or

(ii) the appropriate sentence within the applicable sentencing range; and

(E) identify any basis for departing from the applicable sentencing range.

(2) **Additional Information.** The presentence report must also contain the following:

(A) the defendant's history and characteristics, including:

(i) any prior criminal record;

(ii) the defendant's financial condition; and

(iii) any circumstances affecting the defendant's behavior that maybe helpful in imposing sentence or in correctional treatment;

(B) information that assesses any financial, social, psychological, and medical impact on any victim;

(C) when appropriate, the nature and extent of nonprison programs and resources available to the defendant;

(D) when the law provides for restitution, information sufficient for a restitution order;

(E) if the court orders a study under 18 U.S.C. § 3552(b), any resulting report and recommendation;

(F) a statement of whether the government seeks forfeiture under Rule 32.2 and any other law; and

(G) any other information that the court requires, including information relevant to the factors under 18 U.S.C. § 3553(a).

(3) **Exclusions.** The presentence report must exclude the following:

(A) any diagnoses that, if disclosed, might seriously disrupt a rehabilitation program;

(B) any sources of information obtained upon a promise of confidentiality; and

(C) any other information that, if disclosed, might result in physical or other harm to the defendant or others.

(e) **Disclosing the Report and Recommendation.**

(1) **Time to Disclose.** Unless the defendant has consented in writing, the probation officer must not submit a presentence report to the court or disclose its contents to anyone until the defendant has pleaded guilty or nolo contendere, or has been found guilty.

(2) **Minimum Required Notice.** The probation officer must give the presentence report to the defendant, the defendant's attorney, and an attorney for the government at least 35 days before sentencing unless the defendant waives this minimum period.

(3) **Sentence Recommendation.** By local rule or by order in a case, the court may direct the probation officer not to disclose to anyone other than the court the officer's recommendation on the sentence.

(f) **Objecting to the Report.**

(1) **Time to Object.** Within 14 days after receiving the presentence report, the parties must state in writing any objections, including objections to material information, sentencing guideline ranges, and policy statements contained in or omitted from the report.

(2) **Serving Objections.** An objecting party must provide a copy of its objections to the opposing party and to the probation officer.

(3) **Action on Objections.** After receiving objections, the probation officer may meet with the parties to discuss the objections. The probation officer may then investigate further and revise the presentence report as appropriate.

(g) **Submitting the Report.** At least 7 days before sentencing, the probation officer must submit to the court and to the parties the presentence report and an addendum containing any unresolved objections, the grounds for those objections, and the probation officer's comments on them.

(h) **Notice of Possible Departure from Sentencing Guidelines.** Before the court may depart from the applicable sentencing range on a ground not identified for departure either in the presentence report or in a party's prehearing submission, the court must give the parties reasonable notice that it is contemplating such a departure. The notice must specify any ground on which the court is contemplating a departure.

(i) Sentencing.

(1) In General. At sentencing, the court:

(A) must verify that the defendant and the defendant's attorney have read and discussed the presentence report and any addendum to the report;

(B) must give to the defendant and an attorney for the government a written summary of—or summarize in camera—any information excluded from the presentence report under Rule 32(d)(3) on which the court will rely in sentencing, and give them a reasonable opportunity to comment on that information;

(C) must allow the parties' attorneys to comment on the probation officer's determinations and other matters relating to an appropriate sentence; and

(D) may, for good cause, allow a party to make a new objection at any time before sentence is imposed.

(2) Introducing Evidence; Producing a Statement. The court may permit the parties to introduce evidence on the objections. If a witness testifies at sentencing, Rule 26.2(a)–(d) and (f) applies. If a party fails to comply with a Rule 26.2 order to produce a witness's statement, the court must not consider that witness's testimony.

(3) Court Determinations. At sentencing, the court:

(A) may accept any undisputed portion of the presentence report as a finding of fact;

(B) must—for any disputed portion of the presentence report or other controverted matter—rule on the dispute or determine that a ruling is unnecessary either because the matter will not affect sentencing, or because the court will not consider the matter in sentencing; and

(C) must append a copy of the court's determinations under this rule to any copy of the presentence report made available to the Bureau of Prisons.

(4) Opportunity to Speak.

(A) By a Party. Before imposing sentence, the court must:

(i) provide the defendant's attorney an opportunity to speak on the defendant's behalf;

(ii) address the defendant personally in order to permit the defendant to speak or present any information to mitigate the sentence; and

(iii) provide an attorney for the government an opportunity to speak equivalent to that of the defendant's attorney.

(B) By a Victim. Before imposing sentence, the court must address any victim of the crime who is present at sentencing and must permit the victim to be reasonably heard.

(C) In Camera Proceedings. Upon a party's motion and for good cause, the court may hear in camera any statement made under Rule 32(i)(4).

(j) Defendant's Right to Appeal.

(1) Advice of a Right to Appeal.

(A) Appealing a Conviction. If the defendant pleaded not guilty and was convicted, after sentencing the court must advise the defendant of the right to appeal the conviction.

(B) Appealing a Sentence. After sentencing—regardless of the defendant's plea—the court must advise the defendant of any right to appeal the sentence.

(C) Appeal Costs. The court must advise a defendant who is unable to pay appeal costs of the right to ask for permission to appeal in forma pauperis.

(2) Clerk's Filing of Notice. If the defendant so requests, the clerk must immediately prepare and file a notice of appeal on the defendant's behalf.

(k) Judgment.

(1) In General. In the judgment of conviction, the court must set forth the plea, the jury verdict or the court's findings, the adjudication, and the sentence. If the defendant is found not guilty or is otherwise entitled to be discharged, the court must so order. The judge must sign the judgment, and the clerk must enter it.

(2) Criminal Forfeiture. Forfeiture procedures are governed by Rule 32.2.

Rule 32.1. Revoking or Modifying Probation or Supervised Release

(a) Initial Appearance.

(1) Person In Custody. A person held in custody for violating probation or supervised release must be taken without unnecessary delay before a magistrate judge.

(A) If the person is held in custody in the district where an alleged violation occurred, the initial appearance must be in that district.

(B) If the person is held in custody in a district other than where an alleged violation occurred, the initial appearance must be in that district, or in an adjacent district if the appearance can occur more promptly there.

(2) Upon a Summons. When a person appears in response to a summons for violating probation or supervised release, a magistrate judge must proceed under this rule.

(3) Advice. The judge must inform the person of the following:

(A) the alleged violation of probation or supervised release;

(B) the person's right to retain counsel or to request that counsel be appointed if the person cannot obtain counsel; and

(C) the person's right, if held in custody, to a preliminary hearing under Rule 32.1(b)(1).

(4) Appearance in the District With Jurisdiction. If the person is arrested or appears in the district that has jurisdiction to conduct a revocation hearing—either originally or by transfer of jurisdiction—the court must proceed under Rule 32.1(b)–(e).

(5) Appearance in a District Lacking Jurisdiction. If the person is arrested or appears in a district that does not have jurisdiction to conduct a revocation hearing, the magistrate judge must:

(A) if the alleged violation occurred in the district of arrest, conduct a preliminary hearing under Rule 32.1(b) and either:

(i) transfer the person to the district that has jurisdiction, if the judge finds probable cause to believe that a violation occurred; or

(ii) dismiss the proceedings and so notify the court that has jurisdiction, if the judge finds no probable cause to believe that a violation occurred; or

(B) if the alleged violation did not occur in the district of arrest, transfer the person to the district that has jurisdiction if:

(i) the government produces certified copies of the judgment, warrant, and warrant application or produces copies of those certified documents by reliable electronic means; and

(ii) the judge finds that the person is the same person named in the warrant.

(6) Release or Detention. The magistrate judge may release or detain the person under 18 U.S.C. § 3143(a)(1) pending further proceedings. The burden of establishing by clear and convincing evidence that the person will not flee or pose a danger to any other person or to the community rests with the person.

(b) Revocation.

(1) Preliminary Hearing.

(A) In General. If a person is in custody for violating a condition of probation or supervised release, a magistrate judge must promptly conduct a hearing to determine whether there is probable cause to believe that a violation occurred. The person may waive the hearing.

(B) Requirements. The hearing must be recorded by a court reporter or by a suitable recording device. The judge must give the person:

(i) notice of the hearing and its purpose, the alleged violation, and the person's right to retain counsel or to request that counsel be appointed if the person cannot obtain counsel;

(ii) an opportunity to appear at the hearing and present evidence; and

(iii) upon request, an opportunity to question any adverse witness, unless the judge determines that the interest of justice does not require the witness to appear.

(C) Referral. If the judge finds probable cause, the judge must conduct a revocation hearing. If the judge does not find probable cause, the judge must dismiss the proceeding.

(2) Revocation Hearing. Unless waived by the person, the court must hold the revocation hearing within a reasonable time in the district having jurisdiction. The person is entitled to:

(A) written notice of the alleged violation;

(B) disclosure of the evidence against the person;

(C) an opportunity to appear, present evidence, and question any adverse witness unless the court determines that the interest of justice does not require the witness to appear;

(D) notice of the person's right to retain counsel or to request that counsel be appointed if the person cannot obtain counsel; and

(E) an opportunity to make a statement and present any information in mitigation.

(c) Modification.

(1) In General. Before modifying the conditions of probation or supervised release, the court must hold a hearing, at which the person has the right to counsel and an opportunity to make a statement and present any information in mitigation.

(2) Exceptions. A hearing is not required if:

(A) the person waives the hearing; or

(B) the relief sought is favorable to the person and does not extend the term of probation or of supervised release; and

(C) an attorney for the government has received notice of the relief sought, has had a reasonable opportunity to object, and has not done so.

(d) Disposition of the Case. The court's disposition of the case is governed by 18 U.S.C. § 3563 and § 3565 (probation) and § 3583 (supervised release).

(e) Producing a Statement. Rule 26.2(a)–(d) and (f) applies at a hearing under this rule. If a party fails to comply with a Rule 26.2 order to produce a witness's statement, the court must not consider that witness's testimony.

Rule 32.2. Criminal Forfeiture

(a) Notice to the Defendant. A court must not enter a judgment of forfeiture in a criminal proceeding unless the indictment or information contains notice to the defendant that the government will seek the forfeiture of property as part of any sentence in accordance with the applicable statute. The notice should not be designated as a count of the indictment or information. The indictment or information need not identify the property subject to forfeiture or specify the amount of any forfeiture money judgment that the government seeks.

(b) Entering a Preliminary Order of Forfeiture.

(1) Forfeiture Phase of the Trial.

(A) Forfeiture Determinations. As soon as practical after a verdict or finding of guilty, or after a plea of guilty or nolo contendere is accepted, on any count in an indictment or information regarding which criminal forfeiture is sought, the court must determine what property is subject to forfeiture under the applicable statute. If the government seeks forfeiture of specific property, the court must determine whether the government has established the requisite nexus between the property and the offense. If the government seeks a personal money judgment, the court must determine the amount of money that the defendant will be ordered to pay.

(B) Evidence and Hearing. The court's determination may be based on evidence already in the record, including any written plea agreement, and on any additional evidence or information submitted by the parties and accepted by the court as relevant and reliable. If the forfeiture is contested, on either party's request the court must conduct a hearing after the verdict or finding of guilty.

(2) Preliminary Order.

(A) Contents of a Specific Order. If the court finds that property is subject to forfeiture, it must promptly enter a preliminary order of forfeiture setting forth the amount of any money judgment, directing the forfeiture of specific property, and directing the forfeiture of any substitute property if the government has met the statutory criteria. The court must enter the order without regard to any third party's interest in the property. Determining whether a third party has such an interest must be deferred until any third party files a claim in an ancillary proceeding under Rule 32.2(c).

(B) Timing. Unless doing so is impractical, the court must enter the preliminary order sufficiently in advance of sentencing to allow the parties to suggest revisions or modifications before the order becomes final as to the defendant under Rule 32.2(b)(4).

(C) General Order. If, before sentencing, the court cannot identify all the specific property subject to forfeiture or calculate the total amount of the money judgment, the court may enter a forfeiture order that:

(i) lists any identified property;

(ii) describes other property in general terms; and

(iii) states that the order will be amended under Rule 32.2(e)(1) when additional specific property is identified or the amount of the money judgment has been calculated.

(3) Seizing Property. The entry of a preliminary order of forfeiture authorizes the Attorney General (or a designee) to seize the specific property subject to forfeiture; to conduct any discovery the court considers proper in identifying, locating, or disposing of the property; and to commence proceedings that comply with any statutes governing third-party rights. The court may include in the order of forfeiture conditions reasonably necessary to preserve the property's value pending any appeal.

(4) Sentence and Judgment.

(A) When Final. At sentencing—or at any time before sentencing if the defendant consents—the preliminary forfeiture order becomes final as to the defendant. If the order directs the defendant to forfeit specific property, it remains preliminary as to third parties until the ancillary proceeding is concluded under Rule 32.2(c).

(B) Notice and Inclusion in the Judgment. The court must include the forfeiture when orally announcing the sentence or must otherwise ensure that the defendant knows of the forfeiture at sentencing. The court must also include the forfeiture order, directly or by reference, in the judgment, but the court's failure to do so may be corrected at any time under Rule 36.

(C) Time to Appeal. The time for the defendant or the government to file an appeal from the forfeiture order, or from the court's failure to enter an order, begins to run when judgment is entered. If the court later amends or declines to amend a forfeiture order to include additional property under Rule 32.2(e), the defendant or the government may file an appeal regarding that property under Federal Rule of Appellate Procedure 4(b). The time for that appeal runs from the date when the order granting or denying the amendment becomes final.

(5) Jury Determination.

(A) Retaining the Jury. In any case tried before a jury, if the indictment or information states that the government is seeking forfeiture, the court must determine before the jury begins deliberating whether either party requests that the jury be retained to determine the forfeitability of specific property if it returns a guilty verdict.

(B) Special Verdict Form. If a party timely requests to have the jury determine forfeiture, the government must submit a proposed Special Verdict Form listing each property subject to forfeiture and asking the jury to determine whether the government has established the requisite nexus between the property and the offense committed by the defendant.

(6) Notice of the Forfeiture Order.

(A) Publishing and Sending Notice. If the court orders the forfeiture of specific property, the government must publish notice of the order and send notice to any person who reasonably appears to be a potential claimant with standing to contest the forfeiture in the ancillary proceeding.

(B) Content of the Notice. The notice must describe the forfeited property, state the times under the applicable statute when a petition contesting the forfeiture must be filed, and state the name and contact information for the government attorney to be served with the petition.

(C) Means of Publication; Exceptions to Publication Requirement. Publication must take place as described in Supplemental Rule G(4)(a)(iii) of the Federal Rules of Civil Procedure, and may be by any means described in Supplemental Rule G(4)(a)(iv). Publication is unnecessary if any exception in Supplemental Rule G(4)(a)(i) applies.

(D) Means of Sending the Notice. The notice may be sent in accordance with Supplemental Rules G(4)(b)(iii)–(v) of the Federal Rules of Civil Procedure.

(7) Interlocutory Sale. At any time before entry of a final forfeiture order, the court, in accordance with Supplemental Rule G(7) of the Federal Rules of Civil Procedure, may order the interlocutory sale of property alleged to be forfeitable.

(c) Ancillary Proceeding; Entering a Final Order of Forfeiture.

(1) In General. If, as prescribed by statute, a third party files a petition asserting an interest in the property to be forfeited, the court must conduct an ancillary proceeding, but no ancillary proceeding is required to the extent that the forfeiture consists of a money judgment.

(A) In the ancillary proceeding, the court may, on motion, dismiss the petition for lack of standing, for failure to state a claim, or for any other lawful reason. For purposes of the motion, the facts set forth in the petition are assumed to be true.

(B) After disposing of any motion filed under Rule 32.2(c)(1)(A) and before conducting a hearing on the petition, the court may permit the parties to conduct discovery in accordance with the Federal Rules of Civil Procedure if the court determines that discovery is necessary or desirable to resolve factual issues. When discovery ends, a party may move for summary judgment under Federal Rule of Civil Procedure 56.

(2) Entering a Final Order. When the ancillary proceeding ends, the court must enter a final order of forfeiture by amending the preliminary order as necessary to account for any third-party rights. If no third party files a timely petition, the preliminary order becomes the final order of forfeiture if the court finds that the defendant (or any combination of defendants convicted in the case) had an interest in the property that is forfeitable under the applicable statute. The defendant may not object to the entry of the final order on the ground that the property belongs, in whole or in part, to a codefendant or third party; nor may a third party object to the final order on the ground that the third party had an interest in the property.

(3) Multiple Petitions. If multiple third-party petitions are filed in the same case, an order dismissing or granting one petition is not appealable until rulings are made on all the petitions, unless the court determines that there is no just reason for delay.

(4) Ancillary Proceeding Not Part of Sentencing. An ancillary proceeding is not part of sentencing.

(d) Stay Pending Appeal. If a defendant appeals from a conviction or an order of forfeiture, the court may stay the order of forfeiture on terms appropriate to ensure that the property remains available pending appellate review. A stay does not delay the ancillary proceeding or the determination of a third party's rights or interests. If the court rules in favor of any third party while an appeal is pending, the court may amend the order of forfeiture but must not transfer any property interest to a third party until the decision on appeal becomes final, unless the defendant consents in writing or on the record.

(e) Subsequently Located Property; Substitute Property.

(1) In General. On the government's motion, the court may at any time enter an order of forfeiture or amend an existing order of forfeiture to include property that:

(A) is subject to forfeiture under an existing order of forfeiture but was located and identified after that order was entered; or

(B) is substitute property that qualifies for forfeiture under an applicable statute.

(2) Procedure. If the government shows that the property is subject to forfeiture under Rule 32.2(e)(1), the court must:

(A) enter an order forfeiting that property, or amend an existing preliminary or final order to include it; and

(B) if a third party files a petition claiming an interest in the property, conduct an ancillary proceeding under Rule 32.2(c).

(3) Jury Trial Limited. There is no right to a jury trial under Rule 32.2(e).

Rule 33. New Trial

(a) Defendant's Motion. Upon the defendant's motion, the court may vacate any judgment and grant a new trial if the interest of justice so requires. If the case was tried without a jury, the court may take additional testimony and enter a new judgment.

(b) Time to File.

(1) Newly Discovered Evidence. Any motion for a new trial grounded on newly discovered evidence must be filed within 3 years after the verdict or finding of guilty. If an appeal is pending, the court may not grant a motion for a new trial until the appellate court remands the case.

(2) Other Grounds. Any motion for a new trial grounded on any reason other than newly discovered evidence must be filed within 14 days after the verdict or finding of guilty.

Rule 34. Arresting Judgment

(a) In General. Upon the defendant's motion or on its own, the court must arrest judgment if the court does not have jurisdiction of the charged offense.

(b) Time to File. The defendant must move to arrest judgment within 14 days after the court accepts a verdict or finding of guilty, or after a plea of guilty or nolo contendere.

Rule 35. Correcting or Reducing a Sentence

(a) Correcting Clear Error. Within 14 days after sentencing, the court may correct a sentence that resulted from arithmetical, technical, or other clear error.

(b) Reducing a Sentence for Substantial Assistance.

(1) In General. Upon the government's motion made within one year of sentencing, the court may reduce a sentence if the defendant, after sentencing, provided substantial assistance in investigating or prosecuting another person.

(2) Later Motion. Upon the government's motion made more than one year after sentencing, the court may reduce a sentence if the defendant's substantial assistance involved:

(A) information not known to the defendant until one year or more after sentencing;

(B) information provided by the defendant to the government within one year of sentencing, but which did not become useful to the government until more than one year after sentencing; or

(C) information the usefulness of which could not reasonably have been anticipated by the defendant until more than one year after sentencing and which was promptly provided to the government after its usefulness was reasonably apparent to the defendant.

(3) Evaluating Substantial Assistance. In evaluating whether the defendant has provided substantial assistance, the court may consider the defendant's presentence assistance.

(4) Below Statutory Minimum. When acting under Rule 35(b), the court may reduce the sentence to a level below the minimum sentence established by statute.

(c) "Sentencing" Defined. As used in this rule, "sentencing" means the oral announcement of the sentence.

Rule 36. Clerical Error

After giving any notice it considers appropriate, the court may at any time correct a clerical error in a judgment, order, or other part of the record, or correct an error in the record arising from oversight or omission.

Rule 37. Ruling on a Motion for Relief That Is Barred by a Pending Appeal

(a) Relief Pending Appeal. If a timely motion is made for relief that the court lacks authority to grant because of an appeal that has been docketed and is pending, the court may:

(1) defer considering the motion;

(2) deny the motion; or

(3) state either that it would grant the motion if the court of appeals remands for that purpose or that the motion raises a substantial issue.

(b) Notice to the Court of Appeals. The movant must promptly notify the circuit clerk under Federal Rule of Appellate Procedure 12.1 if the district court states that it would grant the motion or that the motion raises a substantial issue.

(c) Remand. The district court may decide the motion if the court of appeals remands for that purpose.

Rule 38. Staying a Sentence or a Disability

(a) Death Sentence. The court must stay a death sentence if the defendant appeals the conviction or sentence.

(b) Imprisonment.

(1) Stay Granted. If the defendant is released pending appeal, the court must stay a sentence of imprisonment.

(2) Stay Denied; Place of Confinement. If the defendant is not released pending appeal, the court may recommend to the Attorney General that the defendant be confined near the place of the trial or appeal for a period reasonably necessary to permit the defendant to assist in preparing the appeal.

(c) Fine. If the defendant appeals, the district court, or the court of appeals under Federal Rule of Appellate Procedure 8, may stay a sentence to pay a fine or a fine and costs. The court may stay the sentence on any terms considered appropriate and may require the defendant to:

(1) deposit all or part of the fine and costs into the district court's registry pending appeal;

(2) post a bond to pay the fine and costs; or

(3) submit to an examination concerning the defendant's assets and, if appropriate, order the defendant to refrain from dissipating assets.

(d) Probation. If the defendant appeals, the court may stay a sentence of probation. The court must set the terms of any stay.

(e) Restitution and Notice to Victims.

(1) In General. If the defendant appeals, the district court, or the court of appeals under Federal Rule of Appellate Procedure 8, may stay—on any terms considered appropriate—any sentence providing for restitution under 18 U.S.C. § 3556 or notice under 18 U.S.C. § 3555.

(2) Ensuring Compliance. The court may issue any order reasonably necessary to ensure compliance with a restitution order or a notice order after disposition of an appeal, including:

(A) a restraining order;

(B) an injunction;

(C) an order requiring the defendant to deposit all or part of any monetary restitution into the district court's registry; or

(D) an order requiring the defendant to post a bond.

(f) Forfeiture. A stay of a forfeiture order is governed by Rule 32.2(d).

(g) Disability. If the defendant's conviction or sentence creates a civil or employment disability under federal law, the district court, or the court of appeals under Federal Rule of Appellate Procedure 8, may stay the disability pending appeal on any terms considered appropriate. The court may issue any order reasonably necessary to protect the interest represented by the disability pending appeal, including a restraining order or an injunction.

Rule 39. [Reserved]

Rule 40. Arrest for Failing to Appear in Another District

(a) In General. A person must be taken without unnecessary delay before a magistrate judge in the district of arrest if the person has been arrested under a warrant issued in another district for:

(i)   failing to appear as required by the terms of that person's release under 18 U.S.C. §§ 3141–3156 or by a subpoena; or

(ii)   violating conditions of release set in another district.

(b) Proceedings. The judge must proceed under Rule 5(c)(3) as applicable.

(c) Release or Detention Order. The judge may modify any previous release or detention order issued in another district, but must state in writing the reasons for doing so.

(d) Video Teleconferencing. Video teleconferencing may be used to conduct an appearance under this rule if the defendant consents.

Rule 41. Search and Seizure

(a) Scope and Definitions.

(1)   **Scope.** This rule does not modify any statute regulating search or seizure, or the issuance and execution of a search warrant in special circumstances.

(2)   **Definitions.** The following definitions apply under this rule:

(A)   "Property" includes documents, books, papers, any other tangible objects, and information.

(B)   "Daytime" means the hours between 6:00 a.m. and 10:00 p.m. according to local time.

(C)   "Federal law enforcement officer" means a government agent (other than an attorney for the government) who is engaged in enforcing the criminal laws and is within any category of officers authorized by the Attorney General to request a search warrant.

(D)   "Domestic terrorism" and "international terrorism" have the meanings set out in 18 U.S.C. § 2331.

(E)   "Tracking device" has the meaning set out in 18 U.S.C. § 3117(b).

(b) Venue for a Warrant Application. At the request of a federal law enforcement officer or an attorney for the government:

(1)   a magistrate judge with authority in the district—or if none is reasonably available, a judge of a state court of record in the district—has authority to issue a warrant to search for and seize a person or property located within the district;

(2)   a magistrate judge with authority in the district has authority to issue a warrant for a person or property outside the district if the person or property is located within the district when the warrant is issued but might move or be moved outside the district before the warrant is executed; and

(3)   a magistrate judge—in an investigation of domestic terrorism or international terrorism—with authority in any district in which activities related to the terrorism may have occurred has authority to issue a warrant for a person or property within or outside that district;

(4)   a magistrate judge with authority in the district has authority to issue a warrant to install within the district a tracking device; the warrant may authorize use of the device to track the movement of a person or property located within the district, outside the district, or both; and

(5)   a magistrate judge having authority in any district where activities related to the crime may have occurred, or in the District of Columbia, may issue a warrant for property that is located outside the jurisdiction of any state or district, but within any of the following:

(A) a United States territory, possession, or commonwealth;

(B) the premises—no matter who owns them—of a United States diplomatic or consular mission in a foreign state, including any appurtenant building, part of a building, or land used for the mission's purposes; or

(C) a residence and any appurtenant land owned or leased by the United States and used by United States personnel assigned to a United States diplomatic or consular mission in a foreign state.

(6) a magistrate judge with authority in any district where activities related to a crime may have occurred has authority to issue a warrant to use remote access to search electronic storage media and to seize or copy electronically stored information located within or outside that district if:

(A) the district where the media or information is located has been concealed through technological means; or

(B) in an investigation of a violation of 18 U.S.C. § 1030(a)(5), the media are protected computers that have been damaged without authorization and are located in five or more districts.

(c) Persons or Property Subject to Search or Seizure. A warrant may be issued for any of the following:

(1) evidence of a crime;

(2) contraband, fruits of crime, or other items illegally possessed;

(3) property designed for use, intended for use, or used in committing a crime; or

(4) a person to be arrested or a person who is unlawfully restrained.

(d) Obtaining a Warrant.

(1) In General. After receiving an affidavit or other information, a magistrate judge—or if authorized by Rule 41(b), a judge of a state court of record—must issue the warrant if there is probable cause to search for and seize a person or property or to install and use a tracking device.

(2) Requesting a Warrant in the Presence of a Judge.

(A) Warrant on an Affidavit. When a federal law enforcement officer or an attorney for the government presents an affidavit in support of a warrant, the judge may require the affiant to appear personally and may examine under oath the affiant and any witness the affiant produces.

(B) Warrant on Sworn Testimony. The judge may wholly or partially dispense with a written affidavit and base a warrant on sworn testimony if doing so is reasonable under the circumstances.

(C) Recording Testimony. Testimony taken in support of a warrant must be recorded by a court reporter or by a suitable recording device, and the judge must file the transcript or recording with the clerk, along with any affidavit.

(3) Requesting a Warrant by Telephonic or Other Reliable Electronic Means. In accordance with Rule 4.1, a magistrate judge may issue a warrant based on information communicated by telephone or other reliable electronic means.

(e) Issuing the Warrant.

(1) In General. The magistrate judge or a judge of a state court of record must issue the warrant to an officer authorized to execute it.

(2) Contents of the Warrant.

(A) Warrant to Search for and Seize a Person or Property. Except for a tracking-device warrant, the warrant must identify the person or property to be searched, identify any person or property to be seized, and designate the magistrate judge to whom it must be returned. The warrant must command the officer to:

(i) execute the warrant within a specified time no longer than 14 days;

(ii) execute the warrant during the daytime, unless the judge for good cause expressly authorizes execution at another time; and

(iii) return the warrant to the magistrate judge designated in the warrant.

(B) Warrant Seeking Electronically Stored Information. A warrant under Rule 41(e)(2)(A) may authorize the seizure of electronic storage media or the seizure or copying of electronically stored information. Unless otherwise specified, the warrant authorizes a later review of the media or information consistent with the warrant. The time for executing the warrant in Rule 41(e)(2)(A) and (f)(1)(A) refers to the seizure or on-site copying of the media or information, and not to any later off-site copying or review.

(C) Warrant for a Tracking Device. A tracking-device warrant must identify the person or property to be tracked, designate the magistrate judge to whom it must be returned, and specify a reasonable length of time that the device may be used. The time must not exceed 45 days from the date the warrant was issued. The court may, for good cause, grant one or more extensions for a reasonable period not to exceed 45 days each. The warrant must command the officer to:

(i) complete any installation authorized by the warrant within a specified time no longer than 10 days;

(ii) perform any installation authorized by the warrant during the daytime, unless the judge for good cause expressly authorizes installation at another time; and

(iii) return the warrant to the judge designated in the warrant.

(f) Executing and Returning the Warrant.

(1) Warrant to Search for and Seize a Person or Property.

(A) Noting the Time. The officer executing the warrant must enter on it the exact date and time it was executed.

(B) Inventory. An officer present during the execution of the warrant must prepare and verify an inventory of any property seized. The officer must do so in the presence of another officer and the person from whom, or from whose premises, the property was taken. If either one is not present, the officer must prepare and verify the inventory in the presence of at least one other credible person. In a case involving the seizure of electronic storage media or the seizure or copying of electronically stored information, the inventory may be limited to describing the physical storage media that were seized or copied. The officer may retain a copy of the electronically stored information that was seized or copied.

(C) Receipt. The officer executing the warrant must give a copy of the warrant and a receipt for the property taken to the person from whom, or from whose premises, the property was taken or leave a copy of the warrant and receipt at the place where the officer took the property. For a warrant to use remote access to search electronic storage media and seize or copy electronically stored information, the officer must make reasonable efforts to serve a copy of the warrant and receipt on the person whose property was searched or who possessed the information that was seized or copied. Service may be accomplished by any means, including electronic means, reasonably calculated to reach that person.

(D) Return. The officer executing the warrant must promptly return it—together with a copy of the inventory—to the magistrate judge designated on the warrant. The officer may do so by reliable electronic means. The judge must, on request, give a copy of the inventory to the person from whom, or from whose premises, the property was taken and to the applicant for the warrant.

(2) Warrant for a Tracking Device.

(A) Noting the Time. The officer executing a tracking-device warrant must enter on it the exact date and time the device was installed and the period during which it was used.

(B) Return. Within 10 days after the use of the tracking device has ended, the officer executing the warrant must return it to the judge designated in the warrant. The officer may do so by reliable electronic means.

(C) Service. Within 10 days after the use of the tracking device has ended, the officer executing a tracking-device warrant must serve a copy of the warrant on the person who was tracked or whose property was tracked. Service may be accomplished by delivering a copy to the person who, or whose property, was tracked; or by leaving a copy at the person's residence or usual place of abode with an individual of suitable age and discretion who resides at that location and by mailing a copy to the person's last known address. Upon request of the government, the judge may delay notice as provided in Rule 41(f)(3).

(3) Delayed Notice. Upon the government's request, a magistrate judge—or if authorized by Rule 41(b), a judge of a state court of record—may delay any notice required by this rule if the delay is authorized by statute.

(g) Motion to Return Property. A person aggrieved by an unlawful search and seizure of property or by the deprivation of property may move for the property's return. The motion must be filed in the district where the property was seized. The court must receive evidence on any factual issue necessary to decide the motion. If it grants the motion, the court must return the property to the movant, but may impose reasonable conditions to protect access to the property and its use in later proceedings.

(h) Motion to Suppress. A defendant may move to suppress evidence in the court where the trial will occur, as Rule 12 provides.

(i) Forwarding Papers to the Clerk. The magistrate judge to whom the warrant is returned must attach to the warrant a copy of the return, of the inventory, and of all other related papers and must deliver them to the clerk in the district where the property was seized.

Rule 42. Criminal Contempt

(a) Disposition After Notice. Any person who commits criminal contempt may be punished for that contempt after prosecution on notice.

(1) Notice. The court must give the person notice in open court, in an order to show cause, or in an arrest order. The notice must:

(A) state the time and place of the trial;

(B) allow the defendant a reasonable time to prepare a defense; and

(C) state the essential facts constituting the charged criminal contempt and describe it as such.

(2) Appointing a Prosecutor. The court must request that the contempt be prosecuted by an attorney for the government, unless the interest of justice requires the appointment of another attorney. If the government declines the request, the court must appoint another attorney to prosecute the contempt.

(3) Trial and Disposition. A person being prosecuted for criminal contempt is entitled to a jury trial in any case in which federal law so provides and must be released or detained as Rule 46 provides. If the criminal contempt involves disrespect toward or criticism of a judge, that judge is disqualified from presiding at the contempt trial or hearing unless the defendant consents. Upon a finding or verdict of guilty, the court must impose the punishment.

(b) Summary Disposition. Notwithstanding any other provision of these rules, the court (other than a magistrate judge) may summarily punish a person who commits criminal contempt in its presence if the judge saw or heard the contemptuous conduct and so certifies; a magistrate judge may summarily punish a person as provided in 28 U.S.C. § 636(e). The contempt order must recite the facts, be signed by the judge, and be filed with the clerk.

Rule 43. Defendant's Presence

(a) When Required. Unless this rule, Rule 5, or Rule 10 provides otherwise, the defendant must be present at:

(1) the initial appearance, the initial arraignment, and the plea;

(2) every trial stage, including jury impanelment and the return of the verdict; and

(3) sentencing.

(b) When Not Required. A defendant need not be present under any of the following circumstances:

(1) Organizational Defendant. The defendant is an organization represented by counsel who is present.

(2) Misdemeanor Offense. The offense is punishable by fine or by imprisonment for not more than one year, or both, and with the defendant's written consent, the court permits arraignment, plea, trial, and sentencing to occur by video teleconferencing or in the defendant's absence.

(3) Conference or Hearing on a Legal Question. The proceeding involves only a conference or hearing on a question of law.

(4) Sentence Correction. The proceeding involves the correction or reduction of sentence under Rule 35 or 18 U.S.C. § 3582(c).

(c) Waiving Continued Presence.

(1) In General. A defendant who was initially present at trial, or who had pleaded guilty or nolo contendere, waives the right to be present under the following circumstances:

(A) when the defendant is voluntarily absent after the trial has begun, regardless of whether the court informed the defendant of an obligation to remain during trial;

(B) in a noncapital case, when the defendant is voluntarily absent during sentencing; or

(C) when the court warns the defendant that it will remove the defendant from the courtroom for disruptive behavior, but the defendant persists in conduct that justifies removal from the courtroom.

(2) Waiver's Effect. If the defendant waives the right to be present, the trial may proceed to completion, including the verdict's return and sentencing, during the defendant's absence.

Rule 44. Right to and Appointment of Counsel

(a) Right to Appointed Counsel. A defendant who is unable to obtain counsel is entitled to have counsel appointed to represent the defendant at every stage of the proceeding from initial appearance through appeal, unless the defendant waives this right.

(b) Appointment Procedure. Federal law and local court rules govern the procedure for implementing the right to counsel.

(c) Inquiry Into Joint Representation.

(1) Joint Representation. Joint representation occurs when:

(A) two or more defendants have been charged jointly under Rule 8(b) or have been joined for trial under Rule 13; and

(B) the defendants are represented by the same counsel, or counsel who are associated in law practice.

(2) Court's Responsibilities in Cases of Joint Representation. The court must promptly inquire about the propriety of joint representation and must personally advise each defendant of the right to the effective assistance of counsel, including separate representation. Unless there is good cause to believe that no conflict of interest is likely to arise, the court must take appropriate measures to protect each defendant's right to counsel.

Rule 45. Computing and Extending Time

(a) Computing Time. The following rules apply in computing any time period specified in these rules, in any local rule or court order, or in any statute that does not specify a method of computing time.

(1) Period Stated in Days or a Longer Unit. When the period is stated in days or a longer unit of time:

(A) exclude the day of the event that triggers the period;

(B) count every day, including intermediate Saturdays, Sundays, and legal holidays; and

(C) include the last day of the period, but if the last day is a Saturday, Sunday, or legal holiday, the period continues to run until the end of the next day that is not a Saturday, Sunday, or legal holiday.

(2) Period Stated in Hours. When the period is stated in hours:

(A) begin counting immediately on the occurrence of the event that triggers the period;

(B) count every hour, including hours during intermediate Saturdays, Sundays, and legal holidays; and

(C) if the period would end on a Saturday, Sunday, or legal holiday, the period continues to run until the same time on the next day that is not a Saturday, Sunday, or legal holiday.

(3) Inaccessibility of the Clerk's Office. Unless the court orders otherwise, if the clerk's office is inaccessible:

(A) on the last day for filing under Rule 45(a)(1), then the time for filing is extended to the first accessible day that is not a Saturday, Sunday, or legal holiday; or

(B) during the last hour for filing under Rule 45(a)(2), then the time for filing is extended to the same time on the first accessible day that is not a Saturday, Sunday, or legal holiday.

(4) "Last Day" Defined. Unless a different time is set by a statute, local rule, or court order, the last day ends:

(A) for electronic filing, at midnight in the court's time zone; and

(B) for filing by other means, when the clerk's office is scheduled to close.

(5) "Next Day" Defined. The "next day" is determined by continuing to count forward when the period is measured after an event and backward when measured before an event.

(6) "Legal Holiday" Defined. "Legal holiday" means:

(A) the day set aside by statute for observing New Year's Day, Martin Luther King Jr.'s Birthday, Washington's Birthday, Memorial Day, Independence Day, Labor Day, Columbus Day, Veterans' Day, Thanksgiving Day, or Christmas Day;

(B) any day declared a holiday by the President or Congress; and

(C) for periods that are measured after an event, any other day declared a holiday by the state where the district court is located.

(b) Extending Time.

(1) In General. When an act must or may be done within a specified period, the court on its own may extend the time, or for good cause may do so on a party's motion made:

(A) before the originally prescribed or previously extended time expires; or

(B) after the time expires if the party failed to act because of excusable neglect.

(2) Exception. The court may not extend the time to take any action under Rule 35, except as stated in that rule.

(c) Additional Time After Certain Kinds of Service. Whenever a party must or may act within a specified time after being served and service is made under Rule 49(a)(4)(C), (D), and (E), 3 days are added after the period would otherwise expire under subdivision (a).

Rule 46. Release from Custody; Supervising Detention

(a) Before Trial. The provisions of 18 U.S.C. §§ 3142 and 3144 govern pretrial release.

(b) During Trial. A person released before trial continues on release during trial under the same terms and conditions. But the court may order different terms and conditions or terminate the release if necessary to ensure that the person will be present during trial or that the person's conduct will not obstruct the orderly and expeditious progress of the trial.

(c) Pending Sentencing or Appeal. The provisions of 18 U.S.C. § 3143 govern release pending sentencing or appeal. The burden of establishing that the defendant will not flee or pose a danger to any other person or to the community rests with the defendant.

(d) Pending Hearing on a Violation of Probation or Supervised Release. Rule 32.1(a)(6) governs release pending a hearing on a violation of probation or supervised release.

(e) Surety. The court must not approve a bond unless any surety appears to be qualified. Every surety, except a legally approved corporate surety, must demonstrate by affidavit that its assets are adequate. The court may require the affidavit to describe the following:

(1) the property that the surety proposes to use as security;

(2) any encumbrance on that property;

(3) the number and amount of any other undischarged bonds and bail undertakings the surety has issued; and

(4) any other liability of the surety.

(f) Bail Forfeiture.

(1) **Declaration.** The court must declare the bail forfeited if a condition of the bond is breached.

(2) **Setting Aside.** The court may set aside in whole or in part a bail forfeiture upon any condition the court may impose if:

(A) the surety later surrenders into custody the person released on the surety's appearance bond; or

(B) it appears that justice does not require bail forfeiture.

(3) **Enforcement.**

(A) **Default Judgment and Execution.** If it does not set aside a bail forfeiture, the court must, upon the government's motion, enter a default judgment.

(B) **Jurisdiction and Service.** By entering into a bond, each surety submits to the district court's jurisdiction and irrevocably appoints the district clerk as its agent to receive service of any filings affecting its liability.

(C) **Motion to Enforce.** The court may, upon the government's motion, enforce the surety's liability without an independent action. The government must serve any motion, and notice as the court prescribes, on the district clerk. If so served, the clerk must promptly mail a copy to the surety at its last known address.

(4) **Remission.** After entering a judgment under Rule 46(f)(3), the court may remit in whole or in part the judgment under the same conditions specified in Rule 46(f)(2).

(g) Exoneration. The court must exonerate the surety and release any bail when a bond condition has been satisfied or when the court has set aside or remitted the forfeiture. The court must exonerate a surety who deposits cash in the amount of the bond or timely surrenders the defendant into custody.

(h) Supervising Detention Pending Trial.

(1) **In General.** To eliminate unnecessary detention, the court must supervise the detention within the district of any defendants awaiting trial and of any persons held as material witnesses.

(2) **Reports.** An attorney for the government must report biweekly to the court, listing each material witness held in custody for more than 10 days pending indictment, arraignment, or trial. For each material witness listed in the report, an attorney for the government must state why the witness should not be released with or without a deposition being taken under Rule 15(a).

(i) **Forfeiture of Property.** The court may dispose of a charged offense by ordering the forfeiture of 18 U.S.C. § 3142(c)(1)(B)(xi) property under 18 U.S.C. § 3146(d), if a fine in the amount of the property's value would be an appropriate sentence for the charged offense.

(j) **Producing a Statement.**

(1) **In General.** Rule 26.2(a)–(d) and (f) applies at a detention hearing under 18 U.S.C. § 3142, unless the court for good cause rules otherwise.

(2) **Sanctions for Not Producing a Statement.** If a party disobeys a Rule 26.2 order to produce a witness's statement, the court must not consider that witness's testimony at the detention hearing.

Rule 47. Motions and Supporting Affidavits

(a) **In General.** A party applying to the court for an order must do so by motion.

(b) **Form and Content of a Motion.** A motion—except when made during a trial or hearing—must be in writing, unless the court permits the party to make the motion by other means. A motion must state the grounds on which it is based and the relief or order sought. A motion may be supported by affidavit.

(c) **Timing of a Motion.** A party must serve a written motion—other than one that the court may hear ex parte—and any hearing notice at least 7 days before the hearing date, unless a rule or court order sets a different period. For good cause, the court may set a different period upon ex parte application.

(d) **Affidavit Supporting a Motion.** The moving party must serve any supporting affidavit with the motion. A responding party must serve any opposing affidavit at least one day before the hearing, unless the court permits later service.

Rule 48. Dismissal

(a) **By the Government.** The government may, with leave of court, dismiss an indictment, information, or complaint. The government may not dismiss the prosecution during trial without the defendant's consent.

(b) **By the Court.** The court may dismiss an indictment, information, or complaint if unnecessary delay occurs in:

(1) presenting a charge to a grand jury;

(2) filing an information against a defendant; or

(3) bringing a defendant to trial.

Rule 49. Serving and Filing Papers

(a) **Service on a Party.**

(1) **What is Required.** Each of the following must be served on every party: any written motion (other than one to be heard ex parte), written notice, designation of the record on appeal, or similar paper.

(2) **Serving a Party's Attorney.** Unless the court orders otherwise, when these rules or a court order requires or permits service on a party represented by an attorney, service must be made on the attorney instead of the party.

(3) **Service by Electronic Means.**

(A) **Using the Court's Electronic-Filing System.** A party represented by an attorney may serve a paper on a registered user by filing it with the court's electronic-filing system. A party not represented by an attorney may do so only if allowed by court order or local rule. Service is complete upon filing, but is not effective if the serving party learns that it did not reach the person to be served.

(B) Using Other Electronic Means. A paper may be served by any other electronic means that the person consented to in writing. Service is complete upon transmission, but is not effective if the serving party learns that it did not reach the person to be served.

(4) Service by Nonelectronic Means. A paper may be served by:

(A) handing it to the person;

(B) leaving it:

(i) at the person's office with a clerk or other person in charge or, if no one is in charge, in a conspicuous place in the office; or

(ii) if the person has no office or the office is closed, at the person's dwelling or usual place of abode with someone of suitable age and discretion who resides there;

(C) mailing it to the person's last known address—in which event service is complete upon mailing;

(D) leaving it with the court clerk if the person has no known address; or

(E) delivering it by any other means that the person consented to in writing—in which event service is complete when the person making service delivers it to the agency designated to make delivery.

(b) Filing.

(1) When Required; Certificate of Service. Any paper that is required to be served must be filed no later than a reasonable time after service. No certificate of service is required when a paper is served by filing it with the court's electronic filing system. When a paper is served by other means, a certificate of service must be filed with it or within a reasonable time after service or filing.

(2) Means of Filing.

(A) Electronically. A paper is filed electronically by filing it with the court's electronic-filing system. A filing made through a person's electronic-filing account and authorized by that person, together with the person's name on a signature block, constitutes the person's signature. A paper filed electronically is written or in writing under these rules.

(B) Nonelectronically. A paper not filed electronically is filed by delivering it:

(i) to the clerk; or

(ii) to a judge who agrees to accept it for filing, and who must then note the filing date on the paper and promptly send it to the clerk.

(3) Means Used by Represented and Unrepresented Parties.

(A) Represented Party. A party represented by an attorney must file electronically, unless nonelectronic filing is allowed by the court for good cause or is allowed or required by local rule.

(B) Unrepresented Party. A party not represented by an attorney must file nonelectronically, unless allowed to file electronically by court order or local rule.

(4) Signature. Every written motion and other paper must be signed by at least one attorney of record in the attorney's name—or by a person filing a paper if the person is not represented by an attorney. The paper must state the signer's address, e-mail address, and telephone number. Unless a rule or statute specifically states otherwise, a pleading need not be verified or accompanied by an affidavit. The court must strike an unsigned paper unless the omission is promptly corrected after being called to the attorney's or person's attention.

(5) Acceptance by the Clerk. The clerk must not refuse to file a paper solely because it is not in the form prescribed by these rules or by a local rule or practice.

(c) Service and Filing by Nonparties. A nonparty may serve and file a paper only if doing so is required or permitted by law. A nonparty must serve every party as required by Rule 49(a), but may use the court's electronic-filing system only if allowed by court order or local rule.

(d) Notice of a Court Order. When the court issues an order on any post-arraignment motion, the clerk must serve notice of the entry on each party as required by Rule 49(a). A party also may serve notice of the entry by the same means. Except as Federal Rule of Appellate Procedure 4(b) provides otherwise, the clerk's failure to give notice does not affect the time to appeal, or relieve—or authorize the court to relieve—a party's failure to appeal within the allowed time.

Rule 49.1. Privacy Protection for Filings Made with the Court

(a) Redacted Filings. Unless the court orders otherwise, in an electronic or paper filing with the court that contains an individual's social-security number, taxpayer-identification number, or birth date, the name of an individual known to be a minor, a financial-account number, or the home address of an individual, a party or nonparty making the filing may include only:

(1) the last four digits of the social-security number and taxpayer-identification number;

(2) the year of the individual's birth;

(3) the minor's initials;

(4) the last four digits of the financial-account number; and

(5) the city and state of the home address.

(b) Exemptions from the Redaction Requirement. The redaction requirement does not apply to the following:

(1) a financial-account number or real property address that identifies the property allegedly subject to forfeiture in a forfeiture proceeding;

(2) the record of an administrative or agency proceeding;

(3) the official record of a state-court proceeding;

(4) the record of a court or tribunal, if that record was not subject to the redaction requirement when originally filed;

(5) a filing covered by Rule 49.1(d);

(6) a pro se filing in an action brought under 28 U.S.C. §§ 2241, 2254, or 2255;

(7) a court filing that is related to a criminal matter or investigation and that is prepared before the filing of a criminal charge or is not filed as part of any docketed criminal case;

(8) an arrest or search warrant; and

(9) a charging document and an affidavit filed in support of any charging document.

(c) Immigration Cases. A filing in an action brought under 28 U.S.C. § 2241 that relates to the petitioner's immigration rights is governed by Federal Rule of Civil Procedure 5.2.

(d) Filings Made Under Seal. The court may order that a filing be made under seal without redaction. The court may later unseal the filing or order the person who made the filing to file a redacted version for the public record.

(e) Protective Orders. For good cause, the court may by order in a case:

(1) require redaction of additional information; or

(2) limit or prohibit a nonparty's remote electronic access to a document filed with the court.

(f) Option for Additional Unredacted Filing Under Seal. A person making a redacted filing may also file an unredacted copy under seal. The court must retain the unredacted copy as part of the record.

(g) Option for Filing a Reference List. A filing that contains redacted information may be filed together with a reference list that identifies each item of redacted information and specifies an appropriate identifier that uniquely corresponds to each item listed. The list must be filed under seal and may be amended as of right. Any reference in the case to a listed identifier will be construed to refer to the corresponding item of information.

(h) Waiver of Protection of Identifiers. A person waives the protection of Rule 49.1(a) as to the person's own information by filing it without redaction and not under seal.

Rule 50. Prompt Disposition

Scheduling preference must be given to criminal proceedings as far as practicable.

Rule 51. Preserving Claimed Error

(a) Exceptions Unnecessary. Exceptions to rulings or orders of the court are unnecessary.

(b) Preserving a Claim of Error. A party may preserve a claim of error by informing the court—when the court ruling or order is made or sought—of the action the party wishes the court to take, or the party's objection to the court's action and the grounds for that objection. If a party does not have an opportunity to object to a ruling or order, the absence of an objection does not later prejudice that party. A ruling or order that admits or excludes evidence is governed by Federal Rule of Evidence 103.

Rule 52. Harmless and Plain Error

(a) Harmless Error. Any error, defect, irregularity, or variance that does not affect substantial rights must be disregarded.

(b) Plain Error. A plain error that affects substantial rights may be considered even though it was not brought to the court's attention.

Rule 53. Courtroom Photographing and Broadcasting Prohibited

Except as otherwise provided by a statute or these rules, the court must not permit the taking of photographs in the courtroom during judicial proceedings or the broadcasting of judicial proceedings from the courtroom.

Rule 54. [Transferred[1]]

Rule 55. Records

The clerk of the district court must keep records of criminal proceedings in the form prescribed by the Director of the Administrative Office of the United States courts. The clerk must enter in the records every court order or judgment and the date of entry.

Rule 56. When Court Is Open

(a) In General. A district court is considered always open for any filing, and for issuing and returning process, making a motion, or entering an order.

(b) Office Hours. The clerk's office—with the clerk or a deputy in attendance—must be open during business hours on all days except Saturdays, Sundays, and legal holidays.

(c) Special Hours. A court may provide by local rule or order that its clerk's office will be open for specified hours on Saturdays or legal holidays other than those set aside by statute for observing New Year's Day, Martin Luther King, Jr.'s Birthday, Washington's Birthday, Memorial Day, Independence Day, Labor Day, Columbus Day, Veterans' Day, Thanksgiving Day, and Christmas Day.

Rule 57. District Court Rules

(a) In General.

    (1) Adopting Local Rules. Each district court acting by a majority of its district judges may, after giving appropriate public notice and an opportunity to comment, make and amend rules governing its practice. A local rule must be consistent with—but not duplicative of—federal statutes and rules adopted under 28 U.S.C. § 2072 and must conform to any uniform numbering system prescribed by the Judicial Conference of the United States.

    (2) Limiting Enforcement. A local rule imposing a requirement of form must not be enforced in a manner that causes a party to lose rights because of an unintentional failure to comply with the requirement.

(b) Procedure When There Is No Controlling Law. A judge may regulate practice in any manner consistent with federal law, these rules, and the local rules of the district. No sanction or other disadvantage may be imposed for noncompliance with any requirement not in federal law, federal rules, or the local district rules unless the alleged violator was furnished with actual notice of the requirement before the noncompliance.

(c) Effective Date and Notice. A local rule adopted under this rule takes effect on the date specified by the district court and remains in effect unless amended by the district court or abrogated by the judicial council of the circuit in which the district is located. Copies of local rules and their amendments, when promulgated, must be furnished to the judicial council and the Administrative Office of the United States Courts and must be made available to the public.

Rule 58. Petty Offenses and Other Misdemeanors

(a) Scope.

    (1) In General. These rules apply in petty offense and other misdemeanor cases and on appeal to a district judge in a case tried by a magistrate judge, unless this rule provides otherwise.

---

[1]   All of Rule 54 was moved to Rule 1.

(2) Petty Offense Case Without Imprisonment. In a case involving a petty offense for which no sentence of imprisonment will be imposed, the court may follow any provision of these rules that is not inconsistent with this rule and that the court considers appropriate.

(3) Definition. As used in this rule, the term "petty offense for which no sentence of imprisonment will be imposed" means a petty offense for which the court determines that, in the event of conviction, no sentence of imprisonment will be imposed.

(b) Pretrial Procedure.

(1) Charging Document. The trial of a misdemeanor may proceed on an indictment, information, or complaint. The trial of a petty offense may also proceed on a citation or violation notice.

(2) Initial Appearance. At the defendant's initial appearance on a petty offense or other misdemeanor charge, the magistrate judge must inform the defendant of the following:

(A) the charge, and the minimum and maximum penalties, including imprisonment, fines, any special assessment under 18 U.S.C. § 3013, and restitution under 18 U.S.C. § 3556;

(B) the right to retain counsel;

(C) the right to request the appointment of counsel if the defendant is unable to retain counsel—unless the charge is a petty offense for which the appointment of counsel is not required;

(D) the defendant's right not to make a statement, and that any statement made may be used against the defendant;

(E) the right to trial, judgment, and sentencing before a district judge—unless:

(i) the charge is a petty offense; or

(ii) the defendant consents to trial, judgment, and sentencing before a magistrate judge;

(F) the right to a jury trial before either a magistrate judge or a district judge—unless the charge is a petty offense;

(G) any right to a preliminary hearing under Rule 5.1, and the general circumstances, if any, under which the defendant may secure pretrial release; and

(H) that a defendant who is not a United States citizen may request that an attorney for the government or a federal law enforcement official notify a consular officer from the defendant's country of nationality that the defendant has been arrested—but that even without the defendant's request, a treaty or other international agreement may require consular notification.

(3) Arraignment.

(A) Plea Before a Magistrate Judge. A magistrate judge may take the defendant's plea in a petty offense case. In every other misdemeanor case, a magistrate judge may take the plea only if the defendant consents either in writing or on the record to be tried before a magistrate judge and specifically waives trial before a district judge. The defendant may plead not guilty, guilty, or (with the consent of the magistrate judge) nolo contendere.

(B) Failure to Consent. Except in a petty offense case, the magistrate judge must order a defendant who does not consent to trial before a magistrate judge to appear before a district judge for further proceedings.

(c) Additional Procedures in Certain Petty Offense Cases. The following procedures also apply in a case involving a petty offense for which no sentence of imprisonment will be imposed:

(1) Guilty or Nolo Contendere Plea. The court must not accept a guilty or nolo contendere plea unless satisfied that the defendant understands the nature of the charge and the maximum possible penalty.

(2) Waiving Venue.

(A) Conditions of Waiving Venue. If a defendant is arrested, held, or present in a district different from the one where the indictment, information, complaint, citation, or violation notice is pending, the defendant may state in writing a desire to plead guilty or nolo contendere; to waive venue and trial in the district where the proceeding is pending; and to consent to the court's disposing of the case in the district where the defendant was arrested, is held, or is present.

(B) Effect of Waiving Venue. Unless the defendant later pleads not guilty, the prosecution will proceed in the district where the defendant was arrested, is held, or is present. The district clerk must notify the clerk in the original district of the defendant's waiver of venue. The defendant's statement of a desire to plead guilty or nolo contendere is not admissible against the defendant.

(3) Sentencing. The court must give the defendant an opportunity to be heard in mitigation and then proceed immediately to sentencing. The court may, however, postpone sentencing to allow the probation service to investigate or to permit either party to submit additional information.

(4) Notice of a Right to Appeal. After imposing sentence in a case tried on a not-guilty plea, the court must advise the defendant of a right to appeal the conviction and of any right to appeal the sentence. If the defendant was convicted on a plea of guilty or nolo contendere, the court must advise the defendant of any right to appeal the sentence.

(d) Paying a Fixed Sum in Lieu of Appearance.

(1) In General. If the court has a local rule governing forfeiture of collateral, the court may accept a fixed-sum payment in lieu of the defendant's appearance and end the case, but the fixed sum may not exceed the maximum fine allowed by law.

(2) Notice to Appear. If the defendant fails to pay a fixed sum, request a hearing, or appear in response to a citation or violation notice, the district clerk or a magistrate judge may issue a notice for the defendant to appear before the court on a date certain. The notice may give the defendant an additional opportunity to pay a fixed sum in lieu of appearance. The district clerk must serve the notice on the defendant by mailing a copy to the defendant's last known address.

(3) Summons or Warrant. Upon an indictment, or upon a showing by one of the other charging documents specified in Rule 58(b)(1) of probable cause to believe that an offense has been committed and that the defendant has committed it, the court may issue an arrest warrant or, if no warrant is requested by an attorney for the government, a summons. The showing of probable cause must be made under oath or under penalty of perjury, but the affiant need not appear before the court. If the defendant fails to appear before the court in response to a summons, the court may summarily issue a warrant for the defendant's arrest.

(e) Recording the Proceedings. The court must record any proceedings under this rule by using a court reporter or a suitable recording device.

(f) New Trial. Rule 33 applies to a motion for a new trial.

(g) Appeal.

   (1) From a District Judge's Order or Judgment. The Federal Rules of Appellate Procedure govern an appeal from a district judge's order or a judgment of conviction or sentence.

   (2) From a Magistrate Judge's Order or Judgment.

      (A) Interlocutory Appeal. Either party may appeal an order of a magistrate judge to a district judge within 14 days of its entry if a district judge's order could similarly be appealed. The party appealing must file a notice with the clerk specifying the order being appealed and must serve a copy on the adverse party.

      (B) Appeal from a Conviction or Sentence. A defendant may appeal a magistrate judge's judgment of conviction or sentence to a district judge within 14 days of its entry. To appeal, the defendant must file a notice with the clerk specifying the judgment being appealed and must serve a copy on an attorney for the government.

      (C) Record. The record consists of the original papers and exhibits in the case; any transcript, tape, or other recording of the proceedings; and a certified copy of the docket entries. For purposes of the appeal, a copy of the record of the proceedings must be made available to a defendant who establishes by affidavit an inability to pay or give security for the record. The Director of the Administrative Office of the United States Courts must pay for those copies.

      (D) Scope of Appeal. The defendant is not entitled to a trial de novo by a district judge. The scope of the appeal is the same as in an appeal to the court of appeals from a judgment entered by a district judge.

   (3) Stay of Execution and Release Pending Appeal. Rule 38 applies to a stay of a judgment of conviction or sentence. The court may release the defendant pending appeal under the law relating to release pending appeal from a district court to a court of appeals.

Rule 59. Matters Before a Magistrate Judge

(a) Nondispositive Matters. A district judge may refer to a magistrate judge for determination any matter that does not dispose of a charge or defense. The magistrate judge must promptly conduct the required proceedings and, when appropriate, enter on the record an oral or written order stating the determination. A party may serve and file objections to the order within 14 days after being served with a copy of a written order or after the oral order is stated on the record, or at some other time the court sets. The district judge must consider timely objections and modify or set aside any part of the order that is contrary to law or clearly erroneous. Failure to object in accordance with this rule waives a party's right to review.

(b) Dispositive Matters.

   (1) Referral to Magistrate Judge. A district judge may refer to a magistrate judge for recommendation a defendant's motion to dismiss or quash an indictment or information, a motion to suppress evidence, or any matter that may dispose of a charge or defense. The magistrate judge must promptly conduct the required proceedings. A record must be made of any evidentiary proceeding and of any other proceeding if the magistrate judge considers it necessary. The magistrate judge must enter on the record a recommendation for disposing of the matter, including any proposed findings of fact. The clerk must immediately serve copies on all parties.

   (2) Objections to Findings and Recommendations. Within 14 days after being served with a copy of the recommended disposition, or at some other time the court sets, a party may serve and file specific written objections to the proposed findings and recommendations. Unless the district judge directs otherwise, the objecting party must promptly arrange for transcribing the record, or whatever portions of it the parties agree to or the magistrate judge considers sufficient. Failure to object in accordance with this rule waives a party's right to review.

(3) De Novo Review of Recommendations. The district judge must consider de novo any objection to the magistrate judge's recommendation. The district judge may accept, reject, or modify the recommendation, receive further evidence, or resubmit the matter to the magistrate judge with instructions.

Rule 60. Victim's Rights

(a) In General.

(1) Notice of a Proceeding. The government must use its best efforts to give the victim reasonable, accurate, and timely notice of any public court proceeding involving the crime.

(2) Attending the Proceeding. The court must not exclude a victim from a public court proceeding involving the crime, unless the court determines by clear and convincing evidence that the victim's testimony would be materially altered if the victim heard other testimony at that proceeding. In determining whether to exclude a victim, the court must make every effort to permit the fullest attendance possible by the victim and must consider reasonable alternatives to exclusion. The reasons for any exclusion must be clearly stated on the record.

(3) Right to Be Heard on Release, a Plea, or Sentencing. The court must permit a victim to be reasonably heard at any public proceeding in the district court concerning release, plea, or sentencing involving the crime.

(b) Enforcement and Limitations.

(1) Time for Deciding a Motion. The court must promptly decide any motion asserting a victim's rights described in these rules.

(2) Who May Assert the Rights. A victim's rights described in these rules may be asserted by the victim, the victim's lawful representative, the attorney for the government, or any other person as authorized by 18 U.S.C. § 3771(d) and (e).

(3) Multiple Victims. If the court finds that the number of victims makes it impracticable to accord all of them their rights described in these rules, the court must fashion a reasonable procedure that gives effect to these rights without unduly complicating or prolonging the proceedings.

(4) Where Rights May Be Asserted. A victim's rights described in these rules must be asserted in the district where a defendant is being prosecuted for the crime.

(5) Limitations on Relief. A victim may move to reopen a plea or sentence only if:

    (A) the victim asked to be heard before or during the proceeding at issue, and the request was denied;

    (B) the victim petitions the court of appeals for a writ of mandamus within 10 days after the denial, and the writ is granted; and

    (C) in the case of a plea, the accused has not pleaded to the highest offense charged.

(6) No New Trial. A failure to afford a victim any right described in these rules is not grounds for a new trial.

Rule 61. Title

These rules may be known and cited as the Federal Rules of Criminal Procedure.